P. 17

Utility
Role of Party

Efficiency

THE DISCONNECTED

THE DISCONNECTED

Penn Kimball

COLUMBIA UNIVERSITY PRESS
NEW YORK AND LONDON ▪ 1972

Library of Congress Cataloging in Publication Data

Kimball, Penn.
    The disconnected.
    1. Voters, Registration of—United States. 2. Voting—United States.
3. Political participation—United States. 4. Minorities—United States.
I. Title.
JK2160.K54   324'.24'0973   72-6349
ISBN 0-231-03696-5
ISBN 0-231-08315-7 (pbk.)

FOR BARRY AND ROB

ACKNOWLEDGMENTS

The research and travel required to write this book were made possible by a grant from the Ford Foundation to the Graduate School of Journalism, Columbia University. The responsibility for the contents, however, is the author's alone. Generous cooperation and assistance was furnished by election officials, candidates and their staffs, research organizations, scholars, journalists, and political buffs. Some of their names appear in these pages; most do not. My appreciation extends to them all.

Penn Kimball

CONTENTS

THE DISCONNECTED

INTRODUCTION

The reporting of politics presents multiple challenges. No single approach is totally adequate to the dynamics, the subtleties, the obscurities of the political process. When the focus is upon vast metropolitan areas and largely anonymous masses of the disadvantaged poor, it is especially difficult to net the slippery eel of truth.

This book employs a variety of reporting methods in an effort to triangulate the facts about the participation of the urban poor in the American electoral process. Portions might be described as straight journalism, a term which enjoys a differing reputation among various audiences. And yet, the eye of a careful and sensitive reporter can, at times, be more accurate than an assemblage of scientific apparatus. The systematic disciplines of survey research have also been employed, most particularly for analyzing the backgrounds, opinions, and attitudes of voters as compared to nonvoters.

It is customary among pollsters to cut off their interviewing when they encounter probable nonvoters, for the simple reason that the answers of those who do not turn out to vote will skew any attempt to project an accurate prediction of election results. The study here of the 1970 election in Newark, N. J., for example, was specifically designed to probe the facts about those who rarely take part in the political process—the ones we have chosen to call disconnected.

That word carries some important distinctions. Apathetic is the adjective most commonly attached to those who for one reason or another fail to make their way to the polls. The term implies a lumpen indifference arising from some alleged deficiency of character in the individual. The data gathered in this study suggest that the feeling of powerlessness among the urban poor is often an accurate reflection of the institutional bias actually at work in our political system. Alienation is another popular word for describing the supposed embittered state of those who withdraw from the political mainstream. That image also does an injustice to many persons whose sincere efforts to participate are thwarted by roadblocks capable of discouraging those whose resources have not been so limited in life. Disconnected—cut off, turned off—is a less normative and more accurate word, and also more suggestive of a system gone dangerously wrong.

The analytic skills of the academic political scientist are a third valuable means to isolate patterns and identify trends from a large mass of electoral data. While not pretending to special qualification in that field, the author has made case studies and assembled statistical data to measure the political impact of registration activities among minority groups across the country in such places as New York City, Cleveland, Ohio, Los Angeles, California, New Orleans, Louisiana, and San Antonio, Texas. The hard realities of statistical findings in these instances were not always acceptable to those who had invested so much energy and hope in the hard tasks of voter organization. The conventional myths of politics die hard.

The purpose, in general, was to examine a broad spectrum of America's minority poor—Blacks and Puerto Ricans in New York, Newark, and Cleveland; Chicanos in Los Angeles and San Antonio; Indians in Arizona; Southern Blacks in New Orleans and Atlanta—in the context of their past and present participation in the electoral process. It was not a surprise to verify that their rates of voting registration and turnout were distressingly low. It was more unexpected to discover how stubbornly this condition resisted the conventional forms of political organization and activity.

ᒪ The persistent isolation of disadvantaged minorities from the American political process is a serious matter. If the usual techniques of partisan politics and mass communication make so little practical dent on this condition, something needs to be done. It is incumbent upon us, however, to search out the reasons before we can prescribe the remedy. ᒧ

The main thrust of the findings in the pages to follow is that the failure of the American political system to engage millions of potential voters is the product of the institutional structure by which persons can qualify to vote. That structure discriminates most particularly against the poor. And there will probably be no significant improvement in public participation in the electoral process until the federal government takes the initiative to qualify eligible voters rather than place the onus upon individuals thwarted by outmoded state and local regulations. Voting in America is enmeshed in a spider's web of prior restraints.

In recent years two dramatic thrusts have been launched to enlarge registration among disenfranchised sectors of the population: first, the drive across the Deep South in the sixties to place Blacks on the voting rolls for the first time; more lately, the campaign to qualify as voters throughout the country the young people between the ages of eighteen and twenty made eligible by the ratification of the 26th Amendment to the federal Constitution. The successes and disappointments of these two historical events help to illuminate the even more difficult tasks faced by those who have attempted to activate urban minorities under present state regulations.

Universal Voter Registration, similar to that practiced in Britain or Canada, is an idea whose time appears to be coming. In addition, a movement has sprung up in the country to challenge such restrictions as residence requirements and registration closing dates in the courts. The League of Women Voters is monitoring administrative obstacles to registration and voting. The National Municipal League has undertaken a comprehensive analysis of the legal structure of the fifty state election systems in the preparation of model registration and voting codes. A joint venture by these two organizations is aimed to focus national attention, if possible, on the need for electoral reform.

Meanwhile, the 1972 Presidential contest, along with the accompanying congressional, state, and local elections, would probably have been decided without the participation of millions of Americans eligible to share in a system supposedly predicated on the ideal of one man-one vote.

The requirement for an individual to register in order to vote was not introduced into the American political system until late in the nineteenth century. Its emergence coincided with the mass immigration of foreign-born newcomers into American cities and the move to disenfranchise Blacks in the South. Although the rationale included the elimination of fraud by big-city political machines or county courthouse gangs, the Anglo-Saxon majority in a rapidly growing America was also seeking bulwarks against unpalatable change. Mixed in with a Puritanical zeal for civic reform were a whole set of WASPish prejudices about who should be permitted to vote.

In the Presidential election of 1876, when any American wishing to vote simply showed up at the polls, the turnout of potential voters came to 82 per cent. Between 1864 and 1900 the average Presidential turnout was 76.8 per cent of those eligible. Since formal registration requirements were introduced throughout the land, turnout in Presidential elections in the twentieth century has averaged only 59.2 per cent—a drop of over twenty points, or one of every five Americans.

Whatever its original intent, voter registration operates as an effective system of political control. As the pages to follow will document, those who neither register nor vote are drawn disproportionately from the ranks of the nation's poor, from ethnic minority groups, from disadvantaged residents of our largest urban centers.

Those who control the administration of local election laws have usually won their jobs through political patronage and are not anxious to water down the party lists with strangers. The laws themselves are drawn to favor those with White, middle-class skills; oftentimes the process is unconscious, sometimes not. Where the courts or Congress have struck down such direct obstacles as literacy tests and poll taxes, the registration lists have continued to be manipulated indirectly by administrative inconveniences involving the location and hours of registration points.

When a new class of voters between the ages of eighteen and twenty was made eligible by the 26th Amendment, those young citizens immediately ran afoul of restrictive residency require-ments, obscure registration regulations, and uncooperative local registrars. This new minority, of course, also threatened the polit-ical status quo in thousands of American communities, hundreds of Congressional districts, and scores of states—providing they could and would exercise the right to vote. Their frustrations with the country's complicated and diverse election systems might serve to be the final spark to ignite the fires of genuine reform.

The pragmatic approach of Americans to politics has made voter registration a staple of most progressive movements. The assumption has been that with a sufficient expenditure of effort, time, and money few political goals would be incapable of achievement. Registration drives have also been an important rallying ground for new recruits into politics. They have served, in addition, as a relatively noncontroversial device for attracting political contributions. The mass media have contributed gener-ously in the dissemination of registration information, and civic groups have endorsed various types of local registration efforts. Yet, as will become apparent in the case studies to follow, the results of most registration drives have been extremely disappointing. A single conspicuous exception was the effort in the 1960s to enfranchise Blacks across the South; but indications are that once the extraordinary gap initially created by overt forms of intimidation had been closed, the percentages of voter registration in the South also stalled at the same critical plateau which seemed to be the ceiling for participation rates in the urban North. A point of swiftly diminishing returns seemed to set in for the registration of ethnic minorities beyond a limit of about 60 per cent of the voting-age population.

This raised the question of whether the time and money poured into voter registration activities might not better be invested in providing more and better information to qualified voters about issues and candidates. If the quantitative base of American democracy could be otherwise guaranteed, then rewarding activity might be focused on improving its quality.

One risk of diverting energy from helping the disadvantaged poor to become eligible to vote, however, is the familiar phenomenon of how fast one must run merely to stand still. The combination of institutional bias in our electoral process and the psychological damage delivered daily upon urban minorities has made the pool of qualified voters resemble a bucket with a thousand leaks at the bottom for every dipper pouring into the top. The real need is for fundamental rebuilding of the system, more than this frantic patchwork to stay even, important as is the latter to preserving some semblance of economic and social balance on the political scales.

Up to now there seems to have been more energy expended in the precincts in the not always successful attempt to rouse nonvoters to register than in trying to focus popular attention on the urgency of revising the basic registration structure. The results of this research point toward the need for different priorities. The optimistic hope that sheer effort could one day reconnect the Disconnected to the political fabric of our society is not borne out by the data. The time has perhaps arrived to mobilize our resources in a more productive attack on the barriers against full participation in our political process.

The assumption that voting is a privilege to be selectively earned has left the most fundamental act of citizenship at the mercy of a whole series of discretionary obstacles. Once voting is regarded instead as an inherent attribute of citizenship, the ideals of democracy can be more effectively realized. Universal Voter Enrollment is fundamentally a proposal to involve every citizen in the representative system from the beginning instead of harnessing so much official effort toward narrowing the franchise. It is one step, if only the first step, by which millions of Americans might be reconnected to the democratic process in the United States.

PART ONE

PARTICIPATION AT THE POLLS: NEWARK, N. J.

A case study of minority registration and voting in the 1970 mayoralty election in Newark, New Jersey, using the methods of survey research.

Chapter One

AN IMPERFECT DEMOCRACY

Political participation in the United States is selective, which is to say that everyone does not take part in the political process, and those who do participate do so at different levels of interest. This statement is obvious to all who have ever become involved in political campaigns. But, of course, only a fraction of the public does. Some never bother to vote. The turnout in Presidential elections in this country compares unfavorably with major contests in other countries of the Western world. In the 1964 national election, only about 63 per cent of those who could have voted did. In 1968 only 61.4 per cent of the voting population went to the polls. In the Congressional election of 1966, the turnout was only 46.3 per cent.

The report of the President's Commission on Registration and Voting Participation issued in 1963 estimated that one-third of the voting-age population in the United States is not even registered. This is partly because state laws governing the right to vote make it very burdensome to qualify, especially if one is timid, unschooled, poor, different, or new to the neighborhood, city, or region. There is a structural, institutional bias to most of our election regulations, going back to their origins when many Americans really did not believe in universal suffrage.

Women, after all, have been allowed to vote only during the

last fifty of the Republic's 200 years. Property and religious qualifications were characteristic at the outset. There remains, in
this most mobile of societies, an institutionalized hostility toward
changes in voting residences. The administration of voting rights
is usually controlled by local, political party organizations, whose
enthusiasm for expanding the rolls is conditioned by factors of
self-interest and control.

Since fraud at the polls has not been rare historically, voting
regulations tend to invite official challenges, an ancient device
of the middle classes for making maximum use of their superior
bureaucratic skills. The way to catch a thief is to choke him
to death with red tape. It can also be expedient for frustrating
honest folk whose enfranchisement would threaten the relative
distribution of political power.

Of 29 million Americans of voting age who were eligible but
not registered in 1968, half were under thirty years of age. Some
of the reasons for this, as we shall see shortly, are psychological,
social, and economic. Lack of interest among some types of
young adults, however, is not the whole story. The problems
are both motivational and mechanical.

In 32 states, one year of residence was required to register
and vote until the Supreme Court ruled, on March 25, 1972,
that Tennessee's 90-day residence requirement was unconstitutional. Mississippi required two years. A survey by Dr. George
Gallup found that four of ten persons between the ages of twenty-
one and thirty had changed their residence at least once during
the preceding twelve months. The impact of mobility as a deterrent to voter registration was illustrated by the Gallup figures
for unregistered homeowners and renters. The poll found that
16 per cent of those who owned their own homes were not on
the voting lists, while 44 per cent of the renters were not registered.

The significance of these trends as they have affected minority
groups is immediately apparent when one considers the statistic
that more than one-half of the Black population is under twenty-

two years of age, besides being involved in one of the great population movements in this country and being under-represented in the proportion able to buy their own homes.

The defeat of proposals in referenda in Ohio, Connecticut, Oregon, New Jersey, and elsewhere in the late sixties to lower the voting age to nineteen or eighteen turned out not to have been of such far-reaching consequence as some disappointed proponents charged at the time. The 26th Amendment to the U.S. Constitution was passed and ratified within two years. However, the politics of Georgia, Kentucky, Alaska, and Hawaii—states where voters under twenty-one had been previously authorized—had not undergone any documented, dramatic changes as a result. The character of the *potential* vote might be more drastically altered, particularly insofar as minority groups are concerned, by a basic revision of the institutional bias against mobility in our election laws.

Voter registration laws in the United States constitute a major exception to the practice in most democracies of placing the responsibility for updating registration lists on the government rather than on the individual. The American system fits the Anglo-Saxon ethic of rugged individualism better than the realities of universal participation. By contrast, in Britain government officials canvass local communities to see that every eligible voter is recorded on the voting registry. Even where voting is not compulsory, the proportion of nonvoters for major elections in Europe tends to run only one-half to two-thirds as large as the nonvote proportions most typical for American Presidential elections, according to the University of Michigan Survey Research Center.

In European countries where high turnout is typical, it is difficult for the individual to get himself *off* the registration rolls which legitimatize his vote. He is automatically entered on the rolls when he reaches voting age, and various social registration mechanisms serve to keep him on the appropriate voting lists despite changes in residence and the like. In the United States, however, the burden is typically on the individual to make an initial registration when he comes of age, and to keep himself registered in the face of changes in residence, and insofar as the law permits him to remain registered.

The legal barriers preventing the citizen from exercising the franchise become particularly important among those classes in the population whose motivation to take part in the political process may otherwise be impaired. It is comparatively difficult not to know that it is Election Day, but relatively easy to miss the days set aside for voter registration, especially in states where the registration periods are far removed from the time of political campaigns.

For most people, neighborhood polling places are easier to find than more distant central registration points in unfamiliar quarters of the city. Registration procedures in urban centers sometimes include follow-up visits from the police to verify addresses, official mailings from the Board of Elections, or other communications that are threatening to those who stand in awe or terror of the law. Optional registration also weighs the scales against those whose economic circumstances make them anxious to avoid the attention of bill collectors or requirements of jury duty.

Although a great deal of the thrust of voting reform has gone into the elimination of poll taxes and literacy requirements, as well as the substitution of permanent for periodic registration, most Americans encounter a vexing succession of obstacles in order to get themselves registered. Mobile registration, taking the service to the neighborhood and to the job as a function and responsibility of the government, would seem as central to the public interest as taking the census or delivering the mail.

The rationale behind residence requirements was to identify the voters within particular jurisdictions, to give them time to inform themselves of local issues and candidates, and to reduce the incidence of fraudulent misrepresentation at the polls. Before the Supreme Court interceded, some states had reduced the residency requirement to no more than six months in the state and one-to-two months in the county, town, or election district; special provisions had shortened residence requirements in some states for casting a vote for Presidential and Vice Presidential electors. Modern communications make it possible for the motivated person to prepare himself adequately to cast a vote within a relatively short period of time; the unmotivated voter is no better off after ten years of residence than he is after ten days.

Much well-intentioned effort to improve the scale of popular participation in politics has been thwarted by underestimating the more subtle discriminations within our election laws. The matter of national standards of reform may become imperative if the decision is made to abandon the Electoral College for the direct election of the President by popular vote. Minority groups who have enjoyed a bargaining advantage under the winner-take-all system of state electoral votes would then be forced to compete on a straightaway one man-one vote basis.

The theoretical interplay of rival interests in a pluralistic society depends on a rough equality between the competing factions. When a group at the margin contains members who are also only marginally involved in the political process, the inequities take a quantum jump. The Puritan ethic may demand that elections be banned on Sunday, for example, but the practical effect has been to penalize and inconvenience the working classes. The registration of new voters at infrequent intervals, in the political off-season and at hard-to-find locations, discriminates against Blacks and Hispanics as effectively as do the impediments proscribed by the Federal Voting Rights statutes.

In the delivery of services for which we hold the government responsible, comparatively little has been done to ease the exercise of the franchise. The concept of "citizen duty" deeply ingrains the values idealized by most formal instruction in American democracy. Voting is portrayed as an act of individual conscience, almost as if its redemptive qualities required testing to be realized.

As every small-town New Englander learns, direct democracy in the form of a free-wheeling town meeting contains its own seeds of tyranny; the loud and the lengthy can drain the stamina of the meek. Character is perceived as the persistence to last out the ritual, even as faith is measured by attendance at Sunday services. Voting thus becomes more of a privilege to be earned through sacrifice than a right to be enjoyed naturally.

One problem has been that the practice has never equaled the rhetoric. Less than half the eligible adults in the United States get themselves onto the voting lists and into the polling booths for our most important national elections. In 1968 there was a good deal of praise for the virtues of "participatory democracy" in making political parties more responsive to the rank-and-file. The followers of Senator Eugene McCarthy, however, made one of their best showings in winning delegates in New York, a primary where fewer than 25 per cent of the state's registered Democrats came out to vote. The doctrine of "maximum feasible participation" by residents of poverty neighborhoods in programs aimed at their problems has resulted in community "elections" involving fewer than 5 per cent of the eligible.

This suggests that something deeper is at issue than the inflexibility of the power structure, or the admitted shortcomings of election law, or the need for more organization at the grassroots. Senator McCarthy's crusade was least successful in the cities. Various schemes to involve the urban poor in elections to "control" their own schools or their own community development have been engulfed in apathy.

Voter participation has always exhibited a high correlation with education and income, two spheres of urban disadvantage. It is also a fact of life that the poorly educated young tend to tune out on political dialogue. This is accentuated by the higher proportion of the young among urban minorities, the high rate of school dropouts, and the growing number of dependent children carried on welfare rolls. Tenements, rooming houses, and housing projects—the dormitories of the ghetto electorate—

provide, furthermore, a shifting, changing human environment instead of the social reinforcements that encourage political involvement in more stable neighborhoods. And the immediate struggle for subsistence drains the reservoirs of emotional energy available for the distant and complex realm of politics.

The environment of the city is thus an inhibiting factor in itself to individual involvement and participation in elections. In the last century, the political machine helped the immigrant to bridge the gap between duty and necessity by relating one's vote to the receipt of specific, practical rewards. The modern bureaucracy of welfare and social service seems to operate independently of political turnover, so that the vote has lost its meaning as an instrument for survival. Elections come and go, and the life of poverty goes on pretty much as before, neither dramatically better nor dramatically worse. The posturing of candidates and the promises of parties are simply irrelevant to the daily grind of marginal existence.

If one is Black or Puerto Rican, Italian-American or Mexican-American, is foreign-born, or speaks a minority tongue, the psychological adjustments sometimes run directly counter to the Anglo-Saxon model of citizen behavior. One can react to prejudice and discrimination by actively rejecting the White man's system or passively withdrawing from the pain of contact.

A third alternative is the production of personality structures with such damaged self-esteem as to preclude all confidence in one's ability to penetrate the mysteries of political decision. In each case, the result is to reduce the rate of participation below that which might be expected of middle-class Whites, regardless of literature extolling the power of the vote.

The power of the individual to control one's own destiny at the polls is not self-evidently clear in the American federal system, with its overlapping jurisdictions (eighty-seven governments on the average per standard Metropolitan Statistical Area), its system of checks and balances, and its nonideological competition between the two major parties. The formal, rational table of organization found in civics books fails to explain most that actually goes on in the urban environment.

The scope of the social problems of the cities is matched by the fragmentation of the decision-making process. Governments, quasi-governments, private interests, and public lobbies compete for power in a structure never designed to produce the services now demanded of it. The definition of goals and allocation of resources is inadequate. In such a system the premium is on the organization and application of collective political skills, bringing pressure to bear on the sensitive points in a power structure. That is a process carried on independently of the simplified choices at campaign time—a process involving technical expertise, propaganda, or financial resources not usually available to the poor.

This gap between the simple ideal of a visible authority controlled by the will of the people and the complex reality of diffuse power centers buffeted by rival interest groups has strained the comprehension of even favored members of our society. The politically indifferent among the educated and affluent continually complain of the absence of neat issues, clear choices, popular mandates, and public goals. They question whether the act of voting is really meaningful or perhaps one more instance of mindless, mass conformity.

We live in a cultural climate where politicians are scorned, corruption is assumed, and cynicism about politics is the rule—all communicated with the fierce efficiency of modern technology. It is a wonder that the idea of popular sovereignty exercised at the ballot box shows as much vigor as it does.

Representative democracy is an imperfect instrument. There is frequently some gulf between the preference of voters and the policies executed by public servants. Elections provide a periodic review of popular consent or dissatisfaction with only the broadest questions of government, and even these are often ambiguous. The issues most intensely felt by some are sometimes blunted or eclipsed by the multitude of issues collapsed into the choice between two party nominees; third parties fare badly not only under the mechanical forces of a system of single-member, Congressional districts, but also because extreme advocacy of a single cause deprives too many people of their preferences on other issues. It is rare that the winner of an American election can claim a direct transmission of policy from his victorious constituency.

The most powerful force for sustaining voters through these frustrations has been loyalty to party. Political parties have a mysterious life for an institution so frequently denounced. The average voter will claim that he "votes for the man, not the party," whatever the reality of his past history. Parties never live up to what is expected of them when they choose their candidates, adopt their platforms, or staff their administrations. Yet, strong partisanship and stability in their party preferences at the polls are characteristic of those American voters who vote most regularly, are best informed on issues, care the most about politics, and involve themselves most deeply in the political process.

So-called independents, the swing voters and ticket splitters who switch their allegiances most readily from election to election, are likely to be the least interested and least likely to show up when a campaign lacks drama. Even when their educational level is high, they can be shockingly ill informed. The declining role of the old political parties in today's urban affairs, therefore, raises serious problems for programs to activate the inactive.

The appeal of political parties has been aimed directly at the self-interest of individual voters, whereas nonpartisan movements to register new voters must usually depend on invocations of civic duty in order to skirt the penalties of controversy. When "nonpartisan" efforts are directed at specific ethnic or social groups, they have not been effective without sub rosa focus upon programs of specific political action or the fortunes of particular candidates. This has stimulated opposition from rival political interests. Truly "nonpartisan" drives are most effective where they are least needed—among the educated and well-to-do, with a prevailing bias favoring the Republican party.

The problem of bringing nonvoters into an active political role is largely a question of matching the obstacles to voting with a motivational state sufficient to overcome those barriers. The best stimuli must be relevant, easily understood, and emotionally rewarding. Party allegiance—transmitted through the family, through regional heritage, through ethnic and class consciousness—has been a powerful motivator. When it is absent, issues must be polarized or candidates charismatic in order to arouse the voting interest of the indifferent.

A sense of political efficacy on the part of the individual voter has a high correlation with his fulfillment of opportunities to vote, according to the findings of the Survey Research Center at the University of Michigan, which has studied voter turnout in Presidential elections since 1952. The Center defined political efficacy as "the feeling that political and social change is possible, and that the individual citizen can play a part in bringing about this change." Five items were asked of a national cross section of citizens of voting age to produce a Political Efficacy Scale. "Disagree" responses to items 1, 3, 4, and 5, and an "agree" response to item 2 were coded as "efficacious."

1) I don't think public officials care much about what people like me think.

2) The way people vote is the main thing that decides how things are run in this country.

3) Voting is the only way that people like me can have any say about how the government runs things.

4) People like me don't have any say about what government does.

5) Sometimes politics and government seems so complicated that a person like me can't really understand what's going on.

The Michigan researchers found that the higher a person's subjective confidence in his own competence for influencing government the more likely he was to vote. A sense of political efficacy generally increased with income, education, and high-status occupations, and the spread between scores was largest among those with lowest socioeconomic status. Blacks scored lower than Whites.

A comparable series asked of a national sample by Louis Harris produced these percentages of replies among low-income Black respondents:

"The people running the country don't care what happens to me"—62 per cent of low income Blacks agreed.

"What I think doesn't count much"—58 per cent agreed.

"Few people understand how it is to live like I live"—67 per cent agreed.

A feeling of separation from the mainstream of American life, coupled with a sense of political powerlessness, is a potent combination working against political participation by the urban poor.

The demographics of urban America follow a pattern of inmigration by Blacks, Mexican-Americans, and Puerto Ricans accompanied by out-migration on the part of middle-class Whites. In voting terms, this means that the cities are filling up with minorities who ordinarily participate least in electoral politics, while the social classes with the highest rate of political participation are moving away. The net loss in political involvement shows up in declining turnouts in the cities for national, state, and local elections at the very same time that nationwide educational levels are rising and exposure to political materials in the mass media, television in particular, has become nearly universal. A reduction in the average analytic skills of the pool of active voters, furthermore, suggests that city politics is increasingly vulnerable to polarized appeals and emotional demagoguery.

The reduction in the proportion of city dwellers who register to vote and turn out at the polls is not surprising in the light of what has been learned about the nature of political participation in the population at large. Dr. Philip E. Converse, a staff member of the University of Michigan's Survey Research Center, in a report prepared in 1963 for the American Heritage Foundation, pointed out that "nonvoting is relatively common among the cohorts of young people who have been eligible to vote only a short period of time" along with a decline in voting turnout that also takes place in the twilight years after retirement, reflecting the "onset of physical infirmities and a narrowing of psychological participation in the broader life of the society."

In view of the fact that the growing proportions of minority groups in our central cities also have an average age considerably below the national norm, a general tendency toward nonvoting among the young would work with distorted effect among Blacks and Spanish-speaking citizens. At the same time, the residual Whites left behind in the cities contain an over-representation of the old and retired, reaching the point in life where their interest in politics begins to lag. Without any change in the factors producing these age differentials in political activity, the politics of the city would simply become more and more removed from a substantial body of its inhabitants.

There are two views of such a possibility. One is to argue that to raise the brute size of the electorate without increasing its competence to vote intelligently is actually counterproductive, and that leadership by an educated elite is to be preferred over the mobocracy of the uninformed. The weakness in that position is the growing social and economic crisis in our cities and its possible consequences when the inhabitants no longer regard a system of representative democracy as either relevant or viable.

The other alternative is to try to understand what it is that keeps people outside the electoral process and to encourage their entry on the assumption that participation in itself can be an educational and beneficial experience. Another reason for arguing the latter is that the most urgent problems facing government concern the minority groups whose influence is further diluted when their potential voting power cannot be mustered at the polls, the classic means by which newcomers have gained access to political power in America.

The critical, although not the only, factor identified by Dr. Converse in his study of nonvoting among the young was education. The young person who goes to college comes out to vote at only slightly lower rates than older people with college educations—better than 90 per cent in a Presidential year, although their interest flags substantially more in off-year state and local elections. The young person who fails to finish high school, on the other hand, does not catch up with his elders of comparable education until middle-age, and even then one out of four does not vote for President. Converse pointed out that.

It is among the poorly educated that the difference by age becomes extreme. Therefore, if we were to imagine two campaigns to improve vote participation, one directed at the college-educated and one tailored to people of grade school education, and if both campaigns succeeded in bringing the level of turnout among the young up to that of older people of the same education, the campaign directed at the people of grade school background would prod about six times as many citizens to the polls as would the campaign directed at the college-educated young.

Easier said than done.

While a successful campaign tailored to the poorly educated might produce six times as many voters as an equally successful campaign aimed at college-educated young people, it would not be at all surprising to discover that it would be more than six times as difficult to achieve the same impact with poorly educated people. This is in many ways the hub of the problem of non-voting among the young.

Young people, when poorly educated, are highly inaccessible to most of the simpler large-scale efforts toward deliberate change, for they are relatively inaccessible to contact through any channels of "serious" or purposive social communication. They are functionally illiterate: they read little in totum, and almost nothing of a serious nature. They appear, furthermore, to do quite an effective job of ignoring the more serious material which might confront them over the airwaves. Their non-voting is no more than one symptom of a broader insulation from the public affairs of the society.

The effort to improve the quality of education in the ghetto has encountered the same maddening circle; the environment, which is a symptom of conditions that need to be corrected, also inhibits the success of attempted remedies.

Parents of large families have less time to spend with each child and maintain the relationship which internalized the politics of most Americans. A broken family not only diminishes the influence of adult models, but it also spurs the attention of young offspring toward immediate personal economic and social survival at the expense of such deferred rewards as education and politics. Shortages of housing accelerate mobility, increasing the investment of effort necessary to remain eligible to vote while decreasing the chances of being reached by social contact with politically active friends or groups. Early marriage and childbearing escalate the toll on time and energy, leaving a limited attention span for the complexities of political discourse.

A proper school education in the meaning and opportunities of political participation, even if it were made stimulating and relevant, would conflict with the anxieties of young adulthood in the slums. But education for citizenship is one of the casualties of the general breakdown of ghetto school systems.

Some of the lessons of educational experiments conducted in poverty areas have application, perhaps, in trying to motivate individuals over the threshold between voting and nonvoting. The minority child, for example, seems to respond more readily to tangible, external rewards to motivate the learning process, rather than to the value system internalized by White teachers. Free movie tickets or coupons to be exchanged at the supermarket might spur more new voters than printed propaganda. (In the affluent suburbs, blood banks make their quotas by combining appeals to good neighborliness with door prizes exchangeable at local stores.) Children in the ghetto schools enjoy contests that goad the learning process and are especially responsive to public praise. Why not make a virtue of the multitudinous church parishes in the minority neighborhoods of urban America, stimulating them to competition in making new voters and affording them public recognition?

Although the setting and the problems are quite different, it has been the groups organized through the Black churches of the South that have stimulated the political revolution in that section. Some political experts contend that the growing exercise of Black voting rights in the South is governed by a Newtonian law: increases in Black registration stimulate countervailing registration among poor Whites, thus maintaining the balance of power regionally, in spite of dramatic changes in jurisdictions with concentrated Black populations. The data on this point will be examined in a subsequent chapter.

The unexpected social development of the 1950s and 1960s was that the major enlargement of voting rights in the United States took place not in the North, where the legal status of Blacks was comparable to that enjoyed by Whites, but in the South, where the barriers of discrimination were supposedly most formidable. Professor Carl N. Degler of Stanford University, writing in *The New York Times Magazine,* has explained that this was a result of (1) an underestimation by scholars, including Gunnar Myrdal in the classic study *An American Dilemma,* of the "virulence and persistence" of racism in the North; and (2) a misunderstanding of the role of the Southern Black church "as a focus of Negro equalitarian aspirations and organization."

The religious framework and leadership of the Black drive for political participation in the South, as evidenced by the late Martin Luther King, Jr., and other ministers of the Southern Christian Leadership Conference, was of a different style than the political rise of the late Adam Clayton Powell, Jr., formerly pastor of Harlem's Abyssinian Baptist Church. The intervention in the South was a group witness, appealing to the activity of the whole membership in the confrontation in behalf of first-class citizenship.

The Powells and Dawsons in the North profited not by enlarging the involvement of their constituents but by obtaining their proxies, a process of bargaining in the back room rather than role-playing in the streets. The result in the South was an indigenous organization capable of risking life and safety together for the nonviolent pursuit of Constitutional prerogatives. The pattern in the North added nothing to the social fabric, leaving it to the Black militants to try to rouse support in a virtual political vacuum.

A significant new development in recent years has been the emergence of Black candidates contesting for the office of mayor in large urban centers with sizeable minority group populations, The opportunity to elect one of their own number has added a new dimension to the importance of mobilizing the participation of Blacks, Puerto Ricans, and Mexican-Americans in the electoral process. Special efforts have been organized to increase their registration on the voting rolls and to increase their turnout on Election Day. Such situations provide an excellent laboratory for study of the participation process.

With this in mind, a survey in depth was made of the 1970 election for the mayoralty of Newark, New Jersey, where the incumbent, Hugh Addonizio, was originally challenged by six other candidates, including City Engineer Kenneth Gibson and two other Blacks. The remainder of Part I is devoted to an analysis of what happened in Newark and what that hotly contested election revealed about registration and voting among urban Blacks.

Chapter Two

THE SETTING AND THE STUDY DESIGN

The setting

The city of Newark is a prototype of the urban crisis in America. The 1970 census confirmed that a clear majority of its 400,000 inhabitants is now Black. Every day an army of White commuters advances into the downtown business area and retreats again in the evening to "dormitories" in the suburbs. Large areas of the central city look like devastated hamlets in Vietnam—partly the result of bulldozers that cleared acres of tenements for urban renewal tracts which have yet to progress beyond controversial and unfulfilled plans, partly the still unretouched scars of one of the worst of the urban riots during the long hot summer of 1967.

A blanket of pollution rises from the chemical plants and foundry furnaces along the Penn Central and Lackawanna tracks that crisscross the neighborhoods, although many manufacturing jobs must be sought elsewhere. The racket of jets landing and taking off from Newark Airport bounces off the splendid new office buildings along Broad and Market streets, hives full of female white-collar workers filing insurance premiums and invoices for the old firms of the Newark establishment. The brave facade cannot conceal the tackiness of the once fashionable department stores now converted into discount centers, the run-down movie houses and vacant premises dotting the commercial district. The leading local newspaper, recently sold by its local family owners, thereupon removed "Newark" from its logotype in its search for a more metropolitan and prosperous identity.

Within walking distance of the business center are some of the worst slums in the country. The Central Ward, decimated by urban renewal and highway routes, is a Black hole of over-crowded and undermaintained housing, idleness and drug addiction visible in its littered streets. The inadequate school buildings are relics of nineteenth-century, White Newark, abandoned to a new generation of migrants from the South and from Puerto Rico. Police prowl by the pair, in squad cars more often than on foot.

Once a relative stronghold for the Democratic party, a coterie of Black bosses dispensing patronage and favors in return for light but monolithic turnouts in state and national elections, the political structure of the Central Ward was torn apart along with its buildings. The fractionalization process included the community action groups spawned by federal poverty programs, a Black cultural movement headed by militant Black poet and playwright Le Roi Jones (now known by his Muslim name, Imamu Amiri Baraka), traditional civil rights organizations such as the N.A.A.C.P. and Urban League, neighborhood cadres formed to resist the encroachments of urban renewal, plus the personal entourages of Black members of the Newark City Council and Black appointees in the then city Administration of Mayor Hugh J. Addonizio.

How deeply all this competition for leadership at the top actually reached the rank and file of Newark's Black community was a matter of some conjecture. Although no reliable figures existed, knowledgeable persons on the local political scene seemed to agree that the Black and Puerto Rican majority in the total population was only a minority on the lists of eligible voters. A consensus estimate just prior to the 1970 city election was a population 50 per cent Black and 10 per cent Puerto Rican, but only 45 per cent combined in the registration figures. In addition, turnout in White precincts on Election Day habitually exceeded the proportions going to the polls in minority neighborhoods. When Kenneth Gibson, a Black city engineer, ran for mayor in 1966 against Addonizio and former Mayor Leo Carlin, he received 16,114 against 64,577 votes for the two White candidates drawn from the Italian-American and Irish-American enclaves battling for political control of the city.

The election of Addonizio, a former seven-term Democratic Congressman, had culminated the political *Risorgimento* of Newark's 100,000 residents of Italian descent, most of them concentrated in the North Ward. There, the Black and Puerto Rican blocks close to the central city pressed against the well-tended row houses and gardens of first- and second-generation immigrants. Although much of the housing was modest, though well maintained, the area also contained the better residential neighborhoods taken over from the Anglo-Saxon families that had moved to the suburbs. Property, family, security loomed large in the scale of values, and the North Ward Citizens Committee formed by Councilman Anthony Imperiale symbolized the strength of territorial imperatives. Extra street lights and volunteer public safety patrols testified to the tensions and fears felt in an era of racial and social change. Backlash and polarization, the vocabulary applied to the state of mind of Middle America, festered in a political atmosphere also poisoned by counter-allegations of Mafia influence.

Following the 1967 riots, a special commission, established by then Governor Richard J. Hughes, reported that "a pervasive feeling of corruption" in Newark's city administration was a contributing factor to the events which cost twenty-six lives and more than $10 million in property damage. On December 17, 1969, a federal grand jury indicted Mayor Addonizio with fourteen other persons on sixty-five counts of extortion and evasion of income taxes. One of those indicted along with the Mayor was Anthony (Tony Boy) Boiardo, allegedly a Mafia member, whose father had been convicted of conspiracy to operate a multimillion-dollar numbers racket in Newark. One of the accusations against the Mayor was that he had participated in kick-backs extorted from contractors doing business with the city, along with three members of the Newark City Council, two of them Black and the third a distant relative of the Mayor, plus several Addonizio appointees.

In this setting of urban decay, characterized by problems beyond the city's capacity to cope with them alone, by a pessimism unresponsive to the Chamber of Commerce's predictions of a brave new tomorrow, by uncertainties concerning public safety and relations between the races, by disillusion not only with the integrity of local government but also with the moral fiber of the whole society, the schedule of the democratic process called for a citywide election in 1970. The election of Black mayors previously in Cleveland, Ohio, and Gary, Indiana, as well as the recent defeat of a Black candidate in Los Angeles, focused special attention on the possibility of a Black-White political confrontation in Newark. Kenneth Gibson, now thirty-eight, had been preparing for a year to make the race, and, if possible, to unite the Black and Puerto Rican communities behind a single standard bearer. Mayor Addonizio was seeking vindication from the voters on the slogan, "Peace and Progress." The business community, it was rumored, was eager to remove the stigma of the riots and scandals under Addonizio, but not yet prepared to vacate in favor of a Black coalition. Tony Imperiale, a former private investigator, promising law and order and buoyed by a smashing victory the year before in a special election for Councilman-at-large, entered his name in the race, as did two other White hopefuls—Republican State Senator Alexander J. Matturi and Irish-American John P. Caufield, former city Fire Director. Under Newark's "nonpartisan" system, the top two finishers in a preliminary election would qualify for a run-off a month later unless one candidate polled an absolute majority of the votes cast.

A "Black and Puerto Rican Convention" was organized among minority groups to try to agree on a single entry into the mayoral field and to pick a slate of minority candidates equal to the number of vacancies for Councilman-at-large and in wards with the largest concentration of Black and Puerto Rican voters. Although the "delegates" gave a majority to Gibson, two other Black candidates, State Assemblyman George C. Richardson and Harry F. Wheeler, a former school teacher, refused to withdraw. Thus, a field of seven candidates—three Italian-Americans, one Irish-American, and three Blacks—would appear on the May 12 ballot in the race to a run-off on June 16, 1970. Thirty-one candidates filed for four Councilman-at-large seats. All told, there were seventy-two candidates for ten positions.

Thus, the reputed alienation and resultant political apathy engendered among potential voters in Newark might be balanced by the intensity of the issues, ethnic polarization, and competition among a large roster of candidates for mayor. The election would certainly receive attention from the national mass media. The self-conscious search for "Black power" versus White militancy promised a test of the thesis of two Americas as advanced by the findings of the Kerner Commission. On the other hand, Newark, like other central cities throughout the country, had turned out poorly to participate in the 1968 Presidential election. Occasional registration drives failed to stem the steady attrition of a declining population on the voting rolls as well. In four years total registration in the city had dropped more than 20,000, and in the last previous contest for mayor only 62 per cent of those eligible had bothered to go to the polls.

The economic and political poverty in Newark raised the question of the vitality of the election process in the disadvantaged sectors of our society. Who participates? Who does not? And what accounts for the selective involvement of such individuals in the democratic process? The election of mayor in Newark was a kind of laboratory demonstration for representative government, participatory democracy, and the role of disadvantaged minorities in the competition for power within the system.

The test was made even more interesting by the local decision to launch an ambitious progran of voter education, registration, and turnout aimed at mobilizing the theoretical strength of Blacks and Puerto Ricans in the city's balance of power. As early as February, 1968, the Committee for a Unified Newark—drawn from twenty-nine separate organizations, including the N.A.A.C.P., the Urban Coalition, and the Interreligion Foundation for Community Organizations—began preparing an elaborate blueprint for attaining this objective and projected a budget of over $500,000 in a proposal circulated among prospective donors.

"The 1970 municipal election in Newark," a 1969 memorandum stated,

could see the actual emergence of Black political power in this city, a city that just two years ago was almost destroyed by the explosion of Black political desire in conflict with an unchanging, backward, local governmental structure. The 1970 election is crucial because it can be a test of how political power can be gained legitimately by Black people in our time. Newark must serve as an example of positive Black change and give the promise that the just decaying cities of America can be salvaged.

Equally important and inseparable, Newark can serve as a teaching experiment to Black people in methods of organizing and moving to secure political power for Black communities all over America. . . . We say the problem of the cities is the powerlessness of their residents.

The idea of a Black and Puerto Rican Convention "to make the Black community aware that the fewer candidates who ran representing it, the more certain we would be of success" was advanced from the outset, as well as "circulation of materials designed to inform the powerless Black citizens of Newark of their political potential." The table of organization called for twenty door-to-door street workers in each ward, a timetable calling for personal contacts with 3,000 persons per month, and an all-out drive to register the unregistered before the May 12 and June 16 elections.

These plans went through several metamorphoses along the way, and how much was actually spent on their execution is not firmly established. An initial kitty of $75,000 was raised in 1968, including contributions from the Black United Brothers, the Presbyterian Board of Missions, the Episcopal Diocese, Sidney Poitier, and Sammy Davis, Jr. The New Ark Fund, an outgrowth of Le Roi Jones's United Brothers, was said to have raised $162,000 all told for voting registration.

Project Vote, an umbrella operating organization including the N.A.A.C.P. and the League of Women Voters, set a 1970 goal of 25,000 new registrants and went to thhe courts to force the Essex County Board of Elections to provide off-site registration in supermarkets, department stores, and housing projects. Board fences and telephone poles throughout the city were papered with color reproductions of a *Life* photograph, published after the 1967 riots, showing a wounded Black boy lying in a pool of blood before a White policeman with a shotgun under his arm. "Don't let this happen again. Register—Vote," the caption read. Ads in the newspapers urged every citizen to "make yourself count." A coloring book on registration was distributed through all the schools and posters to all the churches. Film strips were shown in downtown stores by suburban volunteers from the League of Women Voters, who also canvassed shoppers to register at card tables manned by election officials.

In Black neighborhoods, teenagers recruited at the High Street headquarters of Le Roi Jones worked for $2.50 an hour ringing doorbells and passing out leaflets and buttons with the inscription, "Vote, Baby, Vote." Volunteers from Rutgers and Seton Hall joined with paid field organizers from the United Auto Workers under ward captains picked by Project Vote. Behind the scenes, the campaign staff of Kenneth Gibson helped with lists of unregistered prospects and telephone numbers for pulling out sympathetic voters on Election Day.

The institutional arrangements for qualifying voters in Newark were relatively liberal by American norms. A citizen was then required to have been a resident in New Jersey for at least six months, and in Essex County for at least forty days before the date of the election. His name was entered in the poll books of the voting district where he resided and kept there permanently until he moved. Registration was permitted any day of the year either at City Hall or the County Building, including nighttime hours just before the deadline for registering for the next election. Election Commissioners were empowered to establish registration centers at other sites from time to time. There was no literacy test nor poll tax, although persons who failed to vote for four years were removed from the lists. Sample ballots were sent out by mail to each voter prior to each election as a method for confirming the correctness of the lists.

This system was more open, for example, than the one then in effect in Texas, in which residents were required to re-register for every election no later than the preceding January. It was less flexible than the one in California, in which deputies could canvass door-to-door and register new voters on the spot. The exclusionary provisions of most state registration laws are in contrast to practices abroad, such as in Great Britain, where it is considered a government function and responsibility—like taking the census—to place all eligibles on the official voting lists. New Jersey excludes all those convicted of felonies, of which there were 25,000 in Essex County, a high proportion of them Black.

The Puritan ethic was apparent in an Essex County Deputy Election Commissioner's remark that neighborhood registration was the "lazy man's way" of becoming eligible to vote. The extra expense involved in a total registration budget of $15,000 for the whole county (twenty-two municipalities) also weighed heavily on the bureaucratic ledger. (Registration officials are paid $3 an hour—two to a registration location plus a driver.)

When Project Vote brought suit for additional off-site registration days, county officials predicted meager results. "We gave them ten spots in each of the five wards in February and March," one official said, "to take the steam out of the pickets. What happened? Between 4 and 8 P.M. in one public housing project only one person showed up. Nobody does the work the party organizations used to do. People living out of wedlock or deadbeats dodging bill collectors don't want their names on the voting lists anyway. When we analyze the off-site registration, 10 to 20 per cent are no good because of criminal records or duplications.''

Registration workers in the neighborhoods charged that mail deliveries of registration verifications failed to reach residents of slum tenements and that bureaucratic interpretation of the laws governing previous registrants who had moved to new addresses was unfairly denying the right to vote. This was especially true, they said, among Blacks forced to move more frequently than Whites in Newark because of substandard housing, urban renewal, and superhighways routed through the ghetto. Such obstacles compounded the problem of motivating the poor and uneducated. ''Some thought they had registered when they signed a petition to get Gibson's name on the ballot,'' reported a canvasser in the Central Ward. ''Some are fearful that they will have to pay a poll tax. And, of course, there is the guy who just don't give a damn, who says, 'politics stinks'.''

Although Newark has no television channel of its own (those nominally assigned have long since become New York metropolitan area stations), the newspapers carried the daily releases from each candidate, scrupulously balanced in space and display. On their editorial pages, both the *News* and the *Star-Ledger* endorsed Kenneth Gibson and applauded the registration drive. Comedian Bill Cosby and author Claude Brown came to the city to give Gibson their personal endorsement and to appear at a benefit along with film star Dustin Hoffman for the registration campaign.

Mayor Addonizio bought spot announcements on television, even though most of the audience reached did not even live in New Jersey, but he refused to appear on the debate programs offered as a public service. Anthony Imperiale toured the city in a flat-bed truck, holding old-fashioned street-corner rallies until he was stricken with influenza midway through the campaign. An Oliver Quayle poll taken for the Chamber of Commerce in January showed him running nearly ten percentage points ahead of Addonizio, and nearly two-to-one ahead of the Mayor among White voters. But at that stage, one-third of the electorate was still undecided.

Significantly, the January Quayle poll showed Addonizio drawing 12 per cent of the Black preferences, a sign of the Mayor's policy of mending fences through Black appointments at City Hall and alliances with Black ward politicians. It was rumored that at least one of the Black candidates opposing the endorsed selection of the Black and Puerto Rican Convention was being financed from sources friendly to the Mayor.

The incapacity of Imperiale at a critical point in the campaign coincided with the peaking of the Mayor's own well-financed and well-organized drive, including almost nightly appearances in Italian neighborhoods. Gibson headquarters complained that the presence of three Black candidates in the race was handicapping their fund-raising efforts, especially from outside the city. Gibson, himself, a quiet, heavy-set man, was a low-key campaigner, and squirmed with obvious embarrassment at a rally addressed by Adam Clayton Powell, Jr.

His public campaign manager was a White New Yorker and his chief aide and schedulemaker at headquarters a White Princeton senior receiving course credit for a study of Newark politics. Strategy sessions in the Gibson camp involved the relative merits of attracting a significant percentage of White voters, as Mayor Carl Stokes had successfully done in achieving re-election in Cleveland, or going all-out for a solid Black majority on Election Day. Actually, the decision was to try for both, but to control the rhetoric which might alienate White voters while pursuing Black votes with neighborhood organization efforts within the Black community.

The allocation of the candidate's time and effort in White areas of the city, however, was a controversial matter within the Gibson camp throughout the whole campaign. The debate was compounded by the fact that advisers differed in their estimates as to whether Black and Puerto Rican voters constituted a majority or minority on the voting lists. In the end, the counsel of those who believed Gibson could not win without White support prevailed in the overall strategy.

An unexpected factor turned out to be the role of John Caufield, who alone in the field seemed to generate personal charisma during the campaign. Handsome, warm, a former fireman and the father of nine children, Caufield caught the fancy of local reporters on the political beat, some of whom tabbed him as the dark horse to watch when the returns came in on May 12. The lone non-Italian White in the field, he was judged to possess potential pulling power among the blue-collar workers in Newark's other ethnic enclaves: Irish, Polish, German, and Portuguese, many of them in the predominantly White neighborhoods in the East and West wards.

A former member of the Addonizio Administration for seven years, he had been fired by the Mayor shortly after he announced he could no longer support him following the federal indictments. He openly campaigned on the "corruption" issue, sparing Gibson the possible antagonism of racial reactions and focusing public attention on the trials scheduled to begin on June 2, two weeks before the date of the final runoff.

On Gibson's other flank was Assemblyman George Richardson, a one-time sponsor of Gibson's 1966 mayoralty effort but now charging that Gibson was the prisoner of Le Roi Jones and other militant elements in the Black community. Richardson, serving his third term in Trenton, had been active in civil rights drives and had once set up his own maverick ticket for state and local office. An urbane politician, attractive in appearance, his recognition quotient was high in the Black community of the South and Central wards.

The third Black candidate, Harvey Wheeler, announced his

withdrawal as a candidate on the final weekend before the May 12 election, but his name remained on the ballot in the voting machines.

In this racially divided and subdivided setting the Newark city election appeared to be of more than average interest to local residents as well as to students of urban politics. The nonpartisan structure and run-off provision afforded a favorable opportunity to measure individual political behavior in a dynamic situation, especially those factors which might be found to be significant as regards registration and voting. The issues in Newark were the relevant issues to be found in cities all over America, manifested there in sharper relief. Accordingly, under a research grant from the Ford Foundation to the Graduate School of Journalism of Columbia University, a public opinion survey was designed and conducted by the author with the assistance of a field interviewing staff supplied by Louis Harris and Associates in May and June, 1970.

The Study Design

To focus upon the disadvantaged sectors of Newark's population rather than a mirror image of the city's entire voting population, the sample for field interviewing was designed to concentrate on low-income neighborhoods. Forty points (with an interviewing quota of ten to eleven per point, one-half men, one-half women) were randomly chosen from a list of every Newark census tract with 50 per cent or more Black heads of household, twenty additional points were randomly chosen from a list of census tracts with at least 50 per cent White heads of household, but also a median income under $5,454 (Newark's 1960 census median income per family).

After canvassing Newark, additional tracts were added and some were eliminated when they were found to have undergone economic or ethnic change since the 1960 census and others because of the removal or destruction of housing.

In a first wave of interviewing, before the May 12 preliminary election, interviews were secured from 419 Blacks and 205 low-income Whites. In a second wave of interviewing, before the June 16 run-off election, additional interviews were obtained from 409 Blacks and 211 low-income Whites. The total sample, 1,244 cases, 828 Black (66 per cent) and 416 low-income Whites, lived in the inner-city sections of the Central and North wards and included both registered voters and unregistered residents.

Because an unexpectedly high proportion of the sample reported themselves to be registered to vote during the first wave of interviewing (73 per cent), a minimum quota of nonregistrants was assigned to each interviewer in the second wave. This produced a final raw count of 535 (65 per cent) Black and Puerto Rican registered voters as against 293 unregistered Blacks and Puerto Rican (35 per cent). Among low-income Whites, the raw split was 291 (70 per cent) registered and 125 (30 per cent) not registered. For statistical purposes, the raw results were weighted to achieve registration ratios of 50 per cent among Blacks and Puerto Ricans and 60 per cent among Whites.

The forty Black interviewing points and twenty White points in the second wave came from the same sixty tracts randomly chosen for the first wave. New blocks, however, were chosen. Black and Puerto Rican interviewers did the interviewing in Black and Puerto Rican areas, while Whites interviewed White respondents. Validation procedures were followed.

In addition to the unanticipatedly high proportion of respondents claiming to be registered, requiring the adjustments described above to achieve sufficiently large cells of unregistered residents for meaningful analysis, the completed survey contained a smaller proportion of Puerto Ricans (5 per cent) than estimates of Newark's total population would indicate. One-third of the White households were Italian-American, the largest ethnic group in that portion of the sample.

Total households contained in the completed survey had a median total income in the range of $5,000 to $7,000 per year, with 65 per cent of Blacks and 54 per cent of Whites reporting family incomes less than $7,000. Forty-one per cent of Black households in the sample and 34 per cent of Whites reported incomes below $5,000. National data on distribution of income for 1969 show 41 per cent of all Blacks and 18 per cent of all Whites with incomes under $5,000. Thus, the Newark sample conformed exactly to national norms on Black income and produced, as designed, a concentration of low-income Whites. The median income for the sample bordered on the poverty line for Northeastern cities (27 per cent of Blacks and 8 per cent of Whites were receiving welfare).

As a check on reliability, candidate preferences expressed by eligible voters before both the initial and run-off elections were matched against a reconstruction of the actual vote in those precincts in which the survey sample points fell. The margin of difference for the six candidates who remained in the May 12 election averaged less than two percentage points per candidate, with the exception of George Richardson, who scored five points better in the survey than on Election Day, when most of his support shifted to Kenneth Gibson. In the run-off, the margin of difference between the survey results and actual Gibson-Addonizio returns in the survey precincts was 2 per cent, well within the margin of error for a sample of this size.

Chapter Three

THE STATE OF MIND IN THE INNER CITY

Mobility

The residents of Newark's inner core reflected the mobile pattern of urban life in the 1970s. Thirty-nine per cent of the Blacks interviewed in the survey had lived in the city no more than ten years; one out of four had arrived within five years. Low-income Whites were significantly more stable. Forty-four per cent had lived in Newark all their lives and an additional 38 per cent more than ten years.

Two out of every three migrant Blacks had moved to the city from the South and 2 per cent of those in the sample had moved there from Puerto Rico. In the White population, one out of four new arrivals were immigrants from abroad. About half of both Blacks and Whites had moved from other cities and had spent all of their formative years up to the age of eighteen in cities.

The Blacks who had migrated to Newark from the South, however, were markedly less citified than the rest of their Newark neighbors. Over 20 per cent came from rural areas, three times the rate in the White population. As many had lived in small towns as in cities.

A majority of Blacks had moved three or more times during their residency in Newark and nearly one in five had changed housing over five times. Even among Whites, 42 per cent in the central city had moved three or more times during their stay in Newark, although one in four had never moved at all.

This picture of a newly arrived, ever-moving Black population living alongside a relatively permanent but nonetheless internally mobile population of Whites posed the question of how much such factors influenced the rates at which each group chose to register to vote and thus become eligible to participate in the electoral process.

In general, it appeared to make relatively little difference on registration whether one had been brought up in the South or the North or outside the mainland United States. This held for both Blacks and Whites. Those brought up in cities—Black or White—were somewhat less likely to become voters than those who had spent their childhood in nonurban areas. Blacks from the rural South and small-town Whites were more likely to be registered, but the margins were barely significant.

More important than any of these considerations was how long an individual had lived in the city of Newark and, even more markedly, how long he had been in his present neighborhood. Despite the re-registration burden when shifting residence from one part of the city to another, moving, as such, did not emerge as a significant factor in voter registration among those included in this survey.

The following table shows the distribution of the White and Black respondents in this survey according to length of residence. Alongside are the figures showing the distribution of registered voters and unregistered. By comparing the percentages registered against the proportion in the same category for each ethnic group, the registration correspondence can be derived.

It is clear from these figures that length of residence in the city and the neighborhood is positively correlated to the decision to become a registered voter whereas no such distinction can be discerned from the frequency of household movement within the city.

MOBILITY AND REGISTRATION

	White				Black-PR			
	Total	Regis-tered	Unregis-tered	Registration Corres-pond.	Total	Regis-tered	Unregis-tered	Registration Corres-pond.
	%	%	%	%	%	%	%	%
Lived in Newark								
Under 6 years	10	2	24	−8	23	13	33	−10
6 to 10 years	8	5	12	−3	16	17	15	+1
Over 10 years	82	93	64	+11	61	70	52	+9
Lived in Neighborhood								
Under 6 years	26	17	43	−9	63	51	75	−12
6 to 10 years	16	16	18	0	18	22	13	+4
Over 10 years	58	67	39	+9	19	27	12	+8
Number of times moved in Newark								
0 to 2 times	56	56	55	0	42	42	43	0
3 to 5 times	31	31	31	0	38	39	35	+1
Over 5 times	11	10	12	−1	17	17	17	0
Not sure	2	3	2	+1	3	2	5	−1

The sample was evenly split between movers (three or more times) and stable residents (two or fewer moves.) Registration rates did not vary from the norm in either group. On the other hand, very long residence (over ten years) in the city or neighborhood proved to be a definite spur to registration, whereas recency (under six years) was a discouraging factor. The middle range of household stability (six to ten years) seemed to produce only a slightly better than average rate of registration among Blacks and little, even negative, results among Whites.

The relative longevity in Newark and in their home neighborhoods among White residents helps to account for the fact that a higher proportion of Whites than Blacks was qualified to vote in the 1970 election, and that although Whites were outnumbered in the population they maintained a majority among those eligible to vote.

Perceptions of the Power Structure

In an attempt to establish how these inner-city residents perceived the pattern of personal influence in their home neighborhoods, each was read a list of fifteen different types of individuals and organizations during the first wave of interviewing. In each case they were asked: "How important do you feel ――― is/are in influencing what goes on in this neighborhood—very important, somewhat important, or not important at all?"

Political figures—such as mayor and councilman—ranked near the top in importance among Whites, but only in the median ranges among Blacks, who placed ministers or priests, policemen, teachers, landlords, and businessmen at the top of their list of neighborhood influentials. While Whites gave the police and clergy "very important" ratings, along with their mayor and councilman, all others scored poorly. At the bottom of the list for both races were the Mafia, numbers operators, and Black Panthers, although Blacks viewed all three as more important than did Whites.

HOW IMPORTANT IN THIS NEIGHBORHOOD?

	Black-PR		White	
	Very Important	Not Important	Very Important	Not Important
	%	%	%	%
Minister or priest	48	13	30	18
Policemen	42	22	37	19
Teachers	42	20	20	28
Landlords	40	25	17	31
Businessmen	39	21	15	31
Mayor	39	23	40	18
Councilman	35	12	34	16
Democratic Ward Leader	36	15	15	23
Social workers	35	21	15	38
Black and Puerto Rican Convention	33	21	4	47
Insurance companies	32	29	15	37
North Ward Committee	24	32	15	26
Mafia	23	41	5	55
Numbers Operators	19	49	6	41
Black Panthers	15	40	4	60

Registered Black voters, but not Whites, rated politicians as somewhat more important than they were perceived to be by the unregistered.

Political action groups—the Black and Puerto Rican Convention and the predominantly Italian North Ward Citizens Committee—seemed to be discounted by their natural adversaries more than they seemed to be perceived as powers in the community. Only 2 per cent of the Italians surveyed thought the Black and Puerto Rican Convention "very important"; the North Ward Citizens Committee was judged "not important at all" by 55

PERCEPTION OF POLITICIANS

	Black-PR		White	
	Regis-tered	Unregis-tered	Regis-tered	Unregis-tered
	%	%	%	%
Mayor				
very important	42	35	40	40
Councilman				
very important	39	36	34	34

per cent of those who said they intended to vote for Kenneth Gibson during the first round of balloting.

The role of the church in the social action of the ghetto, as well as the intensity of such issues as crime, education, housing, welfare, and economics, are reflected in these judgments. At the same time, the temptation to overstate the alienation of the poor, and the Black poor especially, from the political system should be resisted.

Hopes for the Future

Respondents were asked to react to a theme sometimes reiterated in the mass media: "No matter who is elected, Newark is a dead city." One in five agreed with that statement, but three times as many disagreed. Among registered Blacks and Puerto Ricans, 72 per cent said "no" to that idea, compared with 66 per cent of registered Whites. Nonparticipants in the voting process mustered a clear majority, nonetheless, against total pessimism about Newark's future after Election Day.

Making allowance for local pride—an American phenomenon encompassing even Newark—respondents were given two other opportunities to evaluate their personal stake in the mayoralty contest when they were asked to agree or disagree with these statements:

1) "If the election turns out right, I might be better off."

2) "No matter who is elected, nothing is going to get better for me".

This graph indicates their feelings.

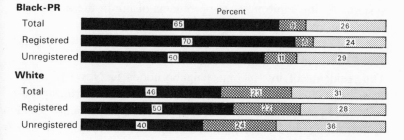

"MIGHT BE BETTER OFF"

Black-PR   Percent
Total   65   9   26
Registered   70   6   24
Unregistered   60   11   29

White
Total   46   23   31
Registered   50   22   28
Unregistered   40   24   36

"NOTHING GOING TO GET BETTER"

Black-PR   Percent
Total   19   63   18
Registered   14   69   17
Unregistered   24   56   20

White
Total   37   43   20
Registered   36   44   20
Unregistered   39   40   21

Agree   Disagree   Not sure

The most interesting aspect of these reciprocally consistent figures is the fact that Blacks much more than Whites expressed optimism about a better life for themselves in the future. Although registered Blacks were considerably more hopeful than unregistered Blacks, both were more positive about their prospects than the low-income Whites in the sample.

Italians felt particularly discouraged, as did those over fifty years of age. Among whites, the differences in outlook between the registered and unregistered were less pronounced than for Blacks and Puerto Ricans.

Even in the despairing circumstances of poverty, social tension, and political corruption it could not be said that the residents of Newark were yet prepared to give up on the democratic system. At the same time, the problems of life in the inner city registered vividly on their collective consciousness.

The Problems Mentioned Voluntarily

The residents of low-income neighborhoods in Newark in the Spring of 1970 found little difficulty in thinking of "serious problems facing people like yourself that the city government should do something about." The pattern of spontaneous replies to that question was broad and varied: better police protection against robberies and muggings; more effective control of the sale of drugs and better programs for the rehabilitation of drug addicts; improved housing and lower rents; newer schools with more competent and understanding teachers; cleaning up the litter and junk from city streets and vacant lots; more efficient and frequent garbage collection; air pollution control; expanded job opportunities plus the training necessary to qualify for good jobs; better race relations; and elimination of political corruption from Newark's city government.

The roster of Newark's urban problems as volunteered by these residents of the inner city was a litany of inadequate public services—each requiring vast new expenditures of public funds from a barren city treasury. Paradoxically, the public demand for these services was accompanied at the same time by a widespread demand for lower taxes. Aside from the special local factor involving charges of corruption in the awarding of municipal contracts, the urban dilemma in Newark was similar to that in metropolitan centers across the nation—a populace groaning under the burden of rising local taxes but frustrated and dissatisfied over the quality of the essentials of life.

The saliency and intensity of Newark's problems were viewed

differently in the White and minority communities, although there was common agreement among all races that crime, drugs, and public safety on the streets were top priority items on Newark's political agenda.

Among Blacks, however, housing inadequacies ranked even higher than the desire for more police protection. Among Whites, the issue of safety in the streets far outstripped all others, but in second place, rather surprisingly, came a substantial level of dissatisfaction with ineffective removal of garbage, litter, and abandoned cars, as well as concern with the whole question of municipal filth and pollution. Blacks and Whites stood together on this issue, suggesting that whoever was eventually elected Mayor of Newark might enjoy an opportunity to take dramatic action in this area, which would cut across ethnic divisions in the city, as indeed would a bold shakeup of a police department held at a low ebb in public confidence.

The urge to cut taxes and control spending was present in all racial groups, but significantly higher among Whites, even though the sample was drawn from the lower end of the White income spectrum. In the Slavic and Italian neighborhoods of Newark's inner city, home ownership, and thus real estate tax liability, was common even among families of comparatively modest incomes. One out of every three Italian-Americans interviewed volunteered that taxes were a serious personal problem. There was obviously a great deal of political potential present if some future city administration could shift some of the tax burden to the daytime army of workers who came to jobs in downtown Newark. And the backlash on taxes and welfare costs was by no means an exclusively White phenomenon in Newark.

Concern over the state of Newark's schools and the extent of job opportunities was primarily centered in the Black and Puerto Rican community. The corruption issue—involving Black members of the City Council as well as the White incumbent mayor—triggered more reaction among Whites than among non-Whites. This was a reflection, perhaps, of the cynicism of the

SERIOUS PROBLEMS FACING NEWARK

	Total	Black-PR	White
Public Safety	%	%	%
More police protection on streets	28	24	36
Crack down on drugs	15	16	12
More drug treatment	7	9	3
Too many robberies and muggings	7	6	9
More law and order	3	1	4
Better relations with police	2	3	2
Total	62	59	66
Housing			
Better housing conditions	28	35	14
Lower rent/more low income	14	18	6
Build more, more quickly	13	18	4
Total	55	71	24
Education			
More schools, improve	14	17	8
Better teachers	8	9	6
More recreation areas	5	6	3
Total	27	32	17

ghetto. A future mayor would need to employ some dramatic symbol of public rectitude to convince people in Newark that honest government was in fact within the realm of the possible. Those Whites who said they intended to vote for Kenneth Gibson, moreover, mentioned corruption twice as often as did the general run of Whites interviewed. These same voters—Black or White—were the most sensitive of all about the need for better public safety and cleaner streets.

Voluntary mention of racial tensions was comparatively small in light of Newark's history of riot as well as vigilante organiza-

SERIOUS PROBLEMS FACING NEWARK —(Continued)

	Total	Black-PR	White
Sanitation	%	%	%
Clean up streets, move abandoned cars, garbage and litter	20	19	24
Improve sanitation department	4	4	4
Stop pollution	1	1	2
Total	25	24	30
Taxes and Spending			
Lower taxes	13	9	22
Cut welfare	3	2	6
Total	16	11	28
Jobs			
More and better jobs	12	17	3
Better training centers	3	4	1
Total	15	21	4
Other Issues			
Race relations	9	7	12
Corruption in government	8	7	11
More welfare	3	4	3
Control kids	2	3	1
Total	22	21	27

tion. The subject ranked well down on the list of things persons were willing to talk about. We shall return later to the question of the extent and severity of the racial polarization in Newark during this election contest between White and Black candidates in an ethnically divided city.

"Big Problem" vs. "No Problem"
As an additional measure of local issues during the early stages of the campaign, those interviewed before the May election were asked to rate a series of statements about life in Newark as a

"big," "little," or "no problem" at all to them personally. The results correlated closely with spontaneous expressions volunteered without such prompting.

HOW MUCH A PERSONAL PROBLEM?

	"Big Problem"		"No Problem"	
	Blacks-PR	Whites	Blacks-PR	Whites
	%	%	%	%
Going out on the streets at night	65	66	18	22
How much you pay in taxes	61	64	17	21
Getting a decent place to live in	71	35	16	51
Urban renewal and new highways that force people out of their neighborhood	61	30	18	52
Getting a good education for the children	59	40	17	40
Getting a good job	56	21	24	62
Feeling you are not represented in the city government	49	33	19	41
Being treated like a human being	38	15	35	64
Getting along with other people in this city	24	12	49	71

The pattern of replies to these closed-end statements confirmed the relevance of the public safety and tax issues to Blacks and

Whites alike. As can be seen from the figures above, Blacks were deeply concerned and Whites less so with problems of housing, relocation, and jobs. Education was rated a "big" problem by a three-to-one margin among Blacks, while Whites were evenly split over whether it was a big problem or no problem at all.

Those questions touching upon human relationships triggered relatively milder reactions than the bread-and-butter controversies of life. Nearly half of the Blacks and Puerto Ricans conceded strong feelings of being "unrepresented" in city government as opposed to only one in five who dismissed representation as a problem. They split down the middle over whether they felt problems about "being treated like a human being." Whites, on the other hand, divided most evenly over the representativeness of City Hall, but tended to dismiss the issue of being treated with dignity.

Both Blacks and Whites expressed faith in their ability to get along with other people in the city of Newark, Whites even more emphatically than non-Whites. Those under thirty in the sample were least optimistic in this regard, 29 per cent saying it was a "big problem" as opposed to only 15 per cent of those over fifty years of age. At the other end of the scale, 65 per cent of those over fifty saw no problem, as opposed to 41 per cent under thirty. Income or education had only minor influence on such attitudes in comparison with the negative effect of being Black or, more particularly, being young and Black.

These same young, at the same time, felt most strongly about being "unrepresented," about not being treated as human beings, and about their frustration over lack of jobs and decent housing.

Polarization

The cross-pressures between people's problems and the ability of the political machinery to deliver needed services were intensified by the facts that the electorate was divided nearly in half by racial background and that the final choice for mayor rested between a White incumbent and a Black challenger. How much did these factors polarize opinion in Newark beyond the moderate levels indicated in the previous data?

White and Black respondents were asked on both waves of interviewing to respond to each of the following questions:

"If a White candidate is elected mayor, do you feel both Whites and Blacks will get equal treatment from Newark's city government, or do you feel Whites will get better treatment than Blacks?"

"If a Black candidate is elected mayor, do you feel both Blacks and Whites will get equal treatment from Newark's city government, or do you feel Blacks will get better treatment than Whites?"

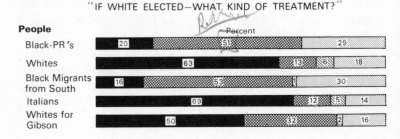

"IF WHITE ELECTED—WHAT KIND OF TREATMENT?"

People	Equal treatment	Blacks better	Whites better	Not sure
Black-PR's	20	51		29
Whites	63	13	6	18
Black Migrants from South	16	53	1	30
Italians	69	12	5	14
Whites for Gibson	50	32	2	16

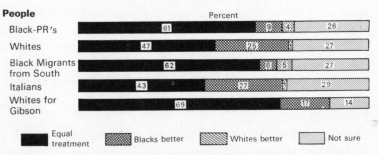

"IF BLACK ELECTED—WHAT KIND OF TREATMENT?"

People	Equal treatment	Blacks better	Whites better	Not sure
Black-PR's	61	9	4	26
Whites	47	25	1	27
Black Migrants from South	62	6	5	27
Italians	43	27	1	29
Whites for Gibson	69	17		14

■ Equal treatment　▨ Blacks better　▧ Whites better　□ Not sure

The questions showed that a relatively high proportion—about one in four—could not give a firm answer on how the races might fare depending on whether a Black or White was elected. But Whites registered overwhelmingly their conviction that a White Mayor would treat all races equally while Blacks felt equally strongly that a Black mayor would do the same. When asked to judge a mayor of a race different from their own, however, there were interesting differences in the attitudes expressed.

Whites generally expressed more confidence in the racial impartiality of a Black mayor than did Blacks about a White mayor, By better than two-to-one, 51 per cent to 20 per cent, more Blacks and Puerto Ricans said Whites would get better than equal treatment under a White mayor. By nearly two-to-one, 47 to 25 per cent, most Whites said a Black mayor would treat all alike rather than favor members of his own race.

The relative disposition of Whites to trust a Black mayor was even more pronounced among those Whites (54 cases) who favored Kenneth Gibson, the Black candidate, in the election. On the other hand, Blacks who had been brought up in the South (462 cases) were the least confident in a chief executive of another race. Italian-Americans (137 cases) were most sure of Mayor Addonizio's fairness toward Blacks, although 12 per cent conceded Whites might get a better than even break from an Administration headed by him.

One would have to conclude either that Blacks were more frank in their distrust, or equated their problems with the fact of a White incumbent, whereas Whites had less to lose from discrimination in a situation which was as yet only theoretical. Mayor Addonizio had indeed gone out of his way to give highly visible representation to some Black politicians, but rank-and-file members of the Black and Puerto Rican communities were largely unimpressed. The comparatively bland personality of Kenneth Gibson may have lacked charisma in Black precincts, but it was reassuring to at least some Whites contemplating the consequences of a Black takeover in City Hall.

Since Blacks felt more intensely about such gut issues as housing, education, and jobs than did Whites, and since the prospect of a Black mayor in Newark was only recently a practical possibility, it was understandable that the Black and Puerto Rican communities should rally their perceptions as well as their hopes around a symbol of Black political power. To that degree it would be fair to say that Blacks in Newark were polarized by the 1970 election.

Although the whites represented in this survey came from low-income areas, were not highly educated, and included a generous proportion of blue-collar workers of Italian, Irish, Polish, and similar ethnic origins, their antagonism toward the idea of a Black mayor was confined to a minority. Whites were only slightly more concerned than Blacks and Puerto Ricans over the lack of safety in Newark streets, and all felt discouraged over the rising cost to the taxpayer of inadequate municipal services. In these White households of the central city, where contact between the races was most frequent, the so-called backlash within polarized segments of White society was less than one might have been led to expect from treatises about hard-hats or White ethnic America.

This is not to say that White Newark was ready to flock aboard the campaign trucks of the Black candidate for mayor. But neither was the stage set for a monolithic clash between the races. Civic pride still flickered, even among the povery-stricken. A certain faith in the system and one's neighbors managed to prevail, despite the pall of corruption and violence. Those willing and able to participate in the political process looked forward with some degree of anticipation to the possibility of better days for Newark.

Chapter Four

THE ELECTORAL PROCESS

In theory, the political process in the United States is a system of participatory democracy. Authority is supposed to rest on the consent of the governed. Representatives are periodically held to account at the polls. The franchise is universally distributed among the great mass of the populace.

The institutions of government are expected to expedite the free flow of information so that the electorate can intelligently appraise their performance. The citizen not only enjoys the right to vote for candidates for local, state, and federal office, but he is also free to engage actively in the organization and direction of political parties. He is encouraged to communicate his views on public policy to all levels of government.

Frequently voters are asked to serve in an advisory capacity to public officials or public agencies, to study policy problems and to make recommendations, or to assemble expert opinion outside the corridors of the governing bureaucracy. Even more frequently, voters organize themselves into groups to advocate and press particular interests upon the centers of power. The resultant picture is that of a citizenry in charge of the state and engaged in the rational exchange of diverse views until a consensus can be ratified by a working majority of the total populace at the polls.

The assumptions beneath this appealing structure are not always made explicit and are sometimes glossed over without reference to the realities. One reason is that the image of participatory democracy, if true, is so highly complimentary not only to individual egos but also to the legitimacy of those who hold power. Paradoxically, it is also the perennial rallying slogan of newcomers to the political scene who seek to overturn those in command of the government. If one is supremely convinced of the rectitude of one's cause, then participatory democracy is certain to deliver victory to the deserving. When this fails to happen the flaw must be in the performance of the system rather than the conviction. Thus, all energy is directed toward energizing hitherto passive and indifferent citizens to make themselves felt in the arena of politics.

There is an intellectual school which argues that this is a very dangerous notion. Millions of Americans, they point out, do not care enough about most elections to bother going to the polls, even though permitted and persuaded to register. These occasional participators, studies have shown, tend to have the least knowledge about candidates and issues. As a group they have low exposure to citizen activity of any kind and much less political experience. Their education is below average, their social disorganization above average. Where that is not the case, they are often so preoccupied by business or personal affairs, so withdrawn by temperament, so alienated from the dominant values of our society, that they cannot truly by reached by rational discourse. Thus, when they do exercise their franchise, they are likely to be motivated by emotional appeals or swayed by demagoguery. Since active participants in politics are the most stable in their long-term party loyalties, the argument runs, the pendulum between victory and defeat is swung by the indifferent and uninformed who sporadically take part in elections.

The logic of this type of analysis would suggest that the public interest is actually better served by the selective participation in politics of the most educated, most active, most "qualified" of the potential electorate. The effort to register the unregistered or activate the apathetic to go to the polls is seen in this context as a counter-productive, even dangerous, form of political meddling.

The egalitarian ideal of the American tradition makes such an argument unpalatable. If all men were indeed created equal, the fact that some appear to be more equal than others is an unsatisfactory hypothesis for perpetuating the unequal distribution of power. Who is to say that the radical zealot with a Ph.D. is a more sensible voter than a field hand in Mississippi whose life may be threatened for the expression of the simplest freedoms? Or a less sensible one? A Nobel Prize in physics carries no guarantee of competent insights into the complexities of foreign policy any more than a childhood of poverty and discrimination has precluded the development of exquisite talent in literature, art, and music. The measurement of political behavior is necessarily subjective. The definition of a "qualified" voter depends largely on the image of politics possessed by the person making the definition.

In practice, the political process in the United States varies enormously from the hypothetical model of a participatory democracy. Suffrage is not universal. The institutional arrangements for becoming eligible to vote are biased in favor of a mercantile ethic of individual enterprise, bolstered by a Protestant conscience and a middle-class sense of civic duty.

The state takes minimum initiatives to keep the voting rolls congruent with the eligible adult population. Only comparatively recently in the United States did the courts intervene to reorder representative constituencies on the principle of one man-one vote, as opposed to systems which permitted certain groups an influence beyond their true proportion of the electorate. Even so, the United States Senate and the Electoral College, neither of which was designed to carry out one man-one vote assumptions, have remained beyond the reach of judicial reform.

The system of checks and balances written into federal and

state constitutions was no accident. The presumption behind some of the oldest American political institutions is that full-blown popular democracy contains reckless possibilities, and not the least of the enemies of freedom might be a tyranny of the masses.

This contradiction between the democratic and federalist ideals in the American political experience has complicated the question of universal participation. The elitist conception of an educated voting public, with ample time and means to pursue politics as an avocation and sufficient security to insulate itself against unworthy emotions, is simply out of touch with reality. It was never true, even for the favored classes.

Self-interest has frequently triumphed over social responsibility within the psyche of the well-to-do voter in the voting booth. Prejudice is no respecter of status. Education does not guarantee intellectual awareness throughout life, much less growth. But the mythology that government is controlled by a rational, conscientious, well-informed, politically competent public has been a powerful instrument for resisting changes in the rules. If bureaucracy and legislative or executive power are controlled at all—and doubts on this score have achieved growing currency—it is not by the people directly. Should it be? To ask the question is un-American, so strong are the forces of political socialization.

It is not, but it should be, is the conventional reply—subject to certain limitations. Criminals, of course, should not have the right to vote (although the incidence of crime convictions falls unequally in different sectors of society). The illiterate, of course, should be barred (although television and radio have become prime media of political communication). One should live a specified period of time where one votes (although there is little connection between higher offices and neighborhood residence, and the vote falls off sharply the more local the contest). Then there is the question of age (although in some cultures family responsibilities begin in the early teens and in our own there is vast disagreement over when one is old enough to drive, to drink, to marry, or be accountable for one's acts).

Such are the formal limitations. The practical limitations are more subtle.

If casting a vote is the most elemental form of political participation, and if one collects data on who does and does not vote in America, those most often outside the system are the poor, the non-White, the young, and the uneducated. Nonparticipators may belong to one or all of these groups. That is not to say that there are not large numbers of nonparticipators in other groups in our society, but the proportions are significantly larger among these.

There is nothing in the rhetoric of American democracy to condone the idea that the public interest might be served by the deliberate exclusion of voters possessing any one of these attributes. Even when the rules of registration are administered to effectively bar non-Whites, the action is usually rationalized by other arguments.

The social costs of excluding individuals from the political process—directly or indirectly—are the principal arguments against elitist theories of participation. They were documented by the urban riots and campus confrontations that shook the nation in the late 1960s and early 1970s. For the process of selective participation carries within it the seeds of its own destruction.

As long as great segments of the population do not take part in the formal expression of popular participation, their sense of involvement will be minimal. It is not clear whether apathy is the cause or effect of this lack of involvement. Those who are frustrated by the lack of success of conventional methods to spur voter interest among the unregistered poor and unregistered minorities are often harsh in their criticism of the habits and values of the underclasses. But is it really so illogical that urban slum dwellers, enveloped by inferior housing and inadequate schools, beset by crime and political corruption, should take a dim view of the chances of one individual to alter these conditions by choosing between the type of party candidates usually offered on Election Day?

Appeals to the citizen's duty to vote in terms comparable to the pledge of allegiance to the flag are a further reflection of specialized social values, appropriate to the sustenance of a life style foreign to many of the less-favored members of society.

Even a seemingly relevant issue, such as the election of community school board members in New York City following a year of militant confrontations over experimental, decentralized schools, failed to attract as many as two in ten eligible voters, not including the thousands of poverty-area parents who did not bother to register. The slogans of participatory democracy and community control likewise proved to be empty of meaning when applied to small-scale elections for neighborhood poverty boards. The low turnouts in these localized models of representative elections squarely contradicted the civics-book image of the nation-wide political process. And the victories scored by well-organized interest groups in the midst of generalized indifference were only more intense and conspicuous examples of the true nature of American politics.

Popular democracy, even among the selective percentages who go to the polls, is never a matter of 51 per cent monolithically behind a single issue winning a sharply defined victory over the 49 per cent solidly opposed. The truism needs to be restated because so much of the dialogue of democracy infers otherwise.

The mosaic of voting behavior in an actual election can be exposed by the techniques of public opinion research, which is keener at carving out the elements than predicting the result with actual certainty. Ironically, the most troublesome problem of the polls is the question of turnout. Who among those interviewed will actually cast a ballot on Election Day? Thus, selective participation, even among a screened sample of more or less reliable voters, weakens our powers of observation into the dynamics of the election process.

If one could be sure why some register and some do not, why

some turn out to vote and some do not, we not only would better understand the subtle relationship between the individual and politics in our society, but also might be more effective in expanding voter participation.

Most of the arguments urging the superiority of those who do participate in the electoral process do not stand the test of analysis through research into individual attitudes and behavior. The level of information of the most informed voters is not very high by objective standards. The influence of ethnic background, family upbringing, and party inheritance is enormous in comparison to the flow of political debate. The choices in a given situation are rarely clearcut, and the decision to vote for particular candidates can be highly irrational, even at the highest levels of education and experience.

If all this is true, the mystique of selective participation evaporates. Instead, all we know is that the biases inherent among some groups in our society are more systematically represented at the polls than those of the nonparticipators. Low turnout at the polls, as a general rule, was long thought to favor the more conservative side in American elections, as it contributed to the upset Tory victory over Labour in the 1970 British Parliamentary elections. In America, Democratic party faith in this proposition was badly shaken by the low-turnout (53 per cent) victory of Harry Truman over Thomas E. Dewey and the high-turnout (63 per cent) victory of Dwight D. Eisenhower over Adlai E. Stevenson.

Farmers, usually conservative but subject to historical fits of populism, are traditionally among the lowest participators on Election Day. It would be fair to say that the ideological effect of low turnout cannot be predicted with certainty and varies according to the particular situation.

The more significant fact is that the number of nonvoters in the 1968 Presidential election (47 million), for example, was higher than the total number of votes (32 million) cast for the winning candidate. The theoretical possibility, therefore, presents itself that the disfranchised could totally alter the character of American politics if they went to the polls with organized intent.

The drawing power of this idea has resulted in active voting drives in recent years among ethnic groups who enjoy a majority among the local population but are only a minority at the polls because of nonparticipation: Mexican-Americans in southern Texas, Blacks in the urban centers and rural counties of the Deep South, Puerto Ricans and Blacks in some of the largest Northern cities.

Funds to encourage the expansion of the voting rolls have been contributed by labor unions, foundations, civil-rights groups, citizens organizations, and individual candidates for office, as well as political parties where it was judged to be in their interest to add new voters from the ranks of the nonparticipators.

Evaluations of the success or failure of such efforts have been relatively slim. Their impact upon election politics has been obscured by the crosscurrents present in every contest.

The 1970 mayoralty election in Newark promised to be one that might actually be decided by changes in the normal patterns of participation. The success or failure of a Black candidate running for the city's top office was thought by some to depend on his ability to reverse the nonregistration and low turnout customarily observed in the Black precincts of the inner city. However, gains in participation among Black voters could conceivably be canceled out if White voters turned out in larger than normal numbers to resist the idea of a Black chief executive.

As mentioned previously, an elaborate program for the activation of the Black vote had been in preparation for at least two years prior to the 1970 campaign. However, the flight of White voters to the suburbs had caused a steady shrinkage of the total number of eligibles on Newark's voting rolls.

Previous Participation

The rate of participation in previous elections among inner-city residents of Newark in this survey was conspicuously low. Bearing in mind that the difficulty of locating unregistered voters made the latter under-represented in the sample, only 44 per cent of those interviewed claimed to have voted the previous year in the election for New Jersey's governor. Only 52 per cent claimed to have voted in the 1968 Presidential election. Only 43 per cent claimed to have voted in the previous election for mayor in 1966.

Generally speaking, the rates of participation in these elections were highest among those over fifty years of age, with the most education and highest incomes. Men voted at a slightly higher rate than women. Whites voted in significantly higher proportions than Blacks.

These are the reported turnout figures among those currently registered to vote.

VOTER TURNOUT

	1969 Guber- natorial	1968 Presi- dential	1966 Mayoralty
	%	%	%
Registered Blacks and Puerto Ricans	73	81	63
Registered Whites	79	89	78

It is interesting to note that Black turnout dropped approximately ten percentage points at each step as the contest dropped from national, to statewide, to local in scope. The trend repeated itself among Whites, comparing Presidential and gubernatorial turnouts, but then leveled out so that the proportion voting for mayor in 1966 nearly equalled that for the 1969 contest for governor. Normally, therefore, the higher rate of participation among White voters in state and national elections (six to eight percentage points) nearly doubled (fifteen percentage points) when the contest was strictly local.

Political Fragmentation

Politically, the party preference expressed by both Blacks and Puerto Ricans and Whites in those low-income neighborhoods was overwhelmingly Democratic. (The Democratic advantage over Republicans was five to one among Whites and ten to one among Blacks.) And yet the 1969 margin of the Democratic candidate for governor, Robert Meyner, over Republican William Cahill in those precincts had been substantially less than three to one, a pattern contributing to Meyner's statewide defeat. White voters claimed to have cast their ballot for the Republican by a margin of 61 to 39 per cent, while Black voters went Democratic in that election 72 to 28 per cent.

As has been noted already, the White population in the low-income, Newark neighborhoods included in this survey contained a heavy proportion of what are described as White ethnic Americans. Those who said their grandparents had been born abroad mentioned these countries:

Italy	31%
Spain or Portugal	14%
Poland	10%
Ireland	10%
Other Eastern European	6%
Germany	5%

In 1968 these White ethnics indicated how they voted ("not sures" excluded).

Nixon	53%
Humphrey	35%
Wallace	12%
Total	100%

The swing to Nixon and defection to Wallace among voters who classified themselves overwhelmingly as Democrats were signs of the fragmentation of traditional party loyalties going on among White ethnics in Newark. In the same election, Blacks in our sample said how they had voted ("not sures" excluded).

Nixon	13%
Humphrey	85%
Wallace	2%
Total	*100%*

Whatever the reasons, it is apparent that these neighbors were beginning to divide their political loyalties sharply along racial lines. The "nonpartisan" format of the election for mayor (only one of the original seven candidates was a registered Republican, and all ran as individuals without party labels) meant that these tendencies would need to find other means of expression in the 1970 contest under review here.

Italian-Americans had been voting more heavily Republican than the average White (five points higher for Cahill and Nixon), particularly older voters. Although three Black candidates originally offered themselves in the race for mayor, by coincidence the list of those running also included the identical number of candidates from Italian-American backgrounds. The inherent polarization between the two largest ethnic groups involved was to be somewhat fragmented in the first round of voting by this roster of choices (although, as we shall see, Black voters solidified more around Gibson than did White voters choosing among Addonizio, Imperiale, and Matturi).

By happenstance, the seventh candidate, John P. Caufield, was White and Irish-American, occupying a potential mediating position between the confronting Black and Italian-American candidates. Since Irish-Americans represented a dwindling portion of the Newark electorate, Caufield's chances depended on his ability to attract support from both Whites and Blacks. If he were eliminated in the first round, Caufield's support—occupying the bridging area between the Black and Italian-

American voting blocs—might well prove to be the crucial factor in the run-off election.

Registration Factors

The question of who would and who would not be eligible to vote in the Newark election was a matter of prime interest to the managers of all the candidates involved. The exact ethnic composition of the potential electorate was clouded by the fact that it had been ten years since the previous U.S. census. The overall population of Newark had dropped from 439,000 in 1950 to an estimated 402,000 in 1970. Official registration in the city had stood at 136,861 for the Presidential election of 1968, compared with 161,326 for the 1960 election. At the time of the 1969 gubernatorial race, the list of eligibles was down to 130,223, as compared with the 153,373 who had been eligible to vote for mayor of Newark in 1966.

Morris Wurgast, then Deputy Commissioner of Registration for Essex County, estimated that of the city's non-Whites not more than half were over twenty-one years of age, and of these only 50 per cent had registered to vote. Although, according to some, Blacks and Puerto Ricans together constituted perhaps as much as 70 per cent of the city's 1970 population, the actual vote at the polls was 55 per cent White. Hence, a high priority to voter registration had been a key component of the strategy of the Black and Puerto Rican coalition behind Kenneth Gibson.

In view of the fact that the Black and Puerto Rican population was, on the whole, much younger in its general composition than that of Whites, its registration potential was handicapped on two counts. First, a disporportionate share of the minority-group population in Newark was under twenty-one, and therefore too young to qualify in 1970. Second, the data collected in this survey showed that the youngest age group, twenty-one to twenty-nine years, was least inclined to register.

The pattern exhibited by males in the age groups above shows that the highest rate of nonregistration among both Blacks and

AGE AND REGISTRATION (MALE)

	Black-PR	Regis-tered	Un-regis-tered	White	Regis-tered	Un-regis-tered
	%	%	%	%	%	%
21 to 29	16	9	22	9	7	13
30 to 34	7	8	6	4	3	4
35 to 39	6	7	6	5	3	9
40 to 49	8	9	8	9	10	7
50 to 64	9	10	8	15	16	14
65 and over	4	7	1	11	12	8

Whites was in the under-thirty group, but that this was a substantially higher percentage of the total Black universe than of the total White universe. From age thirty to age sixty-five among Blacks, the rate of registration remains more or less constant. For Whites, age forty is a milestone where the disposition to register begins to accelerate, reaching its peak in the age group between fifty and sixty-five.

Sex does not seem to alter this general pattern.

AGE AND REGISTRATION (FEMALE)

	Black-PR	Regis-tered	Un-regis-tered	White	Regis-tered	Un-regis-tered
	%	%	%	%	%	%
21 to 29	16	12	20	9	5	14
30 to 34	8	8	8	5	5	5
35 to 39	7	7	6	4	3	5
40 to 49	9	10	7	10	9	8
50 to 64	6	7	5	11	17	4
65 and over	4	4	3	9	10	8

The figures for both sexes in the two key groups were combined.

AGE AND REGISTRATION (MALE AND FEMALE COMBINED)

	Black-PR	Registered	Unregistered	White	Registered	Unregistered
	%	%	%	%	%	%
21 to 29	32	21	42	18	12	27
40 to 65	32	36	28	45	52	33

Thus, roughly one-third of Blacks and Puerto Ricans fall into the under-thirty age group, but more than 40 per cent of the unregistered Blacks in the Newark sample were under thirty. Forty-five per cent of Whites but only one-third of Blacks were between forty and sixty-five, the ages at which registered voters of both races were more highly concentrated. This registration deficit among young members of minority groups is accentuated by the fact that of those eligible to vote it is also the youngest who turn out to vote in poorest proportions.

For purposes of comparison the sample was divided according to a series of key characteristics, and then those who were registered or unregistered and those who had not voted in the past were examined according to these atrributes: sex; race; those who had completed a high-school education or beyond; those who had not gone beyond the fifth grade; women with children under eighteen in the household; individuals with a family income under $3,000; those over fifty years of age and those under thirty. The number of cases in each category is indicated by the table.

Although some of the under-thirty group were not eligible to vote in earlier elections, it is clear that the cells divided according to the oldest and youngest age brackets seemed to show the most significant variations from the overall averages for the respondents interviewed in this survey.

Age also appeared to be the more decisive factor when compared with income or education in determining the extent of participation in the electoral process. When registered and nonregis-

NUMBER OF CASES IN KEY CATEGORIES

Category	Number of Cases
Overall	1,244
Black-PR	828
Whites	416
Men	609
Women	635
5th grade or less	130
High school or beyond	440
Women with children under 18	348
Under $3,000	185
Under 30	300
Over 50	404

Of all these characteristics, the factor of age seemed to be the most important variable as far as variations in the rate of registration or voting were concerned.

VARIATIONS IN RATE OF REGISTRATION

	Percent	Variation
Overall average	54	—
Men	53	−1
Women	55	+1
Black-PR*	50	—
White*	60	—
5th grade or less	48	−6
High school or beyond	60	+6
Women with children under 18	49	−5
Under $3,000	49	−5
Under 30	35	−19
Over 50	68	+14

*Weighted according to independent estimates of proportion on Newark's roll of registered voters.

VARIATIONS IN RATE OF VOTING (PERCENT OF TOTAL SAMPLE)

	1969 Guberna-torial	1968 Presi-dential	1966 Mayor-alty	Total Election Variation
	%	%	%	%
Overall average	44	52	43	0
Men	45	54	44	+1
Women	43	51	41	−2
Black-PR	41	50	38	−5
White	50	55	51	+8
5th grade or less	37	42	34	−9
High school or beyond	48	56	46	+3
Women with children under 18	41	49	36	−7
Under $3,000	38	46	42	−1
Under 30	21	28	16	−27
Over 50	60	66	60	+17

tered persons were analyzed by various demographic categories, the proportions of registered could not be matched in each case against the average for the appropriate ethnic group as a whole.

The distribution of income among Blacks, Puerto Ricans, and Whites in this sample of Newark's inner-city residents was not dramatically different. At the lower end of the economic scale, registration was somewhat more restricted among Blacks but not among Whites. Being on relief, however, was associated with lower rates of registration among both Blacks and Whites. Registration fell off among Whites in the middle range and improved somwhat at incomes above $10,000 a year. Improved income seemed to have the most positive effect on Blacks once they achieved an income of $5,000. But as an independent variable, income alone did not seem to be a determinant of the decision to register.

The graph also illustrates that the Black high-school dropout was more likely to be unregistered in comparison to his share

INCOME AND REGISTRATION

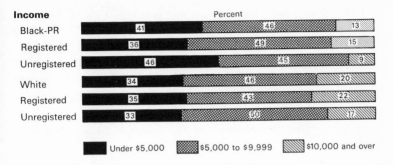

Income

Percent

Black-PR	41	46	13
Registered	36	49	15
Unregistered	46	45	9
White	34	46	20
Registered	35	43	22
Unregistered	33	50	17

■ Under $5,000   ▨ $5,000 to $9,999   ⧄ $10,000 and over

EDUCATION AND REGISTRATION

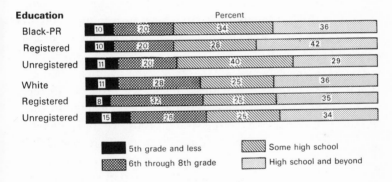

Education

Percent

Black-PR	10	20	34	36
Registered	10	20	28	42
Unregistered	11	20	40	29
White	11	28	25	36
Registered	8	32	25	35
Unregistered	15	26	25	34

■ 5th grade and less   ⧄ Some high school
▨ 6th through 8th grade   ▦ High school and beyond

MARITAL STATUS AND REGISTRATION

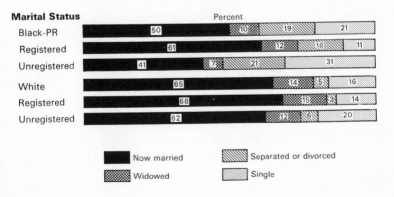

Marital Status

Percent

Black-PR	50	10	19	21
Registered	61	12	16	11
Unregistered	41	7	21	31
White	65	14	5	16
Registered	68	15	3	14
Unregistered	62	12	6	20

■ Now married   ⧄ Separated or divorced
▨ Widowed   ▦ Single

of the population than even those with a very minimum of schooling. Those with at least a high-school diploma registered only slightly more often than their relative share. For Whites, low registration was most likely among those who had stopped school before the sixth grade. Among Whites still living in these low-income neighborhoods in Newark, however, educational levels were actually somewhat inferior to those achieved by Blacks and Puerto Ricans beyond the fifth grade. The few college-educated Whites in the sample had a poor rate of registration, a situation opposite to that for Blacks and the national trends generally.

Other variables included in the analysis suggested that marital status combined with age might have significant effects upon the decision to register. Not only did single persons, Blacks especially, exhibit a relative disinclination to take part in the electoral process, but when family units have been broken up by divorce or separation there was also a negative impact upon the proportion who registered.

The foregoing data indicate that two of the significant variables affecting the disposition of these inner-city residents to register—age and marital status—are more or less immune to short-term drives to increase the registration rolls. There is obviously a relationship between the assumption of family responsibilities and the perception of politics as a relevant activity. The relatively high rate of family breakups among Blacks reported in this survey is, of course, a reflection of the social disorganization that accompanies the life of the urban poor. This, combined with the relative youth of the Black population, thus creates a double blockage operating against voting registration efforts among minority group members in the urban environment.

It has sometimes been speculated that the presence of young children in the home, draining the energies of the mother, is another negative influence on registration. Over a third of the women in this sample had four or more children under the age of eighteen; 13 per cent had six or more. And yet the rates of voter registration among these women did not vary from the norm, positively or negatively, no matter how many children they had.

Respondents in the survey were asked to listen to a series of statements about politics and then to tell the interviewer whether they thought each statement was completely true, partly true, or not true at all. Here is the breakdown of replies to the statement: "By the time I take care of my everyday problems, I don't have much energy left to think about politics."

"DON'T HAVE MUCH ENERGY FOR POLITICS"

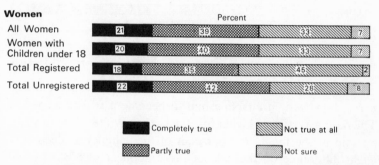

A substantial majority (six out of ten), it should be noted, admitted that the everyday burdens of life in Newark's low-income neighborhoods were an impediment to their ability to think about politics. At that level of physical and emotional debilitation, the problems of child-rearing were not the crucial difference. On the other hand, there was a definite correlation between those who were less inclined to complain about their lack of energy and those who had taken the trouble to register to vote.

The relationship between such attitudes about politics generally and participation in the political system is a matter to which this study will return later in some detail.

Patterns of Influence: Political Party
Whether or not persons interviewed in the survey identified them-

selves with a political party had a visible effect on their tendency to register. Those who were unsure of their party were most likely to be unregistered.

PARTY IDENTIFICATION AND REGISTRATION

Voters	Percent			
Black-PR	67	7	13	13
Registered	76	8	13	3
Unregistered	68	7	14	21
White	49	11	26	14
Registered	55	14	26	5
Unregistered	39	7	27	27

▨ Democrat   ▦ Republican   ■ Independent   ☐ Not sure

Only about one in twelve could recall any help from a political party, however, in enabling him to become a registered voter. The ratio was slightly higher for Blacks than Whites. Union membership in the family (50 per cent of the sample) made only a slight difference on the side of registration among Blacks and even less among Whites. Thus, the organizational attention devoted to voter registration by both political parties and trade unions in New Jersey seemed to have made a minimum impression on this segment of the urban poor in Newark.

The Media
In the period before the first round of voting, respondents were asked if they had been reminded "where and when you could become a voter," and, if so, what medium had been the source of such information. The overwhelming majority either could not remember such registration messages or could not identify their source. To the extent that such communication was recalled (by about 20 per cent of those interviewed), radio was mentioned most often, and by Blacks twice as often as newspapers or television.

People were then asked if they had received any information about the candidates during the campaign for mayor from a variety of sources.

INFORMATION SOURCE ON CANDIDATE

	Total	Registered Black-PR's	Registered Whites	5th Grade or Less	High School or Beyond
	%	%	%	%	%
Newspapers	59	66	66	33	69
Radio	47	69	34	37	50
Television	47	57	44	37	53
Campaign literature	47	58	52	36	57
Sound trucks	46	62	32	42	47
Political meetings or rallies you went to	15	23	18	5	22
Someone coming to your home to talk with you	14	20	11	6	20

Newspapers were the one medium mentioned by Whites with the greatest frequency, particularly by better-educated Whites. (It should be recalled that the Newark television audience was not served by a strictly local station and New York stations allotted only a small portion of their news programs to Newark politics.) Radio topped the list for Blacks, followed closely by newspapers, as a source of information about the candidates for mayor.

The penetration of door-to-door canvassing or neighborhood rallies was relatively small, although substantial numbers said they had been exposed to sound-truck appeals or campaign literature. Those with the least education were not only the least likely to look to the mass media, but they were also the least likely to be reached by person-to-person approaches.

The universal medium of communication about politics to all levels of the Black urban poor in Newark turned out to be the sound truck. They were asked which of the mass media "you rely on most to find out what is going on in this election."

In Newark, newspapers were relied on the most by Blacks and Whites eligible to vote in the 1970 mayoralty election. They were relatively more important to Whites than to Blacks, to older persons, and to those with the most education. Whereas registered Blacks paid more attention to radio than the unregistered, the opposite was true among Whites. Television was more important to participators with the lowest incomes and least education, but it also was closest to newspapers as the prime political medium among those under thirty. Women rated television slightly higher than did men, but there were no substantial differences between the sexes in their reliance on newspapers or radio.

The endorsement of candidates by Newark's two daily newspapers might be expected to have important impact in these circumstances, especially among White voters. The *News* and *Star-Ledger* both endorsed the candidacy of Kenneth Gibson. Television was not an important campaign vehicle, and although Mayor Addonizio did not appear on televised debates among the other six candidates, he, alone, invested in paid political advertisements on New York metropolitan stations.

The mass media did not seem to play a decisive role in stimulating voter registration. The penetration and influence of newspapers was lowest among the unregistered of all races. The possibilities of radio as a medium for Black registration were somewhat dimmed by the fact that unregistered Blacks did not think of radio as a source of political information as much as those already on the voting lists. It is a fallacy to assume that the input into a communication system produces an equivalent impact upon the intended audience. The complications of this process are beyond the powers of the research instruments that were available in this study.

MEDIUM RELIED ON MOST

	Regis-tered Black-PR's	Unregis-tered Black-PR's	Regis-tered Whites	Unregis-tered Whites	Under $3,000	8th Grade or Less	High School or Beyond	Under 30	Over 50
	%	%	%	%	%	%	%	%	%
Newspapers	35	25	50	37	26	8	46	29	34
Radio	19	8	5	13	14	17	9	10	15
TV	21	29	19	20	30	34	22	28	18
All the same	20	18	15	17	21	23	15	19	19
Not sure	5	20	11	13	9	18	8	14	14

Family and Friends

It is an accepted theory of American politics that political predispositions are strongly affected by family upbringing and the circle of friends to whom one is exposed in one's life. Those interviewed in the survey were asked whether their feelings about politics had ever been influenced by family, friends, politicians, fellow-workers, or a teacher. In addition, each was asked to recall whether members of his immediate family had been registered voters during the time "you were a teen-ager."

About half of all Whites in the sample said that their fathers, mothers, or an older brother or sister had been registered. Among Blacks and Puerto Ricans, the pattern of previous family registration was less frequent.

MEMBERS OF FAMILY PREVIOUSLY REGISTERED

	Black-PR		White		Brought up in South
	Regis-tered	Unregis-tered	Regis-tered	Unregis-tered	
	%	%	%	%	%
Father	44	40	59	52	32
Mother	46	41	48	46	33
Brother or sister	35	27	45	34	28

These results show that a history of family registration on the current status of the registered and unregistered had only a slight influence, although the influence is there. Black mothers appear to have been eligible to vote as often as White mothers in families in this survey (there were large numbers of in-migrants in both groups), whereas White fathers were registered more often than Black fathers.

Those brought up in the South, although raised in families where registration was less common, actually had achieved a somewhat better rate of current registration for themselves (by two percentage points) than the average for Newark's Black adults in the sample.

On the broader question of influencing feelings about politics, the results were coded according to the various ways in which registered voters who answered in the affirmative said they had been influenced. Here is the breakdown on how people said they had been influenced on (1) voting or registering; (2) choice of party; (3) choice of candidate; or (4) political thinking.

WHO INFLUENCED FEELINGS ABOUT POLITICS?
(On Voting or Registering*)

	Registered Black-PR	Registered White
	%	%
Someone who held elective office	74	78
Any teacher you had in school	63	19
Your mother and father	43	17
Someone you worked with on a job	34	9
Some friend	29	9
Someone you know who was active in a political party	19	16
Any of your own children	10	17
Your wife or husband	4	2

*Because of comparatively smaller numbers recorded on this question percentages should be construed as suggestive rather than statistically valid for the whole sample.

It is obvious that voters, both White and Black, are candidate-centered when it comes to activating them to register and vote. This personal partisanship operates as a prime motivator even though many registration campaigns in America are organized under nonpartisan auspices and operated as a public service supposedly removed from actual contests for office. It would seem unrealistic, therefore, to conclude that when such campaigns actually succeed in adding new voters to the registration rolls or in bringing out larger numbers to the polls that it is taking place independently of the urge to improve the chances of a specific candidate for office.

Among Blacks in this survey, however, personal influence figured more strongly than for Whites in shaping their feelings about politics. Specifically, registered Blacks rated teachers, parents, fellow-workers, and friends as more influential than party activists of their acquaintance. Whites were less conscious generally of the relation between their participation in the electoral process and their set of personal relationships.

When it came to influencing their choice between political parties, their choice between candidates in a given election, or the general shape of their political thinking, respondents cited different patterns of influence.

WHO INFLUENCED FEELINGS ABOUT POLITICS?

	On Party		On Candidates		On Thinking	
	Black-PR	White	Black-PR	White	Black-PR	White
	%	%	%	%	%	%
Some friend	58	84	10	5	3	2
Fellow worker	51	84	13	3	22	6
Wife or husband	14	7	53	76	17	15
Children	38	46	24	27	17	9
Party worker	32	32	44	47	4	5
Mother or father	25	35	6	13	27	35
Teacher	27	73	6	6	61	21
Elected office holder	23	17	2	4	20	42

Friends and fellow workers played the principal role in determining party, although Whites rated teacher influence highly. Views within the family and party workers were deemed most influential in choice of candidates. Teachers most influenced

Blacks on their general political attitudes, whereas Whites mentioned elected officials and parents most often in this regard.

What emerges from this picture is a diverse and selective pattern of influence on individual political behavior, functioning somewhat differently for various kinds of political acts. The most crucial act—the decision to participate at all—is the one tied most closely to partisan feelings for elected officials. This raises a question concerning the legislative thrust within the Congress to try to divorce voter registration from the supposed taint of partisanship. A possible consequence of such legislation might be to reduce the effectiveness of broad-scaled attempts to enlarge the electorate, or to increase the frustration over the lack of success in registering voters on a nonpartisan basis under present institutions and registration laws, or, worst of all, to encourage further subterfuge in campaign morality already damaged by the gap between law and practice regarding political spending.

The role of the educational process in shaping political attitudes emerges sharply from the importance of teachers in the recollections of these inner-city residents of Newark. A word of warning is called for by these findings. While teachers are rated highly influential by Blacks as to registering and voting and in shaping their political thinking, and highly influential by Whites as to influencing them to vote in a particular party, there is no evidence from this survey as to the direction or content of such political influence. It might be significant that nonregistered Whites cited teachers as an influence four times as often as did those who were eligible to vote. This would seem to confirm suspicions that the teaching of social studies in the public schools might be directly related to alienation, cynicism, and apathy among some nonparticipants in the political process as well as to more positive political behavior engendered in others.

Registered Blacks and Puerto Ricans said teachers influenced their decision to register and vote over three times as often as did registered Whites. The same trend prevailed for teacher influence on individual ways of thinking about politics. White voters, on the other hand, said teachers influenced them to vote in a particular party more often than did Blacks and Puerto Ricans. At the same time, Whites were much more likely than Blacks to classify themselves as "independents." (Comparatively, Blacks and Puerto Ricans in this sample had more years of schooling than did Whites in these inner-city neighborhoods.)

Public school education about the American political process promises to become even more relevant now that the national voting age has been reduced to eighteen. The years before then, studies have shown, are an important part of the political socialization of American boys and girls. How much social studies curricula encourage or discourage participation by the individual in the American political system may be one of the keys to the goal of enlarging the size of the active electorate.

Awareness of Registration Campaign

In light of the special registration efforts being mounted in Newark prior to the 1970 election for mayor, each respondent was asked: "During the last few months were there any special attempts made in your neighborhood to get people registered so they would be eligible to vote? What special attempts were made?"

A majority of registered Blacks and Puerto Ricans—about

1970 NEIGHBORHOOD REGISTRATION

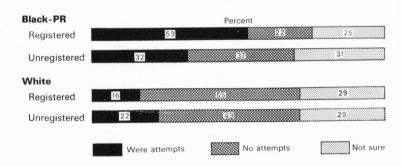

three times as many as registered Whites—said they were aware of special attempts in their neighborhood to register voters. Awareness of such efforts dropped sharply among unregistered Blacks, but one-third of those not on the rolls had been exposed to neighborhood registration efforts. In other words, the drive to register Black and Puerto Rican voters in Newark did not penetrate substantial sectors of the inner-city neighborhoods occupied by minority groups, and many of those reached nevertheless failed to take the sought-after steps to become eligible to vote.

One-third of those Blacks who noticed special registration attempts said canvassers had gone door-to-door in their neighborhood. Another one-third said that they were generally aware of registration workers in the area. One out of every five said that there were representatives of candidates for office working on registration on their block. Thirty-two per cent said a sound truck had passed by. Four per cent said they had been solicited by telephone. The telephone coverage was ten points higher among White registered voters, whereas none of the non-registered Whites received any phone calls.

Actual Results

The situation in Newark as the mayoralty election approached was one of steadily declining registration running parallel with a steadily shrinking White population. The figures since the last previous mayoralty election in 1965 showed the trend of voters eligible for each of three ensuing local, national, and state elections.

Mayor (1966)   153,573
President (1968) 136,823
Governor (1969) 130,223

Newark's Central Ward, in which most of the sample points for this survey were located, had lost a net of 13,000 voters from the registration lists during this period as a result of extensive urban renewal clearance and the damage incurred during the 1967 riots. Nevertheless, a large pool of unregistered Blacks and Puerto Ricans still existed throughout the city.

In order to qualify for the first round of voting it was necessary to have been a resident of the state of New Jersey for at least six months and of Essex County at least forty days prior to May 12. The would-be voter could register at the Hall of Records in the County Office Building or at the office of the Municipal Clerk in City Hall on any business day between 9 A.M. and 4 P.M. Both sites were in the center of the city. Voters who had failed to exercise their franchise at least once during four consecutive years in any election were required to re-register. Voters who had transferred their residence from one district to another in Newark either had to file a notice with the Commissioner of Registration or call in person to be eligible to vote in a new district. Moves within a district required an affidavit of change of residence.

The complexities of these regulations to the uninitiated, the inconvenience and psychic cost of a trip to the central registration points, and the imminence of the cut-off dates moved the sponsors of Project Vote to press for off-site, neighborhood registration days. The Commissioner of Registration for Essex County, with a total budget of $15,000 for all twenty-two municipalities in the county, demurred at the cost of providing extra workers at $3.00 per hour to man such off-site registration points. But it was finally agreed to open ten registration locations from February 14 to April 2 in each of the city's five wards on six selected neighborhood registration days in order, as one staff member explained, "to take the steam out of the pickets." These locations included supermarkets, schools, and public housing projects.

In one such project, open from 4 to 8 P.M. on March 6, only one person registered. It was explained by N.A.A.C.P. officials that a housing project was a poor location for such activity in Newark, because the political arrangements necessary to gain entry into such projects included becoming eligible to vote one's gratitude. Supermarket registration, with manned tables inside the store, produced 200 to 300 registrations on a Saturday, 10 to 20 per cent of which were duplications or defective because of ineligibility, criminal records, and so on. On a single day at the office maintained by the N.A.A.C.P. for off-site registration the top registration figure was 98.

When the cut-off day for the May 12 round of voting, April 2, passed, it was agreed to reopen four sites for two days to make additional voters eligible for the run-off election of June 16—but not until Project Vote filed suit. The target of these efforts had been announced on Martin Luther King's birthday, January 15, as 25,000 new voters in the next fifty days. When the final voting lists for the 1970 mayoralty had been compiled, however, the official number of registered voters eligible for the May 12 and June 16 elections in Newark turned out to be:

May 12, 1970, 133,502
June 16, 1970, 133,823

These figures came to barely 3,000 more than had been registered for the state election the previous fall and 3,000 *less* than had qualified for the 1968 Presidential election. The drop below the registration list for the last previous mayoralty contest in 1966 remained a substantial 20,000 voters. The net gain of 3,000 over 1969, it was estimated, was achieved by adding or restoring about 7,500 names, while 4,500 names were dropped from the official voting list. Although it was an unusual accomplishment to stem a drop in registration in an off-year or local election, the total impact of the money and effort invested in Newark's 1970 registration drive turned out to be disappointingly small, especially considering the drama of the Gibson-Addonizio confrontation. Significantly, registration in the Black Central Ward continued to drop, while the heaviest gains were scored in the predominantly White East Ward. This suggests the possibility that the all-out effort to register Black voters may have activated

Whites to register in even greater numbers than Blacks who managed to get their names added to the 1970 voting lists in Newark.

Institutional Bias

A perusal of the summary of New Jersey election laws distributed by the Commissioner of Registration for Essex County to would-be voters documented the institutional bias of the system, even in a relatively enlightened Northern state. Instructions consisted principally of direct quotations from appropriate legal sources, extremely difficult to follow for even the best-educated laymen.

The use of the mails to notify persons required to re-register because of alleged failure to vote or change of residence overlooked the high percentage of nondeliverability of the mails in blighted neighborhoods.

The governmental locations for registering voters in Newark were difficult to find, forbidding in appearance, and required an investment in time and travel that many individuals lack the motivation to make. The fear of giving signatures felt by members of minority groups makes even off-site registration difficult in inner-city neighborhoods, especially when registration workers are strangers from other parts of the city and of different ethnic groups.

The embarrassments of illiterates and Spanish-speaking residents, the fears of low-income persons regarding debt collectors and social workers, the whole life style of the urban poor, run counter to the red tape and officiousness of a system which places the burden of proof upon the private person who wants to participate in the electoral process.

Explanation for Not Registering

Those who admitted not being registered when interviewed were read "a list of some reasons other people have told us why they are not registered to vote around here" and asked whether "you feel it applies to you or not?" Answers to seven possible reasons for not registering are shown in the graph.

REASONS FOR NOT REGISTERING

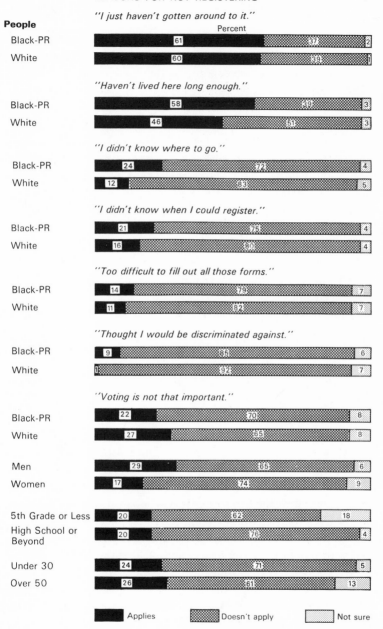

People

"I just haven't gotten around to it."

Percent

Black-PR	61 / 37 / 2
White	60 / 39 / 1

"Haven't lived here long enough."

Black-PR	58 / 39 / 3
White	46 / 51 / 3

"I didn't know where to go."

Black-PR	24 / 72 / 4
White	12 / 83 / 5

"I didn't know when I could register."

Black-PR	21 / 75 / 4
White	16 / 80 / 4

"Too difficult to fill out all those forms."

Black-PR	14 / 79 / 7
White	11 / 82 / 7

"Thought I would be discriminated against."

Black-PR	9 / 85 / 6
White	1 / 92 / 7

"Voting is not that important."

Black-PR	22 / 70 / 8
White	27 / 65 / 8
Men	29 / 65 / 6
Women	17 / 74 / 9
5th Grade or Less	20 / 62 / 18
High School or Beyond	20 / 76 / 4
Under 30	24 / 71 / 5
Over 50	26 / 61 / 13

Applies   Doesn't apply   Not sure

Blacks, Puerto Ricans, and Whites alike admitted in substantial proportions to a low-priority interest in registering. Mobility, on the other hand, was more of a problem to minority group members than Whites, although residence requirements were cited as an excuse by approximately half of these residents of Newark's inner city.

Compared with self-confessed indifference or inadequate residency requirements, the other reasons for not registering drew relatively few affirmative replies. The lack of information claimed by 21 to 24 per cent of Blacks and by 12 to 16 per cent of Whites illustrates, on the one hand, the obstacles inherent in sporadic neighborhood registration and, on the other, the theoretical convenience of Permanent Registration on a daily, year-round schedule. Even fewer unregistered voters would admit that the required paperwork was too difficult for them. Only one in ten Blacks and Puerto Ricans said they had not registered for fear of being discriminated against.

By their own testimony these nonparticipating residents were more prepared to cite their personal indifference than blame the usual list of institutional biases against urban voting. The final statement on the list tested their sense of involvement more directly by asking their reaction to the statement: "Voting is not that important."

Whites discounted the importance of voting more than Blacks, and men did so more than women. The least educated and the oldest in the sample were most unsure. Black women rejected the idea that voting is of secondary importance most overwhelmingly, suggesting the key role of this group in strategies to encourage political participation among Black families.

Low education correlated more closely than sex, income, or age with fears of discrimination and of filling out forms, as well as with a disposition to plead ignorance of the time and place to register. And among the least educated seven out of every ten unregistered persons said they simply hadn't gotten around to it.

Effectiveness vs. Powerlessness

The feelings of persons covered in the survey toward the effectiveness of using democratic procedures to bring about improvements in their neighborhoods were tested in a question asking them to describe their reactions to (1) "electing the right public officials," (2) "speaking out at a public meeting," and (3) "making a complaint to the city officials in charge."

In their judgments on the utility of electing the right public officials there was a substantial difference between those who were registered voters and those who were not.

The reactions of both Blacks and Whites were remarkably similar. Eight in ten registered voters of both races rated local elections an effective means for improving neighborhood problems if the "right" official won. A majority rated such elections "very effective." One in five of those not registered in both races felt such elections would not help at all, as against only one in ten of the registered.

Blacks and Puerto Ricans generally attached greater value to speaking out at public meetings than did Whites. Registered voters of both races thought it more effective than did the unregistered, although the scale of effectiveness was considerably lower than for elections.

Registered Blacks, interestingly, were the only group to come out strongly positive on the effectiveness versus the ineffectiveness of taking neighborhood problems to the city officials in charge. Unregistered Blacks and both registered and unregistered Whites expressed a good deal of skepticism about the responsiveness of city officials to citizen complaints.

A conclusion to be drawn from these data might be that faith in democratic processes does indeed have a good deal to do with the decision to register among those residents of low-income neighborhoods. But disillusion with the system involves less than a majority even of those who do not choose to participate in elections. Blacks had as much confidence in the utility of elections as did Whites, and more than Whites in speaking out at public meetings. In a White power structure tainted by charges of corruption, registered Blacks maintained a faith that political action could be made to work in Newark.

"ELECTING RIGHT PUBLIC OFFICIAL"

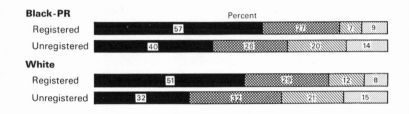

"SPEAKING AT MEETINGS"

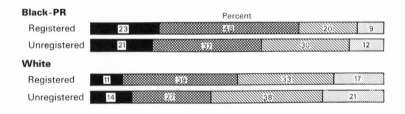

"COMPLAINT TO OFFICIAL"

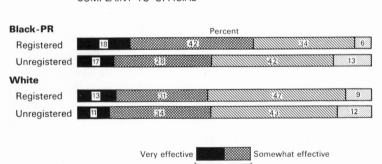

Men interviewed in this survey tended to be more negative than women. Those over fifty were more disillusioned than those under thirty. The very poor, those with incomes less than $3,000 per year, were not far off the norms for their more advantaged neighbors.

Alienation has possibly been overdrawn as a central explanation of the psychological condition of the urban poor, Black or White, and we might look to other feelings to explain what divides those who register and vote from those who show less interest in elections. Later on, we will examine some of these alternative psychological explanations.

Militancy

The assumption that so-called confrontation politics—demonstrations, sit-ins, physical violence—is the alternative chosen by those who have given up on the conventional methods of political participation is not borne out by the findings of this survey.

Respondents were asked this question: "In order to really bring about improvements in the problems facing this neighborhood, would you personally be willing to (list follows), or not?

1) "Join a picket line or demonstration.

2) "Join a sit-in at the office of a high public official such as the Mayor, Board of Education, Governor, etc.

3) "Be arrested and put in jail.

4) "Join a militant organization.

5) "Resort to physical violence if you had to."

It is clear from these figures that Blacks were more ready than Whites to involve themselves personally in various forms of direct action to "bring about improvements in the problems facing this neighborhood." Of the alternatives listed, only picket lines, demonstrations, and sit-ins were acceptable to a majority—Black registered voters. Unregistered Blacks and Puerto Ricans were less willing than the registered to do any

MILITANCY INDEX

	Black-PR		White		Men	Women	5th Grade or Less	High School or Beyond	Under 30	Over 50
	Registered	Un-registered	Registered	Un-registered						
	%	%	%	%	%	%	%	%	%	%
Willing to Demonstrate	57	47	23	23	48	37	35	50	53	28
Sit-in	59	47	18	18	45	38	34	49	52	25
Go to jail	33	26	9	11	29	17	19	26	26	17
Join militants	18	23	4	10	19	13	14	17	26	8
Resort to violence	30	31	7	10	29	17	20	25	32	13

of these things, or to be arrested and put in jail for a neigh' cause.

Large majorities of Whites, registered and unregistered alike, rejected all these forms of community action, even the mildest form of picketing and demonstrating.

It was at the point of being willing to "join a militant organization" or "resort to physical violence" that unregistered Blacks began to surpass the registered, and the same trend was apparent among Whites. Militant organizations had appeal to no more than one out of five Blacks. Only a tiny minority of Whites, one in ten, condoned physical violence when deemed necessary, as compared with nearly one-third of all Blacks in the sample. The better educated the individual the more willing he or she was to demonstrate, nonviolently or otherwise. Men were more militant than women, the young more militant than the old.

Obviously, political action of a direct nature appealed to many of the same persons who also took part in conventional forms of political participation—the "more the more" phenomenon. But minority group members in Newark were significantly more willing than Whites to take neighborhood problems to the streets, at the risk of arrest or violence. Whether this represented a difference of perception in the seriousness of their frustrations, or a difference of assessment in what it would take to move the power structure, cannot be deduced from these data. By the same token, one should not jump to the conclusion that Blacks were more conditioned to a life style of violence and dissent in the urban core then their White, predominantly Catholic neighbors. Blacks brought up in the South were least unwilling to consider resorting to violence or to joining a militant organization, although exhibiting no pattern of their own on the other items on the list. This was the same group that was least confident that a White mayor elected in 1970 would treat Blacks as fairly as members of his own race.

Chapter Five

THE ELECTION

Attitudes Toward Politics

Those engaged in the process of choosing a mayor for Newark, and who lived in the city's central core, entered the process with few illusions.

Respondents were asked to express their feelings about the truth or untruth of these statements: (1) "You can't believe what you see about politics in the press"; and (2) "Politicians never carry out their promises, so it makes no difference who wins an election." The overwhelming majority (better than seven out of ten) said they thought there was some truth in both statements.

Those with the best education expressed the most skepticism about both the press and politicans. The press had even less credibility (defended by about 15 per cent) than did politicians (defended by about 25 per cent). Blacks and Whites showed little difference in their lack of faith in the believability of the media, although registered voters were stronger in their criticism than the unregistered. Registered voters spoke up more for politicians than did the unregistered.

The authoritarian tendencies in Newark's inner-city population were apparent in their replies to this statement: "A few strong leaders would do more for this city than all the laws and talk." Some of these replies, illustrated in the graph, may have been a reflection of both the cloud over the Addonizio Administration and the aftermath of Newark's riots and rising crime rate. The

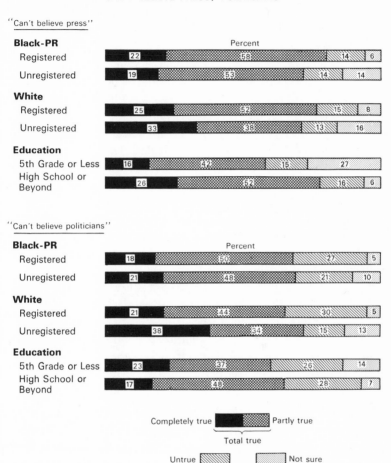

"CAN'T BELIEVE PRESS / POLITICIANS"

"Can't believe press"

Black-PR — Percent

Registered — 22 | 58 | 14 | 6

Unregistered — 19 | 53 | 14 | 14

White

Registered — 25 | 52 | 15 | 8

Unregistered — 33 | 38 | 13 | 16

Education

5th Grade or Less — 16 | 42 | 15 | 27

High School or Beyond — 26 | 52 | 16 | 6

"Can't believe politicians"

Black-PR — Percent

Registered — 18 | 50 | 27 | 5

Unregistered — 21 | 48 | 21 | 10

White

Registered — 21 | 44 | 30 | 5

Unregistered — 38 | 34 | 15 | 13

Education

5th Grade or Less — 23 | 37 | 26 | 14

High School or Beyond — 17 | 48 | 28 | 7

Completely true / Partly true

Total true

Untrue   Not sure

unanimity between the races was surprising, with the Italian-American population, if anything, more restrained than Blacks on this subject.

Also, education was no leavener of the public impatience with the local political dialogue. Newark felt itself in the throes of a leadership gap, accentuated by a deep-seated cynicism toward all politicians. This feeling of pessimism was further reflected in the evaluation of this statement: "The way government works around here, an election is not going to improve things like education and housing." These feelings are summed up in the graph on the facing page.

Thus, feelings were running strongly among Blacks that "It's important for people who are alike to stick together and elect their own":

The urge toward ethnic solidarity and bloc voting was conspicuously stronger among Blacks in Newark than Whites in general or Italian-Americans in particular. The better educated were more ready than the poorly educated to resist the concept of group solidarity. Those not eligible to vote, especially Whites, were less motivated by this ethnic consciousness.

It is sometimes said that the emotional drain of survival in the urban core robs its residents of the stamina to take an active part in an optional activity such as politics. Respondents were closely divided on the proposition: "By the time I take care of my everyday problems, I don't have much energy left over to think about politics." For the sample as a whole, 58 per cent considered this statement to be at least partly true, as against 37 per cent who said it was not true at all. Lack of energy appeared to be a significant factor among those who were not registered to vote, even more for unregistered Whites than unregistered Blacks. Women with young children, on the other hand, showed no more signs of debilitation than other women in the survey. Men testified to having markedly more energy left over for politics than did females.

This combined with the extent to which a personality trait, expressed by a statement such as "I often prefer to say nothing at all about politics than something that will make people angry with me," affects political participation, is shown by the graph on page 100.

Again, education was the key to the greatest feeling of self-confidence about discussing politics. Registered voters were less diffident than unregistered voters. But the fact that majorities

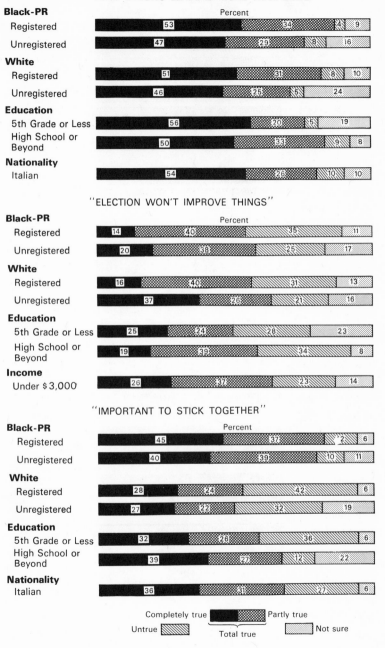

"NEED STRONG LEADERS MORE THAN LAWS"

Black-PR
Registered — 53, 34, 4, 9
Unregistered — 47, 29, 8, 16

White
Registered — 51, 31, 8, 10
Unregistered — 46, 25, 5, 24

Education
5th Grade or Less — 56, 20, 5, 19
High School or Beyond — 50, 33, 9, 8

Nationality
Italian — 54, 26, 10, 10

"ELECTION WON'T IMPROVE THINGS"

Black-PR
Registered — 14, 40, 35, 11
Unregistered — 20, 38, 25, 17

White
Registered — 16, 40, 31, 13
Unregistered — 37, 26, 21, 16

Education
5th Grade or Less — 25, 24, 28, 23
High School or Beyond — 19, 39, 34, 8

Income
Under $3,000 — 26, 37, 23, 14

"IMPORTANT TO STICK TOGETHER"

Black-PR
Registered — 45, 37, 2, 6
Unregistered — 40, 39, 10, 11

White
Registered — 28, 24, 42, 6
Unregistered — 27, 22, 32, 19

Education
5th Grade or Less — 32, 26, 36, 6
High School or Beyond — 39, 27, 12, 22

Nationality
Italian — 36, 31, 27, 6

Completely true / Partly true / Total true / Untrue / Not sure

NOT MUCH ENERGY FOR POLITICS

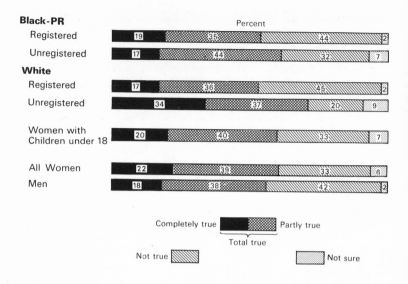

Black-PR
Registered
Unregistered
White
Registered
Unregistered

Women with Children under 18

All Women
Men

Completely true / Partly true
Total true
Not true
Not sure

PREFER TO AVOID CONTROVERSY

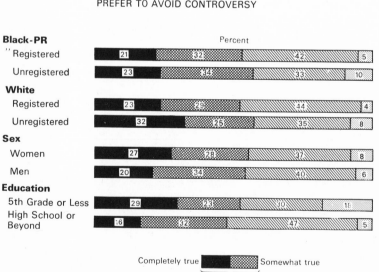

Black-PR
"Registered
Unregistered
White
Registered
Unregistered
Sex
Women
Men
Education
5th Grade or Less
High School or Beyond

Completely true / Somewhat true
Total true
Not true
Not sure

across the board expressed fears of antagonizing others by voicing their political views was a mark of the restraints upon political organization operating in Newark's low-income neighborhoods at the time of the 1970 election.

Within the series of attitudes toward politics tested in this survey was that expressed by the statement: "They make it so hard to register and vote that it is more trouble than it's worth." Inherent in those words were the considerations of cynicism, pessimism, lack of energy, and insecurity that had characterized the thinking of those interviewed in Newark's inner-city neighborhoods. And yet, 68 per cent answered that the idea that it was not worth the trouble to register and vote was "not true at all." The figure rose to 78 per cent among all registered voters combined. (Interestingly, this ten-point range coincided almost exactly with the turnout of voters in the first and second round of the election for mayor.)

NOT WORTH VOTING

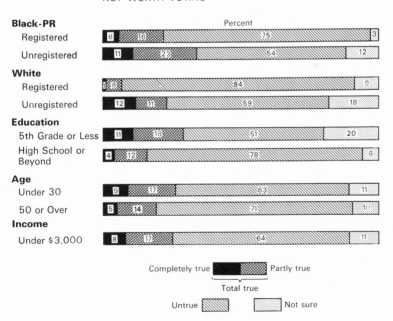

A sense of civic duty to register and vote was operating powerfully among Whites who were already registered, and much less strongly, as one might anticipate, among unregistered Whites. Unregistered Blacks valued participation even less than did unregistered Whites, and registered Blacks were somewhat more skeptical than their White counterparts. Older persons valued voting more than the young; three out of ten of the poorly educated felt it to be at least partly true that registering and voting were more trouble than it was worth.

Yet, on the whole, the answers to this question reaffirmed the existence in the lower-income neighborhoods of Newark of a participating, if unenthusiastic, electorate alongside a substantial population of nonparticipators who, at least outwardly, were not dramatically different from those who placed a higher value on exercising the franchise. The principal differences between Blacks and Whites were the comparatively stronger urge of the Blacks to achieve racial identity at the polls and the more intense commitment of the Whites to the worth of the effort needed to take part in the electoral system.

Thus, the stage was set for an election in which Blacks and Whites held an almost equal balance of power between them. And, since of the seven candidates for mayor three were Black and four were White, the thrust of ethnic solidarity was bound to be important among minority group members seeking to elect the first Black mayor in the city's history. On the other hand, the incumbent Mayor, Hugh Addonizio, had been elected in prior years with the support of substantial numbers of Black voters. The scandals surrounding his Administration probably had something to do with the deep spirit of cynicism expressed in this survey. The sense of political identity, moreover, was also part of the mores of Newark's substantial community of Italian-Americans. The balance of power in the forthcoming election, therefore, might very well be wielded by White voters of other ethnic origins. Their rate of participation was likely to be higher than for Blacks. Whether or not White ethnics would vote only for White candidates contained the key to the outcome of the 1970 race for mayor.

Degree of Interest

As a measure of the degree of popular interest in the specific outcome of the 1970 election for mayor, respondents were asked: "Do you find that you are very interested in the campaign for mayor, only somewhat interested, or does the whole thing bore you?" Sixty-three per cent of registered Blacks said they were "very interested," compared with 50 per cent of registered Whites. Nine out of ten of the registered voters of both races expressed at least some interest in the contest, although 6 per cent of potential Black voters and 8 per cent of potential White voters admitted being bored by the whole thing. Among the unregistered the boredom index rose from 13 per cent among Blacks to 33 per cent among Whites! Italian-Americans were ten points higher than other Whites in the intensity of their interest in the outcome, and a similar margin existed between the better educated and poorly educated in the sample.

Previous Election

Of the registered voters, 68 per cent had voted in the 1966 mayoralty election. Those who could recall whom they voted for indicated their voting histories.

Four years previously Addonizio had carried fellow Italian-

1966 MAYORALTY

	Total	Black-PR's	Whites	Italian-Americans
	%	%	%	%
Addonizio	49	41	58	82
Carlin	15	6	27	5
Gibson	22	36	3	—
Not sure	14	17	12	13

Americans almost monolithically, plus a higher percentage of the Black vote than did Kenneth Gibson, who had been a late entry into the race. Only 3 per cent of the Whites had voted for the non-White candidate.

Perceptions of Candidates

To establish what were the images of the three leading candidates for mayor of Newark in 1970 in the minds of the potential electorate, pairs of statement concerning each candidate, one pro and one con, were read to respondents, who were then asked whether they tended to agree or disagree with each statement.

Regarding City Councilman Anthony Imperiale, for example, the two statements were:

1) "Councilman Anthony Imperiale is trying to bring law and order back to the city so it can be a safe place to live."

2) "Councilman Anthony Imperiale is a White racist who wants to keep Blacks down by force."

White voters perceived Imperiale to be the protector of "law and order" by a two to one margin, whereas Black voters perceived him as a "White racist" by better than four to one. Imperiale, in short, was a polarizing candidate. Whites disagreed that the Councilman was racist, 48 per cent to 15 per cent; Blacks disagreed that he would make the city safe, 60 per cent to 18 per cent. His fellow Italian-Americans were more favorably impressed than other Whites, although 11 per cent conceded he wanted to keep Blacks down by force. Women took a less favorable view of him than did men.

This positive image among Whites and negative image among Blacks contained an important exception—Whites who said they were considering voting for Kenneth Gibson in the first round of voting on May 12. Although their numbers were too small for reliable statistical projection at that stage of the campaign, it was striking that 100 per cent of these Whites for Gibson said that they considered Imperiale to be a force-minded racist. And better than eight out of ten rejected the idea that his kind of law and order would make the city safe. (In a poll taken by Oliver Quayle in January, Imperiale was running second in the race for mayor. He was perceived as "Conservative" by a large majority of voters, and was the overwhelming favorite of Italian-Americans in his home North Ward.)

When voters were asked to express agreement or disagreement with two statements characterizing Mayor Hugh Addonizio, his negative impression on Blacks was even stronger than Imperiale's, whereas his overall impression on White voters was also negative by a small margin.

White voters in Newark disagreed, 40 to 35 per cent, that Mayor Hugh Addonizio did not deserve to be mayor because of his connection with organized crime, although one in four could not express an opinion. By the same token, they rejected the notion, 42 to 34 per cent, that the Mayor had been the victim of a smear campaign. Whites planning to vote for Gibson felt overwhelmingly that Addonizio had been a bad mayor who did not deserve to be reinstated in office. Italian-Americans came down squarely on the Mayor's side, but even three of ten in his own ethnic group indicated their reservations about Addonizio's performance in office.

Black voters agreed more strongly with the negative statement on Addonizio and disagreed more with the positive statement about him than they had in the case of Imperiale. Unregistered persons had a harder time than the registered in making up their minds about him. It remained to be seen, however, whether feelings on racial matters—as evidenced in reactions to Imperiale—cut more deeply than feelings about crime in politics—as evidenced in reactions to Addonizio—when Imperiale and Addonizio competed for a place in the run-off election among those residents of low-income neighborhoods.

In contrast to his two leading White rivals, the overall image of Kenneth Gibson was positive among Newark's White voters in the central city as well as being overwhelmingly positive among fellow Blacks.

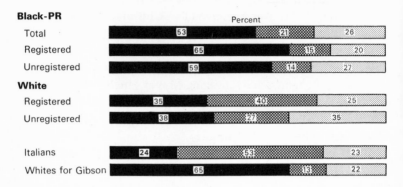

"HUGH ADDONIZIO DOES NOT DESERVE TO BE MAYOR, BECAUSE OF HIS CONNECTION WITH ORGANIZED CRIME."

Black-PR
- Total — 53, 21, 26
- Registered — 65, 15, 20
- Unregistered — 59, 14, 27

White
- Registered — 35, 40, 25
- Unregistered — 38, 27, 35

- Italians — 24, 53, 23
- Whites for Gibson — 65, 13, 22

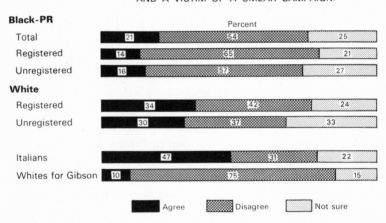

"MAYOR HUGH ADDONIZIO HAS BEEN A GOOD MAYOR AND A VICTIM OF A SMEAR CAMPAIGN."

Black-PR
- Total — 21, 54, 25
- Registered — 14, 65, 21
- Unregistered — 16, 57, 27

White
- Registered — 34, 42, 24
- Unregistered — 30, 37, 33

- Italians — 47, 31, 22
- Whites for Gibson — 10, 75, 15

Agree — Disagree — Not sure

Among registered Black residents of the low-income neighborhoods of Newark, Kenneth Gibson enjoyed overwhelming (thirteen to one) support as a "good mayor for all the people." Charges that he was a "front" for Le Roi Jones and other militants who had attained a great deal of notoriety during the 1967 riots, and who had participated in Gibson's endorsement by the

Black and Puerto Rican caucus, were believed by only 4 per cent of the registered Blacks interviewed in this survey. Unregistered Blacks were slightly less favorably disposed toward Gibson than those who had qualified to take part in the mayoralty election and slightly more prone to believe that he would be controlled by militants.

Although half the Whites were simply "not sure" what to think of Gibson—a mark of the dissonance that occurs when members of one race are exposed to mass media content about politicians of another race—a substantial (29 to 19 per cent) plurality of those with opinions thought he would try to be a good mayor for all the people. These tended to be the same Whites who had answered that they thought Whites and Blacks would get equal treatment under a Black mayor.

This basic reservoir (20 to 30 per cent) of White confidence in Gibson's racial fairness was a critical asset for a Black candidate running in a racially divided city. And those White voters who declared their support for Gibson in the survey came down 100 per cent on the side of the Black candidate on this key issue.

Unregistered Whites were slightly more favorably disposed toward Gibson than those who had qualified to take part in the mayoralty election and slightly less prone to believe that he would be controlled by militants. By a small margin (25 to 23 per cent) those White voters with opinions on the matter rejected the idea of a militant takeover. Whites supporting Gibson rejected the threat of a militant takeover overwhelmingly (76 to 6 per cent) and were as willing as Black voters to take a position on that matter.

Italian-Americans were just as ready to believe in Gibson's performance in office as other Whites, but were more apprehensive over the thrust of a militant "takeover." They agreed, 27 to 18 per cent—55 per cent were "not sure"—with the statement that Gibson was "just a front" for Black militants.

The combination of a small base of confidence among Whites from low income neighborhoods, plus a huge bloc of noncommital

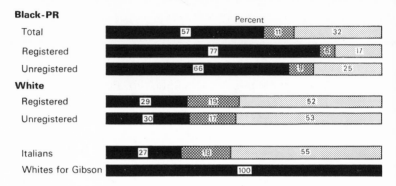

"ALTHOUGH HE IS BLACK, CITY ENGINEER KENNETH GIBSON WILL TRY TO BE A GOOD MAYOR FOR ALL THE PEOPLE."

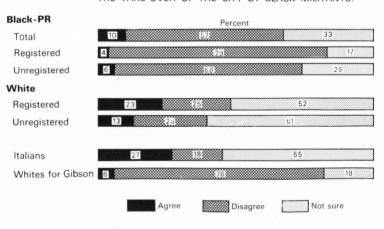

"CITY ENGINEER KENNETH GIBSON IS JUST A FRONT FOR THE TAKE-OVER OF THE CITY BY BLACK MILITANTS."

White voters, indicated that Gibson, if he had chosen to do so, might have successfully carried his campaign directly to the White electorate. The debate over the wisdom of such a course continued within the Gibson camp throughout the campaign. For the first round of voting on May 12 the decision seemed to have been made to minimize his personal appearances before White voters—with consequences we will examine shortly.

Voter Preferences—First Round

The first wave of interviewing in this survey began about two weeks before the initial round of voting and continued until the weekend before May 12, the day of the election. The sample, it should be recalled, was not drawn to represent a cross section of the entire voting population, but was concentrated in the low-income neighborhoods of the central city and controlled to include a two-thirds proportion of Blacks and a one-third proportion of Whites, both registered and unregistered to vote. When the voting preferences expressed in the survey were later compared to the actual election results in the precincts in which the sample points fell, the margins of difference for the six candidates who remained in the race nevertheless turned out to be less than two percentage points per candidate, with the single exception of the second Black candidate, Assemblyman George C. Richardson, most of whose support shifted to Kenneth Gibson in the final hours before the polls opened.

Twenty-eight per cent of those interviewed could express no preference among the candidates, and 1 per cent said they would vote for Harry L. Wheeler, who withdrew at the eleventh hour although his name remained on the ballot.

In this constituency Gibson was close to a majority in his own right, but obviously not by a margin sufficient to overcome possible losses in more affluent sections of the city with larger proportions of White middle-class voters. Putting all the Black candidates and White candidates together, the split for the Black candidates was 57 to 43 per cent, or somewhat below the proportion of Blacks in the sample. This indication that preferences crossed racial lines was borne out by the breakdowns for each candidate.

FIRST ROUND—PREFERENCE FOR MAYOR
(Low-Income Neighborhoods)

	Actual	Not Sures Eliminated
	%	%
Gibson	36	50
Addonizio	12	18
Imperiale	10	14
Caufield	6	8
Richardson	5	6
Matturi	2	3
Wheeler	1	1
Not sure	28	—
Total	100	100

Of the seven candidates in the race, only two—Gibson and Addonizio—attracted significant support from voters of a different race. And at this stage of the campaign Gibson's percentage among Whites (4 per cent) was less than half of Addonizio's share (10 per cent) of the Black vote in these neighborhoods.

Imperiale was the preferred candidate over Addonizio among Italian-Americans (32 to 24 per cent), with 11 per cent going to Republican State Senator Alexander J. Matturi.

John P. Caufield, the Irish-American, former Fire Director in the Addonizio Administration, drew his support almost exclusively from White ethnics outside the Italian-American community. Males outnumbered females among his supporters by two to one.

Among those from households in the acute poverty category (under $3,000) Addonizio made a better showing (19 per cent) than among the sample as a whole (12 per cent). And Addonizio also fared better among those qualified to vote, Black or White, as against those not registered.

Since Gibson was just as popular among unregistered as registered Blacks, and more popular among unregistered than regis-

MAYOR PREFERENCE BREAKDOWN

	Total	Black-PR's		Whites		Italians	Under $3,000
		Regis-tered	Unregis-tered	Regis-tered	Unregis-tered		
	%	%	%	%	%	%	%
Gibson	36	50	49	4	7	3	30
Addonizio	12	10	6	22	15	24	19
Imperiale	10	2	4	24	26	32	7
Caufield	6	1	1	15	13	—	9
Richardson	5	10	6	—	4	3	3
Matturi	2	1	—	8	9	11	3
Wheeler	1	1	2	—	—	—	2
Not sure	28	25	32	27	26	27	27

tered Whites, the arithmetic of a citywide registration drive was on his side despite Addonizio's apparent penetration of the Black voting community. An effort directed exclusively at putting Black voters on the rolls, however, was not necessarily advantageous for the Gibson candidacy, because Addonizio's percentage of support among unregistered Blacks (6 per cent) was outweighed by Gibson's support among unregistered Whites (7 per cent). A selective registration drive among Whites might well have produced significant benefits for Gibson when White candidates other than Addonizio had been eliminated.

Respondents were asked the reasons for backing the candidates of their choice and their answers were organized by various categories. The results are shown in the table.

What emerged from the profile of each candidate in the perceptions of his supporters was this general picture:

Gibson: Perceived as competent, although personal qualities do not project strongly. One in four of his supporters professed verbally his desire for a Black mayor.

Addonizio: Experience in office and defense of his performance in City Hall cited most often.

Imperiale: Exclusive possession of the law and order issue, plus fairly high number of mentions of personal qualities.

Caufield: Projects the strongest of all candidates as a personable and sincere individual. Of all the White candidates he received smallest backing on racial grounds.

In view of the fact that Newark's local political system called for a run-off between the top two candidates in the first round of voting the second choices of those favoring each contestant were of considerable significance. Among those planning to vote for Kenneth Gibson, five in ten said they would vote for George Richardson as their second choice, indicating the high rate of Black identity among Black voters, since Richardson was not considered to be a contender to make the run-off. Addonizio supporters mentioned Imperiale and Gibson, in that order, as

REASONS FOR BACKING CANDIDATES IN FIRST ROUND

	Gibson	Addonizio	Imperiale	Caufield	Richardson	Matturi
	%	%	%	%	%	%
Interested in the people	14	10	15	29	11	20
Competent	9	17	3	15	18	—
Honest and sincere	3	6	11	23	13	26
Will do a good job	27	32	25	13	36	14
Experience	5	23	2	10	9	26
"Need one of us"	—	7	5	3	—	—
"Need a Black"	23	—	—	—	11	—
Law and order	1	1	29	3	—	—
Need a change	10	—	9	5	2	20

their second choices. Sixteen per cent of Addonizio backers said that they were ready to vote for Gibson if the Mayor did not make it into the second round, twice as many as those backing Gibson who listed Addonizio as their second choice. The Mayor himself was not a strong second choice with any other group.

Of all the candidates in the race, Councilman Imperiale loomed as the greatest threat to win a run-off election. He was the leading second choice among supporters of each of the other three White candidates (named by 40 per cent of Caufield's backers and 25 per cent each of those supporting Addonizio and Matturi). Running only slightly behind the Mayor in this inner-city constituency, and running first among White voters in general and Italian-Americans in particular, he stood to gain most as the White survivor in the run-off election. Ironically, it was Addonizio's ability to attract some Black support that kept the Mayor ahead of Imperiale in this pre-election poll. (Imperiale, who had been running ahead of the Mayor in a Quayle poll taken in January, was taken ill in the midst of the campaign. By April he had been passed by Addonizio in telephone call-backs to the same voters, losing eight percentage points, while the Mayor, after an all-out campaign, was gaining nine.)

The sleeper situation in the race was what the Caufield voters might do if Caufield did not make it into the run-off. Comparatively few (5 per cent) named Gibson as their second choice at this stage, as against the 40 per cent who looked to Imperiale if their own man did not make the run-off. But, if neither Caufield nor Imperiale survived the first elimination test, the largest segment of the Caufield vote was up for grabs. Only one in ten of Caufield's backers, and those were mostly Italian-Americans, said they would vote for Addonizio in case of a run-off. How many of the other White Catholics of modest income, from typical blue-collar, "hard-hat" families, would vote for a Black man in a final confrontation with the Mayor? The question became salient when the returns of the May 12 election were tallied.

The May 12 Results

This is how the outcome of the first round of voting for mayor of Newark turned out.

ACTUAL VOTE—MAY 12

	Number of Votes	Percent
Gibson	37,859	43
Addonizio	18,212	21
Imperiale	13,978	16
Caufield	11,950	13
Matturi	4,734	5
Richardson	2,038	2
Wheeler (withdrew)	146	—
Total	88,917	100

Total Black candidates 40,043 = 45%.
Total White candidates 48,874 = 55%.

When the final returns were counted, Kenneth Gibson had swept all but the North Ward, Imperiale's home base, where he ran third behind the Councilman and Addonizio. His total was more than double that for the incumbent Mayor but 8,000 votes short of the majority for election without a run-off. Just as significantly, the total number of votes garnered by the Black candidates came to 40,043 as against a combined total of 48,874 for the four White candidates. The total turnout, 65.37 per cent of the total registered in the city, topped the 1966 percentages by a little more than 3 per cent, but indicated that a good deal of apathy had prevailed despite the large roster of candidates. Turnout in the all-Black Central Ward, where many of the sample points in this survey were located, was 58 per cent, well below that for predominantly White wards in other parts of the city. All six candidates nominated for the City Council by the Black and Puerto Rican caucus, however, made it into the run-off.

Councilman Imperiale, who polled 13,978 votes, when asked

whom he would support in the run-off, said, "I will have to go home and speak with God and my conscience before I make that decision. It will be a matter of choosing between the lesser of two evils." (He eventually endorsed Addonizio.)

John P. Caufield, whose vote if transferred was large enough to put Gibson over the 50 per cent mark, declared for Gibson and assumed an active role almost immediately in the Gibson campaign.

When the survey went back into the field prior to the run-off election, voters were asked how they had voted in the May 12 elections. Their replies confirmed very closely the preferences expressed in the poll prior to the voting on May 12, except for a shift of 5 per cent among Blacks from Richardson to Gibson.

Of the inner-city residents in the sample, 58 per cent had voted for Gibson, 18 per cent for Addonizio, 11 per cent for Imperiale, and 7 per cent for Caufield. Of White voters interviewed, 13 per cent had voted for Gibson in the first round in these low-income neighborhoods; 7 per cent of Black voters had cast their vote for Addonizio. Italian-Americans had split down the middle between Addonizio and Imperiale, although 11 per cent of those interviewed reported voting for Gibson.

Forty-five per cent of the Black sample, before adjusting for registered voters claimed to have voted on May 12, as compared with 53 per cent among Whites, indicating an unexceptional turnout in central-city precincts. Among registered voters the turnout of Whites in the sample was 3 per cent higher than for Blacks. The poorest, youngest, and least educated voted well below the citywide average. Italian-Americans voted well above the citywide average for other Whites, and even farther ahead of the Black turnout.

These figures suggested that a Gibson victory in the final election would depend on what changes occurred in voter turnout between the two elections as well as his ability to improve his showing among White voters, particularly those whose first loyalties had been to his new supporter, John P. Caufield.

The strategy for the Gibson camp in the next phase of the campaign depended on a judgment as to whether there were enough registered Black voters to assure the election of a Black mayor with their votes alone. Robert Curvin, Community Affairs Director for Rutgers University in Newark, estimated the division of registered voters in the city at 50 to 54 per cent White. Others placed the percentage of Black voters at 45 to 53 per cent. (The U.S. census report on the 1968 election estimated that in the North 61 per cent of non-White voters turned out, compared with 72 per cent for Whites.) Eventually, those who believed Blacks were probably the minority prevailed, although Gibson's willingness to take his campaign into White areas seemed dampened by his desire to remain as the symbol of Black identity in Newark.

Some attempt was made, nevertheless, to play down race as a major theme of the Gibson campaign—"Elect Ken Gibson, a man for all the people"—and eliminate references to Black Power from the official campaign literature. However, Gibson campaigned with the Reverend Ralph David Abernathy, Dick Gregory, and Black athletes from the New York Mets, Jets, and Knicks. The organizational effort was stepped up to mobilize a bigger Black vote in the heavily Black Central and South wards. One campaign aide said: "We have got to bring out another 25 or 30 per cent of the registered voters, and if Gibson doesn't get at least 10 per cent of the White registration, it will be a close election." University students, Black and White, came to Newark as volunteers in the canvass effort.

Another line of strategy was to de-emphasize the role of Le Roi Jones and Black militants in light of an Addonizio campaign to portray Gibson as a front for Black extremists and to avoid at all costs any outbreaks of racial disturbance.

Caufield charged that Addonizio had offered him "anything I wanted in City Hall" in return for his support, but he said he was supporting Gibson because "all I want from City Hall is honesty, integrity, efficiency, and a fair deal for all citizens of Newark."

Voter Preferences—Second Round
Now that the choice had been narrowed to Gibson and Addonizio, shifts indeed took place when voters were asked a week to ten days before the June 16 run-off how they intended to vote.

VOTER INTENTIONS IN JUNE COMPARED TO MAY

	Vote May 12		Preference June 16		Change	
	Black-PR	White	Black-PR	White	Black-PR	White
	%	%	%	%	%	%
Gibson	85	13	87	22	+2	+9
Addonizio	7	36	6	60	−1	+24
Not sure	—	—	7	18		

The progression for Gibson had been from the 3 per cent of Whites in the survey who said they had voted for him in 1966 to the 5 per cent who indicated their preference for him a few days before the May 12 round of voting to the 13 per cent who reported they had actually voted for him, then to the 22 per cent who said they now intended to vote for him on June 16. With the "not sures" removed, Gibson's share of the Whites in this survey came to 27 per cent.

Although Gibson's first round percentage (85 per cent) of Black votes was increasing only slightly in these inner-city neighborhoods, his share of the White vote had increased by nearly ten points, with nearly one in five still undecided. Addonizio's small share of the Black vote was holding firm. But the Whites who had voted for Addonizio's opponents in the first round of voting were not all swinging his way in the two-man final.

One reason for this was that the Mayor's trial on charges of extortion and income tax evasion actually began during the second campaign period, despite his efforts to have it postponed, (In the January Quayle poll, 98 per cent of Blacks and 52 per cent of Whites with an opinion had said they thought the Mayor was guilty of the charges.) The timing of these dramatic headlines about political corruption in Newark coincided with the decisions being taken by voters torn between their racial anxieties and disenchantment with the Addonizio Administration.

Of the White voters who said that they intended to vote for Gibson on June 16, 38 per cent had voted for Caufield in the first election. One in three of these said that their grandparents had been born in the United States. But the national origins of the others reflected a broad array of European ethnic groups (15 per cent Polish, 12 per cent Irish, 12 per cent Portuguese, 12 per cent Italian, 7 per cent German). Four out of ten came from families that included a union member. A clear majority of all Whites voting for a Black candidate in these inner-city neighborhoods could be classified as White ethnic Americans.

When asked why he was voting for Gibson, a Polish-American engineer, who had listed planes flying over his home into Newark Airport as the number one problem on his mind, said simply: "I don't think Gibson can do any worse than Addonizio did." A sixty-five-year-old, retired, Irish service worker said: "Gibson will bring in a new group of politicians. Maybe they will have a whole new set of ideas that will bring Newark back on its feet." This from a twenty-five-year-old, married, White factory worker: "I feel he will have better control over his own kind. I feel the Negroes will show greater respect for law and order if they have a Negro mayor." A forty-five-year-old woman, Irish-Catholic and an unskilled worker, cited high taxes as the city's number-one problem: "That's why I'm voting. Addonizio hasn't done anything for the people. Let's see what Gibson can do."

A skilled Polish craftsman shifting from Caufield to Gibson said: "Addonizio doesn't deserve to be re-elected. I think Gibson would do a better job for all the people. What would happen to the city if Addonizio were convicted?" A Portuguese taxi driver: "Newark is so bad now, Addonizio has been mayor a long time. Gibson's more educated and will put all the bad elements in their place, Maybe if we get a new man who really cares and he tries to understand the problems of all the people, maybe Newark might survive."

The importance of these White voters willing to vote for a Black mayor was apparent when the reasons volunteered by respondents for backing their candidate were categorized and examined. Over one in three Addonizio backers volunteered to interviewers that they were voting for the Mayor because he was White, Three out of ten Gibson voters declared that they were voting for the Black candidate because of their desire for a Black mayor, equalled only by the number who said it was "time for a change":

"Black power is getting people in office who will help you," testified a twenty-two-year-old Black clerical worker, "I think Gibson will help us Black people."

"Because I don't want to vote for a colored man, I have to go with my own kind," declared a sixty-year-old Italian craftsman.

"Addonizio helped us," conceded a forty-five-year-old Black salesman, "but he was helping himself at the same time."

"If you put a nigger in," said an Imperiale voter shifting to Addonizio, "you might as well bury the city."

"He's an Italian like I am," said a middle-income construction worker. "That's good enough for me."

When the 1970 voting preferences in the inner city were compared with the actual results of the 1966 contest between Addonizio, Gibson, and Carlin, the movement of voting blocs between the two elections became clear.

The massive shift of Black voters from Addonizio to Gibson, compared to Gibson's showing of four years ago in a three-way

1970 VS. 1966

	White		Black-PR		Italian		All Voters	
	1966	1970	1966	1970	1966	1970	1966	1970
	%	%	%	%	%	%	%	%
Addonizio	70	73	50	7	92	90	59	28
Gibson	3	27	42	93	8	10	17	72
Carlin	27	—	8	—	—	—	24	—

race against two White candidates, is the most conspicuous trend. Italian-Americans, on the whole, retained their loyalty to the Mayor. Carlin's White vote in 1966 exactly equals Gibson's White vote in 1970, following his backing by the heir to the following of Newark's last Irish-American mayor. The vote in the poll of these low-income neighborhoods of Newark showed them going 72 to 28 per cent for Gibson compared to a 58 to 18 per cent split with Addonizio in the first round, Thus, while the Mayor gained ten percentage points with the elimination of his White rivals, Gibson gained fourteen percentage points in spite of the predominance of Black voters in the sample who had turned out almost monolithically for Gibson from the outset.

The Final Returns
This is the citywide vote, as revealed when the final returns were in on June 16.

ACTUAL VOTE—JUNE 16

	Raw Vote	Per cent
Gibson	55,097	56
Addonizio	43,086	44
Winning margin	12,011	100
Turnout 76%		

Sample precincts selected by WNBC, New York, to build a model for election night projections of the voting returns in

Newark, confirmed the fact that Gibson polled better than 20 per cent among White voters in the election. In a precinct in the more affluent section of Vailsburg in the West Ward, Gibson increased a 4 per cent share of White votes on May 12 to 27 per cent on June 16, paralleling almost exactly the swing picked up by this survey in racially mixed, low-income neighborhoods in the central city. According to WNBC projections, Gibson tallied about 95 per cent in all-Black precincts.

In short, the White voters of Newark who voted for the Black candidate for mayor rather than for Hugh Addonizio provided most, if not all, of Gibson's winning margin of 12,011 votes. These included White ethnic Americans of modest income, living in racially mixed neighborhoods. The evidence would indicate that the charges of extortion and income tax evasion, on which Mayor Addonizio was found guilty shortly after Election Day, plus dissatisfaction with governmental services in Newark, motivated these voters more powerfully than racist tendencies supposedly present in such blue-collar groups. The data in this survey also indicated that Whites who voted for Gibson were most prepared to believe that all races would be treated fairly by a Black mayor. Some of this feeling was undoubtedly the result of Kenneth Gibson's positive image among White voters, his bland personality, and his low-key campaign.

Although many who voted for Gibson in the run-off election had supported Caufield in the first round of voting, principally from non-Italian ethnic groups, there was no evidence in the survey that their votes were the result of anti-Italian bias. By the same token, Italian-Americans, like Blacks, showed a strong loyalty to the candidate with whom they felt an ethnic identity.

Bearing in mind that the voters of Newark—Black and White—were urgently concerned over the problems of crime, drugs, and public safety, placing them at the top of their priority lists, it seems likely that Mayor Addonizio's indictment created a credibility gap for him on the city's principal political issues. Six out of ten Whites who said they planned to vote for Gibson cited the need for a change in City Hall, compared with one in six who spoke of his personal qualities and one in ten who thought the time had come for Newark to have a Black mayor.

The increase in turnout between the first round of voting on May 12 to the run-off on June 16 was approximately 8 per cent (7,000 votes), not nearly as sharp as that which had occurred in a similar situation in Los Angeles involving Mayor Sam Yorty and Black Councilman Thomas Bradley. In that race, Bradley led the first round and lost the run-off, although polling 39 per cent of the White vote. (Blacks, of course, are a much smaller proportion of the Los Angeles electorate, and Yorty did relatively well among Mexican-American voters.) The Newark election had fewer open appeals to racist voting. The turnout figure of 76 per cent was very comparable to that in Cleveland the year before when Mayor Carl Stokes was re-elected. But considering the character of the candidates and the intensity of the issues involved in the Newark election plus the special efforts made to involve the population in the election, a turnout of only three out of four registered voters was not very high. The available data do not show whether Blacks and Whites voted at the same rate, although the survey showed that Blacks were more interested than Whites (63 per cent "very interested" versus 50 per cent of Whites). At the same time, as the election neared its climax nearly one in five White voters had been unable to say how they intended to vote and individuals under cross pressures often solve their dilemma by staying at home on Election Day. Women tended to be more undecided than men.

Some of the psychological factors which seemed to effect the disposition of inner-city residents of Newark to participate in the political process will be examined in the next chapter.

Chapter Six

PSYCHOLOGICAL FACTORS

To test the attitudes of those interviewed on a number of matters possibly related to their motivation to participate or not to participate in the electoral process, each was handed a card containing twelve different statements "people have made to us" and asked to indicate whether "you agree strongly, agree somewhat, disagree somewhat, or disagree strongly." Although the statements were listed in random order, they actually represented the positive and negative side of six different states of mind, characterized by the reciprocal descriptions over each set of quotations:

1) *Civic—Uncivic*
   a. "Everyone has a duty to vote even if there isn't much difference between the candidates."
   b. "A good many elections aren't important enough to bother with."
2) *Involved—Estranged*
   a. "Voting is an important way that people like me can have a say about how the government runs things."
   b. "People like me don't have any say about what the government does."
3) *Effectual—Ineffectual*
   a. "If you pay attention, anyone can pick up enough information to vote intelligently."

b. "Politics is just too complicated for people like me to understand."

4) *Connected—Isolated*

a. "This neighborhood is a real home to me."

b. "Nobody around here even knows I'm alive."

5) *Partisan—Non-Partisan*

a."If I don't know anything else, which party a candidate belongs to tells me a lot whether to vote for him."

b. "Political parties don't mean much to me anymore."

6) *Optimistic—Pessimistic*

a. "In the long run things are gradually getting better for people like me."

b. "Nothing will ever happen to make things better for people like me."

The scale of agreement or disagreement with each of these statements could be matched against whether the respondent was or was not a registered voter, thus providing an opportunity to match various states of mind with the decision to become eligible to take part in the election process. The feeling, for example, that "everyone has a duty to vote" provoked agreement from nine out of ten registered voters in the sample, 67 per cent saying they "strongly" agreed with that. A significantly smaller proportion of the unregistered showed this sense of civic duty, and one out of five took open exception to the idea that everyone should vote.

A similar pattern prevailed on the reciprocal side of the question, although only six out of ten registered voters chose to disagree that "a good many elections aren't important" and 34 per cent thought that to be true. A plurality of unregistered (45 to 43 per cent) agreed that elections sometimes aren't important enough to bother with, while an additional 12 per cent weren't sure.

Clearly, both the value attached to the duty to vote and the perception of the saliency of a given election are part of the participation process.

Registered Blacks shared the same sense of civic duty as registered Whites, and the unregistered of both races were equally weaker in their motivations in this sphere. Education and maturity had a significantly positive effect on feelings of civic responsibility.

A scale was constructed on the basis of whether respondents agreed strongly, agreed somewhat, disagreed somewhat or disagreed strongly on each of the pairs of statements. Those, for example, who agreed strongly that everyone has a duty to vote and disagreed strongly that some elections aren't important enough to bother with were rated "high" on being civic and "low" on being uncivic. Those 50 per cent whose answers clustered in the median ranges of agreement or disagreement were rated "medium."

The importance of a value system emphasizing the duty to vote and the importance of elections shows up in the resulting figures.

"UNCIVIC"

	Total	Black-PR		White		5th Grade or Less	High School or Beyond	Under 30	50 and Over
		Registered	Un-registered	Registered	Un-registered				
	%	%	%	%	%	%	%	%	%
High	39	30	52	24	49	45	31	40	38
Medium	39	45	34	42	39	41	43	41	38
Low	22	25	14	34	12	14	26	19	24

Close to a majority of both unregistered Blacks and unregistered Whites have a high "uncivic" score on the scale. Those with the poorest educational background had a strong tendency to have a weak sense of civic duty.

When scales were constructed for all six negative psychological states—(1) uncivic; (2) estranged; (3) pessimistic; (4) inefficacious; (5) nonpartisan; (6) isolated—the top correlation was between the scale for inefficacy and unregistered voters.

PSYCHOLOGICAL STATE AND REGISTRATION

		Black-PR		White	
	Total	Regis-tered	Unregis-tered	Regis-tered	Unregis-tered
High	%	%	%	%	%
Uncivic	39	30	52	24	49
Inefficacious	41	28	53	32	58
Nonpartisan	32	24	32	35	51
Isolated	20	19	28	11	16
Estranged	19	11	24	14	36
Pessimistic	18	10	21	24	20

Among Blacks, unregistered voters are likely to have a low sense of duty and strong feelings of political incompetence. Among Whites, weak attachment to political parties is also characteristic of the unregistered, as well as the other two states of mind. Isolation, estrangement, and pessimism appear to be less involved with participation than the other three factors, although among Blacks and Whites there was a definite relationship between feelings of being isolated or estranged and not being registered to vote. Pessimism is stronger among unregistered Blacks than registered Blacks, but this is not true for Whites.

Blacks in this survey felt more loyalty toward political parties but less estrangement from government than did Whites. Blacks were more optimistic, and Black voters more so than Whites over the possibility of long-run improvements in their lot. Inability to comprehend the complications of politics bothered both Blacks and Whites, and it was the leading characteristic of the unregistered voters of both races.

The sense of being socially isolated in the urban core was less intense than some had anticipated, and it was only half as strong among Whites in low-income neighborhoods in Newark as among Blacks. Education seemed to have no bearing on feelings of isolation, although those with the lowest income felt more isolated than the average. Young people had the strongest sense of being cut off from their neighbors.

Only 8 per cent of the Italian-Americans in the survey scored in the high range on the scale of isolation, as compared with 23 per cent for Blacks. Italian-Americans were twice as pessimistic, however (31 to 16 per cent high on the scale), over future improvements in their lot. Black voters felt more strongly than anyone except White voters backing Gibson that people can have a say about what government does.

The pages to follow show the complete breakdowns for the answers to the six pairs of psychological probes.

The President's Commission on Registration and Voting Participation concluded in 1963 that the reasons for low participation are both legal and psychological. The 1961 Report of the U.S. Commission on Civil Rights advanced the theory of "cumulative deprivation": that is, those who suffer the bias of our formal institutions are usually also the victims of inadequate education, poverty, social disorganization, and an accompanying feeling of psychological inadequacy.

If there is indeed a relationship between education and the motivation to vote, and between political self-confidence and participation generally, strategies to increase participation in the political process cannot be considered apart from the total condition of the urban poor. Voting is part of a social process. The combination of mild motivation and institutional obstacles to vote must be attacked from both ends of the equation. But if one avenue only could be pursued there is probably more to be achieved by breaking down the barriers of institutional bias than in trying to energize the potential electorate beyond present motivational levels.

In Newark, not even the possibility of electing the city's first

CIVIC

"EVERYONE HAS A DUTY TO VOTE"

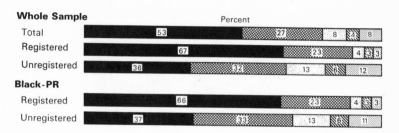

Whole Sample

Percent

Total	53 · 27 · 8 · 4 · 8
Registered	67 · 23 · 4 · 3 · 3
Unregistered	36 · 32 · 13 · 6 · 12

Black-PR

Registered	66 · 23 · 4 · 3 · 3
Unregistered	37 · 33 · 13 · 6 · 11

UNCIVIC

"A GOOD MANY ELECTIONS AREN'T IMPORTANT"

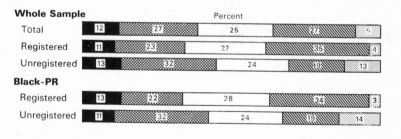

Whole Sample

Percent

Total	12 · 27 · 25 · 27 · 9
Registered	11 · 23 · 27 · 35 · 4
Unregistered	13 · 32 · 24 · 19 · 13

Black-PR

Registered	13 · 22 · 28 · 34 · 3
Unregistered	11 · 32 · 24 · 19 · 14

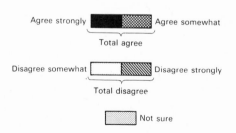

Agree strongly ▮ ▨ Agree somewhat
Total agree

Disagree somewhat ▯ ▨ Disagree strongly
Total disagree

▨ Not sure

INEFFECTUAL

"POLITICS TOO COMPLICATED FOR PEOPLE LIKE ME"

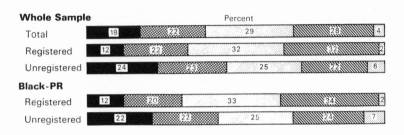

EFFECTUAL

"IF YOU PAY ATTENTION, ANYONE CAN VOTE INTELLIGENTLY"

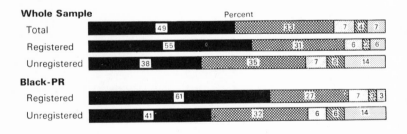

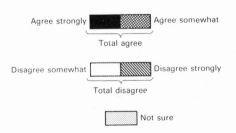

PARTISAN

"WHICH PARTY TELLS ME A LOT"

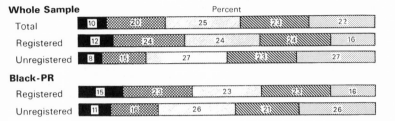

Whole Sample   Percent
Total
Registered
Unregistered
Black-PR
Registered
Unregistered

UNAFFILIATED

"POLITICAL PARTIES DON'T MEAN MUCH"

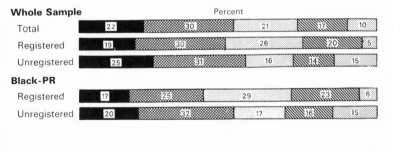

Whole Sample   Percent
Total
Registered
Unregistered
Black-PR
Registered
Unregistered

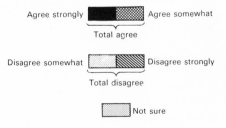

Agree strongly ▮▓ Agree somewhat
⎵ Total agree

Disagree somewhat ▢▨ Disagree strongly
⎵ Total disagree

▨ Not sure

ESTRANGED

"PEOPLE LIKE ME DON'T HAVE ANY SAY"

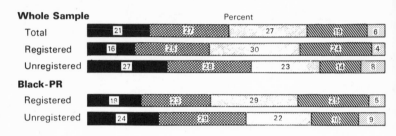

INVOLVED

"VOTING IS AN IMPORTANT WAY TO HAVE A SAY"

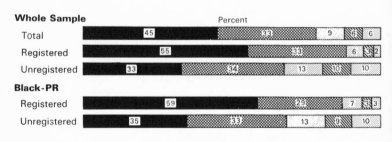

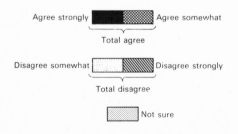

ISOLATED

"NOBODY KNOWS I'M ALIVE"

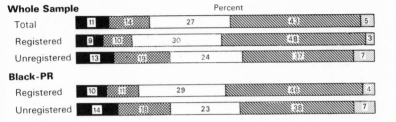

CONNECTED

"THIS NEIGHBORHOOD IS REAL HOME TO ME"

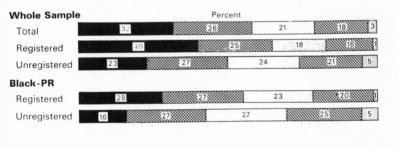

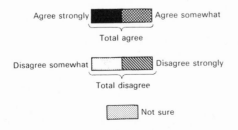

PESSIMISTIC

"NOTHING WILL EVER HAPPEN TO MAKE THINGS BETTER"

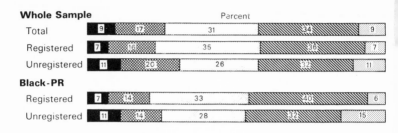

OPTIMISTIC

"THINGS ARE GRADUALLY GETTING BETTER"

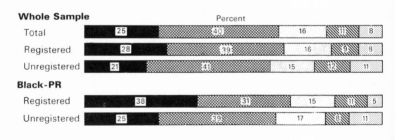

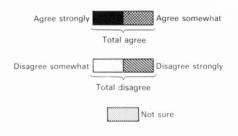

Black mayor triggered an exceptional registration and turnout. As we have seen, this was the result of a system that places the onus on the would-be voter to qualify himself on the registration rolls and of very real psychological barriers that prevent individual residents of low-income neighborhoods of the central city from taking an active part in the system.

We turn now to a similar election in Cleveland, Ohio, in 1969, when that city's first Black mayor, Carl Stokes, sought re-election, and also to the 1969 election for mayor of New York City, where the fate of John V. Lindsay was partially dependent on his ability to rally the participation of Black and Puerto Rican voters.

This tale of two cities further examines the efficacy of organized attempts to increase greatly the registration and turnout of minority group voters in situations where their self-interest would seem to be directly at stake.

PART TWO

A TALE OF TWO CITIES: CLEVELAND, OHIO, AND NEW YORK CITY

An eyewitness account of the 1969 re-election strategies of Black Mayor Carl B. Stokes and White Mayor John V. Lindsay in their racially mixed constituencies.

Chapter Seven

THE POLITICS OF RACE

The plight of the American city became a test of its political spirit in the autumn of 1969. Mayoralty elections in New York City and in Cleveland, Ohio, two polyglot symbols of the old American dream and two urgent examples of the new urban crisis, engaged most of our ideals of democracy at the polls. The tale of these two cities hovered between the spring of hope and the winter of despair. Would the outcome validate fears that it was, indeed, the worst of times? Or was there hope, if not for the best, for better times?

The issue, simply put, involved the relative balance between voters who would use their franchise to express an emotional response to the problems of race and poverty and the countervailing ability of the disadvantaged poor to advance their interests within the electoral system—backlash vs. frontlash, White vs. Black; voters prepared by education and middle-class values to organize an impact on the election returns against the uneducated, disorganized, even apathetic poor.

The social and economic parallels between the situations in New York City and Cleveland were the common denominators of urban social change: a postwar influx of Black and Puerto Rican minorities to a central city blighted by the shift of jobs and White population to the suburbs. Both cities struggled with the inadequate resources available to finance schools, housing, or programs to alleviate the health and welfare needs of the underemployed poor. A deterioration of city services to insure safety, remove garbage, and expedite transportation was accelerating even more rapidly than rising taxes. The frustrations of urban living had triggered violence and disorder in the sprawling ghettos of each, although the scale of outbreaks in the Hough and Glenville areas of Cleveland had attracted more national notoriety than similar disturbances in Bedford-Stuyvesant and Harlem.

Lindsay and Stokes
The political equation facing two incumbent mayors running for re-election was the reverse image of an identical dilemma. In New York, Mayor John V. Lindsay, White, Anglo-Saxon, Protestant, fought a defensive action in the Catholic and Jewish precincts of Queens and Brooklyn against the charge that he had been overly sympathetic to the aspirations of minority Blacks and Puerto Ricans. At the same time, his campaign organization launched a full-scale effort to produce compensating pluralities on Election Day in non-White neighborhoods.

Cleveland's Black mayor, Carl B. Stokes, enjoyed the advantages of racial identification among potential voters within the East Side ghetto, but was handicapped on the opposite side of the city in the White, ethnic enclaves composed mostly of Eastern European stock.

The arithmetic of the ballot box could not produce victory for either candidate, even if he achieved a monumental turnout of the minority vote, without substantial support from the White community. The goal in each case was to maximize one without alienating the other.

Both Carl Stokes, first elected to a two-year term in 1967, and John Lindsay, who won a four-year term in 1965, represented the activist approach to the tough job of urban chief executive. With the help of federal funds from a Democratic Administration in Washington, they had inaugurated new programs and new agencies to tackle the massive problems of poverty, blighted housing, hard-core unemployment, deteriorating schools, drug addiction, and rising crime rates. Stokes, a Democrat, became embroiled in political fights with city councilmen from his own party over such issues as the spread of low-income housing into middle-class neighborhoods. Lindsay found himself in the middle of angry tensions between White teachers and Negro and Puerto Rican parents over his administration's experiments to decentralize the public schools. The concern of both mayors for the needs and aspirations of the minority groups in their respective cities touched off insecurities within the ranks of White voters about jobs, their neighborhoods, and even their personal safety on the streets.

The style of the two candidates for re-election, although reflecting their differing personalities, shared the common attributes of most of new breed of American mayors who had come to the forefront in the era since the inauguration of President John F. Kennedy. Articulate, problem-oriented, young, dynamic, they brought an image of motion to the encrusted interiors of City Hall. Their ideas for saving the cities included high-risk ventures into the established preserves of businessmen and bureaucrats. Their wars against complacency were justified by the extent of the crisis of the city. But the recurring call to battle stations had fatigued the populace, wearing thin its stamina while escalating its emotions.

Stokes, a Black man in a 62 per cent White community, originally had won office in 1967 with the votes of one in five White voters, in addition to the nearly unanimous support of the city's 90,000 Black voters who came to the polls. Stokes defeated Republican Seth Taft by a mere 1,679 votes, although Cleveland had been a Democratic stronghold for years, with better than eight out of ten voters registered Democrats. Although Stokes could not have won without 30,000 White votes, the fact remains that three times as many Whites abandoned their traditional

Democratic ties rather than vote for a Black candidate for mayor. An unusual feature of the 1967 Cleveland election was that the turnout in Black voting precincts *exceeded* by a narrow margin the percentage of eligible voters who came out in White precincts. (When Kenneth Gibson carried Newark three years later, the turnout in Italian-American precincts was 85 per cent, eleven points higher than the 74 per cent turnout in Black areas.)

It is a normal fact of American political life that participation in the electoral process increases in relation to a rise in education and income. It is also true that voters who feel internal conflicts between their normal voting habits and the available choices often resolve these cross-pressures by staying home on Election Day. The overall turnout in Cleveland in 1967 approached 80 per cent—high for a municipal election—but Stokes's victory was fashioned out of a delicately balanced mixture of Black self-consciousness and White forbearance measured against the sum of hostility and apathy.

That equation takes on added significance since the 1970 census showed fourteen major American cities with a Black majority of population and another forty with a non-White proportion of 25 per cent. The interracial characteristics of the urban politics of the future, extrapolated from the experiences of the present, raise questions not only of individual voting behavior but also of the structure of the institutions regulating popular involvement in the electoral process.

The problems presented are not limited to situations where Black candidates must enlist White support in order to be elected, or where White candidates will face Black majorities, but include the fate of White officeholders sensitive to the needs of minority groups in their constituencies but faced with the practical requirements of holding together a biracial coalition to achieve a winning plurality.

Although there has been a good deal of attention paid to "backlash" or polarization among the Whites, and especially the Wallaceite proclivities of lower-income, blue-collar families, the introduction of a potentially large but historically deprived Black electorate into the political systems of American cities remains comparatively unexamined.

Lindsay, a White Protestant and, in 1965, a formal Republican running in an ethnically diverse and predominantly Democratic New York City, duplicated the narrow Stokes victory in Cleveland by formulating many of the same issues in the reverse racial context. He managed to win better than two in five Black votes only a year after Blacks had gone against the Republican Presidential candidate by over 90 per cent. The difference added up to his 100,000 vote margin over two opponents who together outscored him consistently except for his banner pluralities among fellow W.A.S.P.S. and liberally minded Jews in his former Manhattan Congressional District. Turnout was relatively low in White precincts, but lower yet in Black and Puerto Rican areas. The citywide average was less than 75 per cent as against 87.5 per cent in the Presidential election.

The New York equation differed from Cleveland's in that a higher participation by Blacks and Puerto Ricans in 1965 might have hurt more than helped Lindsay, since most who came out then continued to vote the Democratic ticket. Four years later, however, that situation had been spectacularly changed by racial tensions in the city and the nomination of "law and order" candidates by the two major parties to oppose Lindsay, who was now running on the Liberal and Independent lines. Lindsay's polls showed him registering better than 80 per cent among the two non-White minorities. Now his goal was to activate this support, get them on the voting rolls, and turn them out on Election Day—all without further alienating the White majorities who collectively preferred his two opponents.

Thus, for both Carl Stokes in Cleveland and John Lindsay in New York, their 1969 campaigns for re-election became tests of their ability to bring minority-group voters into the system in their fight for political survival. Going for Stokes were the factors of racial and party identification, neither of which was working for Lindsay. Going for Lindsay was a White electorate with a past record of crossing party lines for "liberal" causes and a cosmopolitan tradition of ethnic accommodation, however strained by contemporary upheavals, neither of which could be said of the Midwestern, industrial center on Lake Erie. Against them both was the political apathy of the ghetto.

The eventful 1969 re-election of mayors John V. Lindsay of New York and Carl B. Stokes of Cleveland illustrated the new force of Black voters in American urban politics. The final returns from those cities also documented the capacity of Black voters to polarize their support around a single candidate—apart from party membership and beyond the influence of time-honored methods for organizing voters in city neighborhoods.

Although both Lindsay and Stokes made token gestures toward activating Black voters by direct contact in the precincts, their campaign strategists all but wrote off the worth of standard grass-roots techniques in the asphalt jungles of poverty. The Black vote, however, delivered itself to the polls—motivated more by fear than pride, in response to messages absorbed from television rather than handbills or position papers, and in spite of the institutional bias of American elections against the poor, the uneducated, and the isolated non-White.

Although neither candidate could have won without nearly monolithic pluralities in Black election districts, the turnout of eligible voters in those districts was unexceptional. Although both paid special attention to trying to add Black voters to the rolls before the election, these efforts were, in the main, unsuccessful.

Disconnection, outmoded electoral regulations, and indifference to the practical benefits offered from City Hall all served to keep thousands of potential Black voters outside the system. In the end, Lindsay and Stokes owed their elections not to any success in increasing political participation among the disenfranchised, but rather to the massive, bloc vote of those Blacks interested enough to go to the polls more or less by their own volition. The implications of these facts on the politics of the seventies are worth examination.

What will happen when a White minority of the population enjoys a majority position on local election rolls? Will Black majorities unite only behind Black candidates? How will Black minorities in the cities organize their votes to become an effective balance of power among White candidates? The response of White voters to new patterns of racial balance has attracted the attention of both scholars and the media. The other side of the equation, the response of Black voters, is equally fascinating, and no less significant to the future shape of urban politics.

Taken at face value, the successes of Lindsay and Stokes alleviated some of the concerns aroused earlier in the year, when a Black candidate in Los Angeles led the primary but lost to Mayor Sam Yorty in the runoff. Actually, Councilman Thomas Bradley carried a larger share of the White vote (over 30 per cent) while losing in Los Angeles than did Carl Stokes while winning in Cleveland (24 per cent).

Bradley, it was said by some, ran poorly in Mexican-American districts. Lindsay carried Black areas in New York by better than 80 per cent, although 58 per cent of the city as a whole voted for his opponents. Puerto Rican voters were twenty points lower than Blacks in rallying behind Lindsay. Special factors in each instance make such statistics dangerous foundations for simple generalizations. Not too much is clear, for example, regarding Spanish-speaking "backlash," although Hispanic minorities have been even more outside the political process than their Black counterparts. Political rivalry within minority groups, it is fair to say, can be more fierce than other forms of ethnic conflict. The urban politics of the seventies promises to be a storm test of the willingness of every species of American to make common cause with one another.

Chapter Eight

THE STOKES FORMULA IN CLEVELAND

The Stokes story in Cleveland was that the first Black mayor of a large American city polled fewer Black votes in 1969 running against County Auditor Ralph J. Perk—a White Republican—than he did in 1967, but nevertheless managed to increase his narrow overall plurality. The key was Stokes's ability to increase his small share of White support by some five percentage points between the two elections while holding the almost total backing (97 per cent) of Black voters who came to the polls. That combination gave him a winning margin of 3,753 in 1969 as against 1,679 two years before.

One could take a pessimistic view of the fact that a man who had become a national figure, who was a Democrat in a city where Democrats outnumber Republicans eight to one, who was a personable candidate endorsed by both local newspapers, who enjoyed the backing of the downtown business establishment, and who focused his public statements on biracial cooperation, managed to capture only 5,000 additional White voters between the two elections. The crucial character of this shift is underlined by the fact that had Stokes merely duplicated his 1967 run in all White wards, he would have lost in 1969.

The racial solidarity among Blacks for a Black mayor concealed the absence of any conspicuous effect of his political

breakthrough on rank-and-file political involvement. Total registration in Black wards in Cleveland went down, although it is
difficult to measure the impact of shifting population and blighted
housing on the potential number of eligibles. Since census data
are thought to be unreliable in the central cities (the figures are
quickly out of date and do not conform to voting boundaries),
and since the analysis of voting is a tedious and expensive process, most politicians simply throw up their hands when asked
to estimate the number of nonregistered eligibles.

Cleveland had a system of permanent registration in which
voters were kept on the lists unless they failed to vote in two
consecutive elections. The Black wards of Cleveland turned out
80 per cent of their lists in 1967, higher than the 79 per cent
in White wards. It was one of those rare occasions when low-
income turnout exceeded that in higher-income areas. Participation ordinarily rises with education and income, but the practical
possibility of electing a Black mayor for the first time upset these
patterns among all races in Cleveland in 1967.

During the 1968 Presidential year, on the other hand, only
66 per cent of Cleveland's Black voters had exercised the
franchise, a trend repeated across the country and one which may
well have cost Humphrey the election in such states with large
Black electorates as Ohio, Illinois, Missouri, and California.

In any case, the attrition of eligible Black voters in Cleveland
who sat out these two elections could have been substantial.
The prospect of a member of the Black race in the top post
of the local political structure failed to excite the interest of two
in ten Black voters in 1967. Stokes's local campaign for Hubert
Humphrey failed to activate one in three Black voters in 1968.
The turnout of Black voters in 1969 for Stokes himself fell below
80 per cent of those eligible, a defection more serious because
of the drop in their absolute numbers on the voting lists.

There were noticeable differences in the scale of efforts to
register Black voters in Cleveland during the two mayoralty campaigns. In 1967 Stokes enjoyed the technical assistance of experi-

enced White suburbanites attracted by the opportunity to advance the cause of Black opportunity. They worked on the professional details behind the scenes. Martin Luther King, Jr., and aides from the Southern Christian Leadership Conference came to Cleveland and spoke to rallies in Hough and Glenville, the ghetto areas on the city's predominantly Black East Side.

The local chapter of the Congress on Racial Equality, supported by a $25,000 grant for voter education from the Ford Foundation, made a special effort in 1967 to increase registration in three East Side wards. CORE provided leaflets, neighborhood canvassers, sound trucks, baby-sitters and transportation to the Board of Elections central registration office. Card tables containing information sheets and maps of registration locations were set up in front of supermarkets and discount stores in the area. The drive achieved considerable notoriety in the local press and charges by Republicans in Cleveland and Washington that nontaxable funds were being diverted to the partisan advantage of Democrat Stokes.

When the books closed, the net gain in Black registrants over the year before in the three target wards came to a grand total of 1,147! And this was at a cost of better than $20 per registrant.

Two years later, Martin Luther King was gone and so were the White suburbanite volunteers, banished by Stokes to mollify the party organization. The 1969 registration campaign was run from City Hall and channeled through the ward headquarters of Democratic councilmen. Two veterans of the 1967 effort had gone off to Atlanta to help the cause of a Black candidate for vice mayor there. CORE had shifted its focus to Black nationalism, but its offer to supply experienced paid workers to the Stokes registration drive was refused.

When the books closed this time, the same three wards showed a net loss of 2,912 eligible voters from the 1967 figures. Registration in Black and mixed wards throughout the city in 1967 was down by more than 11,000 as compared with an increase over 1967 in White wards of more than 2,000. Round Two of Carl

Stokes's battle for the mayoralty had obviously generated more heat in Cleveland's White community than any comparable awakening of political involvement among Cleveland's Blacks.

The trend did not escape the attention of the strategists for the Stokes campaign. Two years before they had experienced a rude shock when the turnout in Black wards for his successful primary fight dropped ten points between the primary and the general election. They had geared up the primary to such a pitch that some voters expressed surprise when Stokes was not immediately installed in City Hall after it was over. This time, opposed in the primary by a weaker rival, they decided to try to crank things up only once, saving the big push for the main event.

The Arithmetic of Black and White Votes

But it was not so simple as that. The arithmetic of politics in a city of polarized racial attitudes is a subtle art. If Candidate A, for example, can be expected to win all the Black votes and Candidate B is going to win most of the White votes, the equation for victory becomes highly selective. In Cleveland there were 316,000 registered voters for the 1969 election, 196,000 (62 per cent) White, 120,000 (38 per cent) Black. If everybody voted and everybody voted the straight color line, Stokes would lose by 76,000 notes.

But, of course, everybody was not going to vote and the color line was not going to be drawn 100 per cent of the time. In his first victory Stokes had polled slightly less than 20 per cent of the White vote and an average of 95 per cent in the Black wards. (It was not 100 per cent because an occasional White voter sometimes never escapes the Black ghetto. Also, the poor are most likely to become confused when trying to operate a voting machine. In mixed areas of the North, where race is not part of the official record, estimates necessarily contain a slight margin of error. The most solidly segregated Black ward in Cleveland went 98.2 per cent for Stokes in 1967.)

Professor William Irwin, a member of the political science faculty at Case Western Reserve University, on leave to assist the Mayor, and Professor John F. Burke, Jr., of Cleveland State University set their calculators to work on the raw data of the voting lists. The first calculation to be made was what would happen if the 1969 election turned out to be a carbon copy of the 1967 election except for the inescapable new fact that Black registration had dropped while White registration had risen. Applying the 79 to 80 per cent turnout rate of 1967 to the new numbers on the voting lists, they discovered the bad news that Stokes would lose on that distribution if everything else stayed the same.

Here is some simple arithmetic. Take 79 per cent of the registered Whites and give 80 per cent of those to the Republican candidate; take 80 per cent of the registered Blacks and give 5 per cent away to Stokes's opponent and you end up with an equation looking roughly like this: White vote for Perk (125,000) plus Black vote (4,000) equals 129,000; White vote for Stokes (31,000) plus Black vote (92,000) equals 123,000. Q.E.D. Stokes loses by 6,000!

When Irwin and Burke sorted and re-sorted their numbers against different levels of turnout on Election Day, they could produce a matrix showing just what the result would be for each percentage point change in the number of White and Black voters going to the polls. Holding the Stokes proportion of the White vote at one out of every five and his proportion of the Black vote at better than nine out of every ten, the only combination putting Stokes over the top would be if somehow the percentage of Blacks turning out to vote exceeded the percentage of Whites voting by six points or better—an extremely unlikely eventuality.

If Whites and Blacks turned out in approximately equal percentages, as they had in 1967, Irwin's computations produced another disturbing guideline. Stokes would lose by a bigger margin in a high-turnout election than in a low-turnout election; his deficit increasing as the larger base of White voters in Cleveland gave his opponent bigger pluralities than produced by a smaller base of Black voters, even though the latter gave nearly all their votes to Stokes.

Although the figures seemed complicated and not self-evident to politicians accustomed to cruder methods of calculation, their story was clear enough for the Stokes strategists to grasp. Little was to be gained by cranking up a campaign aimed at urging every voter to do his duty at the polls unless someone could figure out a way to heat up the mostly Black East Side to fever pitch while keeping the mostly White West Side complacently calm. In this era of mass media coverage, that would be a neat trick.

When the professors reworked their figures to indicate what might happen if Stokes could increase his proportion of the White vote, even slightly, the numbers began to dance. Here is some simple arithmetic again. Take 79 per cent of the registered White vote and this time give only 78 per cent instead of 80 per cent to the Republican candidate; leave the Black figures the same. Now the equation becomes: White vote for Perk (122,000) plus Black vote (4,000) equals 126,000; White vote for Stokes (34,000) plus Black vote (92,000) equals 126,000. A dead heat!

Now try it again with Stokes drawing 24 per cent of the White vote. Stokes amazingly wins—no matter what the turnout—as long as White voters and Black voters are going to the polls at approximately the same rate. At 80 per cent turnout the Stokes plurality is better than 6,000 votes. At 70 per cent it is still 5,000 votes. This leaves a cushion, if the Black turnout drops below White turnout, of approximately 2,000 votes per percentage point drop in Black election districts.

The winning formula was clear: put maximum effort into reassuring White voters, even at the expense of running a dull campaign that strikes no extra sparks of enthusiasm among Black voters. And indeed, this became the nub of the 1969 Stokes campaign strategy in Cleveland. On election night it turned out this way: White turnout 74 per cent; Black turnout 78 per cent; Stokes's share of the White vote was 22 per cent, Professor Irwin figures. (Data collected by Burke showed Stokes polling between a low of 18 per cent and a high of 36 per cent in White and mixed wards on the West Side). Stokes's plurality was 3,753 votes.

When the returns were in, Ralph Perk declared that he had "always said that if there was a light vote Carl Stokes would win. If the vote had been heavier, the story would have been different." Perk supporters blamed a cold, persistent rain throughout the afternoon, leading to a monumental traffic jam on Interstate 71, for cutting down the turnout in the White wards on the West Side. The total vote throughout the city was down 20,000 from 1967 and the overall percentage of the registered vote down from 79 per cent to 76 per cent. Perk's best West Side wards, 2 and 9, had turnouts of better than 80 per cent and his poorest, Ward 8 (with a large population of Puerto Ricans), had a turnout of only 67 per cent. This lent some credence to the theory that the hopes of Perk, who, himself, was of Czech descent, depended on a huge backlash of blue-collar voters. Whatever the reason, it failed to materialize in Cleveland. A second White candidate, Sydney Stapleton, of the Socialist Workers' Party, polled 1,476 votes running on a platform against the war in Vietnam and the "oppression of Black people."

Stokes had the nominal support this time of the Cuyahoga County Democratic organization, but several of the White councilmen from the West Side avoided identifying their campaign with his. Council President James V. Stanton, who had been considered to be the natural White leader of the party until the Stokes 1967 victory, was openly hostile. (He was later elected to Congress.)

On Election Day, Cleveland policemen turned up at East Side polling places in Black neighborhoods in civilian clothes with credentials qualifying them as "volunteer challengers" on State Issue I, a referendum on giving nineteen-year-olds the vote. They had met earlier at two East Side halls, the Polish People's Home and the Slovenian National Hall. They brought box lunches and 18,000 registration notices returned because the voter had not been found at the listed addresses. Some carried arms. Obviously the intent was to hold down the turnout in Black precincts.

Stokes ordered his Irish-American police chief (removed after the election) to investigate. At 4:30 P.M. the call went out over the police radio: "The activities of members of the Police Department, wherein, they are reportedly acting as witnesses and challengers for State Issue I in this election, is a violation of the charter of the city of Cleveland, the laws of the state of Ohio, and the rules and regulations of the division of police."

Two of Stokes's strongest East Side wards—17 and 18, where he garnered 96 and 97 per cent of the total vote—turned out only 71 per cent of their registered voters. Wards 24 and 25, on the other hand, where Stokes received 98 per cent of the total vote, had turnouts of 77 and 78 per cent respectively. The highest turnout in the city—85 per cent—was in Ward 13, where Stokes received 90 per cent of the votes cast, and he polled 97 per cent in Ward 10 on the Southeast Side in a turnout of 81 per cent. Obviously, the influences governing the proportion of Black voters who went to the polls in Cleveland in the 1969 mayoralty operated at a variance of ten to fifteen percentage points, with middle class Black areas outvoting the poor and disadvantaged. How much police intimidation contributed to this is difficult to measure.

The fundamental political assumptions underlying the Stokes approach were (1) a Black Democratic candidate running in a Democratic city against a White Republican opponent could count on the solid support of every Black voter who turned out; (2) a rock bottom seven in ten of the eligible Black voters would come out in this type of municipal contest with only a normal amount of organizational prodding; (3) a bedrock two in ten of the eligible White voters would vote for a Black candidate for mayor as long as he seemed more "moderate" than "militant," and this proportion might be improved a marginal amount by careful campaigning; (4) the practical danger of an exceptionally big outpouring of hostile White voters was far more real than the unrealistic dream of an exceptionally large outpouring of dedicated Black voters.

The Stokes Style

The political style of Mayor Carl Stokes suited this script extremely well. He reflected the old rather than the new breed of Black politicians, having served an apprenticeship in the Ohio Legislature. And he dutifully seconded the nomination of his old friend Hubert Humphrey at the uproarious 1968 Democratic national convention in Chicago. The air of the fortress-like City Hall alongside Lake Erie was not unlike that of hundreds like it, except for their White incumbents, across the land. Mayor Stokes was walled off behind a set of partitions guarded by courteous but protocol-minded veterans of bureaucratic service. The table of organization was designed to serve the familiar clients of local politics at a leisurely pace, in contrast to the organized chaos and brash purposefulness one encountered around a Robert Kennedy or Richard Hatcher.

Stokes, himself, was a handsome, friendly appearing figure of a man. And yet his incandescence seemed to light on cue, like a mask beaming at everyone in general but at no one in particular. His natty suits, with colored handkerchiefs tucked just-so in the breast pockets, looked as if they might have come off the rack of Harry Truman's haberdashery, a shade this side of River City. He did not seem a man who would go out of his way to offend anybody, not even an enemy.

Standing in the brisk autumn air at the rapid transit stop on the White West Side, greeting the stoic Slavic faces which were pointed toward home, a can of beer, and a plate of dinner, Stokes was a figure without horns. Among his own in a church basement on the other end of town, he cautioned, "I didn't become mayor to baby-sit for every problem of the Negro people." Appearing at a housing project before an audience of welfare mothers, he clapped his hands for order at the milling band of children. "Sit down, little people," he commanded. "If you want to sit up here, there can't be any talking." His remarks began shakily when he referred to this FDR-vintage project (Valleyview) by the name of the newer, more handsome houses (Riverview) a few blocks away. There was a scattering of hisses, but Carl flashed a broad grin and made a quick recovery. He pledged "decent low-income housing in desirable locations—not the old parts of town where the factories, railroads, and high crime rates are." There were no local reporters present, but he reminded his audience that "I've taken a lot of punishment for saying low-cost housing should not be in the worst sections." (Applause) "I don't want to make a speech," he concluded. "I just want to answer anything that's on your mind. Come down to the Hall. We want to know if we're doing right or wrong. If we don't come to you, you come to see us, heayah."

A close campaign associate of Mayor Stokes said after the election: "The name of the game was to pursue a campaign of low-key reassurance on the White West Side. In the Black wards, on the East Side, the effort was made to stir up as much activity and enthusiasm as possible. The critical matter in the Black wards, of course, was level of turnout, and we used every means at our command to increase it." A hostile witness might describe this strategy as two-faced, but it was dictated by simple political prudence. And Carl Stokes was ideally suited to carry it out.

While the Black-published *Call-Post* was telling its readers that "Perk Plans Racist, Last-Hour Attack!" and "Failure on the part of Cleveland's Negro voters to turn out in massive numbers next Tuesday, November 4, might well cost Mayor Carl B. Stokes, their symbol of dignity and progress, the election...," he was described in the White-owned *Plain Dealer* as "the Great White Hope . . . an affirmation of America's promise that any qualified man can achieve."

On the one hand, Stokes was able to stand as a folk hero

in Black neighborhoods; on the other, his nonthreatening language and impeccable connections in the business community made it possible for some Whites to accept the idea that he might help to keep Cleveland cool. Many of those who could not, apparently, solved the cross-pressures of their dilemma by withdrawal as opposed to crossing over to the Republican party. They chose not to participate at all in the voting.

An Unsuccessful Gambit

Two years later, after two frustrating terms in the Mayor's Office, Carl Stokes chose not to run for re-election. With talk of a national Black Caucus which might back a Black candidate in various 1972 Democratic Presidential primaries as a bargaining card at the national convention, Stokes was anxious, nonetheless, to demonstrate his personal political clout in Cleveland. The experiment involved entering his former campaign director, Arnold R. Pinckney, as an Independent candidate for Mayor.

The Republican nominee was again Stokes's old opponent, Ralph J. Perk. Before backing Pinckney, Stokes had thrown his support in the Democratic primary to the anti-organization candidate, James Carney, who did well in Black wards to win the nomination. With a White Democrat and a White Republican thus nominated by the two major parties, Stokes then switched to Pinckney, who, it was hoped, would win the solid Black vote while the White vote in the city splintered between Carney and Perk.

The gambit failed, and along with it the national political reputation of Carl Stokes was badly damaged. He had violated the principal lessons of his own campaigns—low-profile activity among Black voters while courting a solid minority of Whites. The arrogance of the last-minute attempt to manipulate the Black vote shocked Whites while alienating many Blacks. Pinckney ran far behind Stokes's 1969 count in the Black East Side wards and polled fewer than 200 votes in each of nine White wards.

Although the total vote dropped another 10,000 from the 1969 tally, the turnout in White precincts dropped only half as much as the drop in Black wards. White turnout *exceeded* Black turnout for the first time since the 1965 mayoralty election. Pinckney, running twenty points behind Stokes on the East Side, trailed Perk by 12,579 and the two White candidates together received 80,000 more votes than the Black. According to results from sample precincts analyzed by the NBC elections unit, Pinckney received no more than 77 per cent of the vote in Black precincts while 21 per cent was going to his White Democratic opponent and, as before, only 2 per cent to Republican Perk. More telling, Pinckney received no more than 2 per cent of the vote in all-white precincts. The high-profile campaign, concentrating on Blacks, polarized White voters in a way that had never happened in Carl Stokes's own campaigns. One result was the eclipse of Stokes as a potential leader of Black political aspirations nationally. He left Cleveland to take a job as a television news anchorman on NBC's New York station.

A Ceiling on Participation?

The data from Cleveland suggest that there may be a level of registration and turnout among disadvantaged voters beyond which it is very difficult to go under present institutional arrangements. Methods of grass-roots organization or even the 1969 presence of a relatively charismatic candidate in a polarized election did not greatly alter the rate of political participation. Actually, participation diminished among both Blacks and Whites in Cleveland as they became more accustomed to the actuality of a Black mayor. Small increments appeared to be restricted mainly to areas characterized by higher incomes and education and, to some degree, membership in a politically activated church.

One has to look beyond the limited structure of the present process of registering and voting to make major gains through this ceiling on political participation, which seems to prevail in urban centers across the whole land. The complete roster of our social institutions—education, distribution of income, housing patterns—as well as the workings of our election laws in fifty states and the District of Columbia are all relevant to those who remain disconnected from the electoral process.

Chapter Nine

MOBILIZING MINORITY VOTERS
IN NEW YORK

The 1969 re-election of Mayor John V. Lindsay supplied final proof of the death of clubhouse machine politics in New York City as well as the feebleness of party labels when voters are moved by independent issues.

Party loyalty has traditionally been most unshakable among the poorest and least educated—handed down in the family along with physical features or religion. Since Franklin D. Roosevelt, the allegiance of Black voters to the Democratic party in the North has been one of the constants in the ebb and flow of two-party politics. The Lindsay New York City victory in 1969 showed that Black voters—poor as they were, so cut off from middle-class channels of political dialogue, conditioned by reflex to reach for the Democratic lever on the voting machine—were fully capable of perceiving a new set of self-interests and acting upon them independently at the polls.

Blacks in New York City had given better than 90 per cent of their votes to Democrats Robert Kennedy and Lyndon Johnson in 1964, and again to Democrat Hubert Humphrey in 1968. In his first 1965 campaign, John Lindsay had devoted special attention to Bedford-Stuyvesant and Harlem, the two biggest concentrations of Black population, and earmarked a portion of his sparse media budget for a major effort on radio stations catering to Black audiences. His 1965 mark of polling 40 per cent of the vote in Black precincts was unprecedented for a Republican candidate, twice that polled by the Republican candidate in the mayoralty contest four years before. But the fact remained that a clear majority had stayed within the familiar pattern and pulled the voting machine lever over the name of Democrat Abraham Beame. Even so, Lindsay's margin of increase (twenty percentage points) in the Black electorate represented about 100,000 additional votes—not very far off the exact plurality, 136,144, of his 1965 citywide victory.

In the more polarized atmosphere of 1969, the Black vote was from the outset a high-priority item in the Lindsay re-election strategy. It was an important component of his Manhattan blitz, an all-out drive to extract every last Lindsay vote from his sympathetic home borough to offset the expected defections in alienated Brooklyn and Queens.

Manhattan is smaller than the two boroughs across the East River. But it contains a decisive proportion of upper-income Jews, who in years past had broken party lines to support such liberal Republicans as United States Senator Jacob Javits and Governor Nelson Rockefeller, as well as Lindsay himself, a former Congressman from the "Silk Stocking" District on Manhattan's East Side. The Mayor's private polls showed him relatively strongest from the start among the affluent group dubbed "Manhattan limousine liberals" by the Democratic candidate, Mario Procaccino. By contrast, lower-income Jews living in the racially tense neighborhoods of the outer boroughs had not only been alienated by the Lindsay Administration's role in a series of disputes over neighborhood control of the public schools, but year in and year out had also constituted the most reliable White voting bloc for the Democrats.

The Manhattan arrangement was to be a nonvisible but highly organized drive to pull out a maximum Lindsay vote on Election Day, while the candidate concentrated his public activity in the other boroughs, hitting the issues revealed by his polls as having the most leverage with potential vote switchers. Some Jewish voters, for example, were anti-Lindsay on his handling of the Ocean Hill-Brownsville dispute over "community control" of schools by Black and Puerto Rican parents but pro-Lindsay for his early stand against the war in Vietnam. The argument that Lindsay had put a fourth police platoon on the streets during high crime hours, and over the opposition of backers of Lindsay's two mayoralty opponents, showed unanticipated pulling power.

The defensive strategy in Brooklyn and Queens included nightly forays by canvassers briefed in Manhattan headquarters, loaded into buses, and sent forth to ring doorbells in marginal election districts. The candidate toured synagogues with such regularity that, or so the story ran, Lindsay was a more familiar sight than fountain pens at a Bar Mitzvah. He unveiled a battalion of new snow-removal equipment in Queens (where residents had been stranded for days under the drifts after a blizzard during the winter of 1968-1969) the final week before the election. He haunted the Mets ballpark, although he doesn't care much for baseball, until the day the team clinched the pennant and the players fortuitously poured champagne over his unstuffed shirt to front-page pictures in the newspapers and top play in the evening television newscasts.

While Lindsay was on view in the "provinces," his headquarters in the former DePinna store on Fifth Avenue worked behind the scenes to firm up Manhattan. A technician on loan from the Republican National Committee organized a phone-calling operation to saturate the Upper East Side: first, to amass a list of those for Lindsay; second, to get those not on the voting lists to register; and, finally, to pull out the Lindsay vote on Election Day. The West Side, home territory of the Democratic Reform Clubs backing Lindsay, worked out an experiment with the Board of Elections to permit voters to register during August at card tables set up on the sidewalk. Nearly half the new voters added to the citywide rolls during this period came from Manhattan alone, and most of these from either the phonathon districts on the Upper East Side or in areas on the Lower East Side and West Side where mobile registration was tried.

The telephones and the card tables were marks of the general collapse of door-to-door, organizational politics in the city. Workers were afraid to canvass after dark, when the majority of city voters could be found at home. Doormen barred the entrances of apartment houses and, where there were no security forces, tenants were afraid to open their doors to strangers. The organization of voting lists by party, by ethnic background, and by local address could be assigned to the computers by anyone with sufficient funds to pay the costs. The phone numbers of those in the economic class which possessed private phones could be matched against the voting lists by the use of criss-cross directories. Volunteers to call up voters are recruited most easily from among young college girls—who respond to a charismatic candidate or moral issues, who often find companionship in grassroots politicking, and who, in the words of Senator Eugene McCarthy's former campaign manager, "consume telephone calls like popcorn."

Middle-class voters are still reachable by the technique of private mass communication. The telephone, however, lends itself more to activation than persuasion, offering no friendly cues to the anonymous, and discussion is too easily terminated. One willing to proclaim political fealty on the phone can safely be counted as a top prospect to cast a similar vote on Election Day; heckling him to the polls does not even shatter his allegiance. The good news from Lindsay's Manhattan East Side phone operation was that better than six in every ten persons reached on the phone gave back an affirmative reply. Another two in ten said they were "undecided," a dangerous category when counting noses by phone. But only one in ten turned out to be aggressively hostile. Here was prime territory for a saturation phone campaign on Election Day.

But what about the Blacks and Puerto Ricans? The questions pondered by Richard Aurelio, Lindsay's campaign manager, were: (1) How far could the normally Democratic voting behavior of these minority groups be switched toward a White Anglo-Saxon Protestant running on a third-party ticket? (2) How could Mayor Lindsay meet the fears of White voters over racial tensions without betraying his support of programs for the disadvantaged? (3) If Lindsay could amass substantial support in Harlem and Spanish East Harlem, could it be translated into effective pluralities on Election Day to build up the Manhattan blitz?

Although Aurelio scrapped most of the Lindsay storefront neighborhood headquarters set up by his predecessor four years before in favor of a "media-oriented" campaign, he made exceptions for the West Side, South-Central Harlem, and two pockets of Puerto Rican voters along Columbus Avenue in the West and either side of Park Avenue in the East 100s. These centers for possible volunteer activity, distribution of literature, voter registration, and visibility in the neighborhoods were a grudging concession to the proponents of "participatory democracy," although Aurelio's private opinion was that they would probably cost more than they were worth and should not be allowed to divert important money from the purchase of commercials on television.

A semifinal test of this theory was available for four days in October, when New Yorkers were permitted to add their names or correct their voting residences on the permanent registration rolls. This was done at the same polling places as those used on Election Day, so that a vigorous effort in a specific locality, if it produced results, would show up in the tallies for each Assembly District.

The problem for the storefronts was the difficulty of acquiring accurate information on the eligibles who might not be on the voting lists in a particular area. People do not readily volunteer that they are ineligible to vote. In low-income districts, particularly, the voting lists are seen as a roster for jury duty, bill collectors, and visits from the law. Those who move often are not familiar with the mechanics for maintaining eligibility at a new address. Door-to-door canvassing with the official lists in densely populated housing projects, for example, is a frustrating experience of misinformation, language barriers, hostility, and fright.

An intensive review by staff assistants in the Mayor's office produced 40,000 names in New York housing projects thought not to be on the voting rolls. Postcards were sent to each, urging them to become eligible to vote for the Mayor and to show their support for his housing proposals. No one could figure out the results, except for complaints from the Board of Elections that people already voters had duplicated their names on the lists during the registration period. (The registration inspectors in New York didn't check applicants, for some reason, against the existing list.)

The Drive in the 70th Assembly District

One of the beachheads for the Lindsay forces was the 70th Assembly district, which runs through South Harlem on either side of Lenox Avenue northward from Central Park. The 70th contained every problem associated with the plight of the urban poor and had been designated as a target area for the Model Cities program to be financed from Washington and coordinated from City Hall. Its population was calculated to be 65 per cent Black and 27 per cent Puerto Rican, bridging the area south of 125th Street and the westernmost fringes of Spanish Harlem. Of the population twenty-one years of age and over, as calculated by a Lindsay aide in a special report, entitled "Mounting a Voter Registration Drive," and prepared in the office of the Mayor, only 35 per cent were registered to vote in the 1968 Presidential election: that is, 25,000 out of a possible 70,000.

The inviting prospect of a large pool of potential new voters, responsive to the efforts of the Mayor in behalf of community development, had been heightened by the results from the district in the party primaries earlier in 1969. Although only 930 eligibles had taken part in the Republican primary, they had voted 90 per cent for Lindsay over the conservative G.O.P. winner, State Senator John Marchi. On the Democratic side, 7,465 had voted in that primary, and only 6 per cent for Mario Procaccino, the citywide victor and nominee opposing Lindsay and Marchi in the three-way contest. Better than 70 per cent had voted for the then Bronx Borough President, Herman Badillo, the Puerto Rican leader who, after losing the primary, had bolted his party to endorse Lindsay. All this from a district that had voted 67 per cent of its some 20,000 turnout for Democrat Abraham Beame in his narrow loss to Lindsay four years before.

Thus, the 70th Assembly District, with the second lowest total of eligible voters of all the Manhattan districts, offered two kinds of leverage for maximizing the Mayor's Manhattan margin: (1) a massive shift to Lindsay from voters normally found in the Democratic column; and (2) a substantial addition of new voters ready to vote for the Mayor in overwhelming proportions. In addition to his endorsement by Herman Badillo, the Mayor also enjoyed the public support of Percy Sutton, running for re-election as the city's only Black Borough President, and of Black Congressperson Shirley Chisholm.

Although the organization 70th Assembly District Assembly-man, Hulan Jack, remained loyal to the Procaccino ticket, he was not himself up for re-election. Jesse Gray, head of the Har-lem Tenants Union on Lenox Avenue, had won a spirited Democratic primary for city councilman, and was waging an active campaign in the 70th Assembly District modeled on his rent-strike organizational efforts in years past, but divorced from the contest for mayor. The resultant ferment might be expected to add interest in a registration drive without harming the Mayor's prospects too much.

The command post for the Lindsay campaign in the 70th Assembly District was a second-floor loft at Lenox Avenue and 111th Street, across the street from a public housing project and a few blocks away from the community offices for poverty pro-grams in the neighborhood. "Federation of Negro Civil Servants and Community Organizations for Lindsay'' was lettered on the large sign above the ground-floor entrance, locked against vandals, addicts, and other marauders of the high-crime-rate area and controlled by a buzzer from upstairs. In charge upstairs was Mr. Wittie McNeil, an employee of the Sanitation Department and a community consultant to the Model Cities program in the Assembly District.

The Federation represents the societies of Black civil servants in each of the major city departments, a form of ethnic fraternal organization begun years ago by the Irish and Italian immigrants who made their way into the ranks of the police and fire departments. Political activity is forbidden during civil service working hours, but a volunteer working on his own time under the auspices of his departmental social group theoretically becomes a free agent. The idea of Wittie McNeil was that Blacks who had made it into city employment ''owed something back'' to their Harlem communities as well as to a Mayor who had widened the doors of opportunity. And by organizing them through the Federation he might attract a steady flow of volunteer manpower, familiar with the local territory and accountable through their organizations for the tasks assigned.

The charts and maps on the upstairs walls divided the 70th Assembly District into eight principal areas, each assigned to a particular civil servant society. Each night of the week one or more of these societies pulled the duty of staffing headquarters, in addition to performing the regular tasks out on the blocks under their jurisdiction. ''That way,'' said McNeil, ''we can pinpoint who should get the credit, or the blame, for every job that needs to be done. If the posters are up, we know who did it. If some blocks aren't covered, we know why. When registration is finished, we'll have a box score and a pitcher of record for every E.D. in our area.''

The society names on the duty lists had the ring of heroic deeds: Guardians (Police), Vulcans (Fire), Vanguards (Public Works), Sentinels (Treasury), Praetorians (Housing), Cerbereana (Transit), Aegis (Finance), and Altix (Meter Maids). Lindsay headquarters in Spanish Harlem lent Spanish-speaking workers to help out in the Puerto Rican blocks. The housing projects were papered with registration notices and signs describing the location of registration points. Affidavits were offered to prospective new voters who could claim a sixth-grade education in Puerto Rican schools and thereby be exempted from taking a literacy test.

When October arrived, sound tricks toured the streets, blaring "Brothers and sisters. Today is registration day. Mayor Lindsay needs your vote. El Alcade Lindsay necista tu vote. Tu vote es muy importante." Spot announcements were donated generously by local broadcast outlets. A check was made of all polling places in the Assembly District and reports phoned in to the Board of Elections where inspectors were missing or slow in reporting for duty.

When the four-day registration period had been completed, the new voters added in the 70th Assembly District came to a grand total of 1,962— the second lowest total for an Assembly District in Manhattan, where 55,516 were added to the rolls, and an increase slightly below a citywide average of 8.6 per cent and considerably below the better than 10 per cent scored in the high income areas of the East Side, where registration was heavy to begin with. The special effort in the 70th Assembly District was actually eighty-seven names behind the number added in the adjoining 72nd, Percy Sutton's and Charles Rangel's clubhouse territory in Central Harlem. In the more populous 67th, the center of the Reform Democrat registration effort on the West Side, 3,347 new names were added in the October registration period. On a percentage basis, however, the old hands from the West Side did even more poorly than did the new effort in Harlem.

By almost any standard of measurement, however, the Lindsay special registration drive was a failure, and most of all in failing to recruit large numbers of Blacks and Puerto Ricans. Total registration, when the lists were finally purged of deaths and duplications, was smaller than for any mayoralty election since 1957, when permanent personal registration was instituted.

The lone bright spot was the August period of decentralized mobile registration on Manhattan's West Side and Lower East Side—an experiment cutting the usual red tape by bringing registrars directly to prospective voters on the streets. Out of 65,700 registered in all five boroughs during this period, nearly half —32,457—came from Manhattan alone. The top Assembly Districts in the city were (1) the 67th (80th to 100th St., West Side), which registered 5,480; (2) the 61st (Lower East Side), which registered 4,816; and (3) the 69th (110th to 139th St., West Side), which registered 3,324. The figure in Harlem's 70th Assembly District, where mobile registration was restricted by Election Board officials, was 1,680.

Since the Board of Elections had not gotten around to compiling and publishing these additions according to Election Districts by the end of 1970, there was no immediate way of telling how much of this overall dent was among minority groups. But that early advantage made Manhattan second only to Brooklyn in the final number of new 1969 registrants, less than 10,000 behind a borough with a third of a million more population, and well ahead of Queens and the Bronx. The voting trends on Election Night were to make this registration situation even more significant.

Election Day in Harlem
Election Day, November 4, 1969, in Harlem turned warm and dank after early morning showers, the kind of autumn weather one associates with the smell of burning leaves and the tang of fresh cider in the country. The players in the sidewalk craps game at Lenox and 112th rolled the red dice in their shirtsleeves, clutching dollar bills in their fists and imploring the fates. There was not a cop in sight the length and breadth of the main avenue

slicing through the storefronts, housing projects, and blighted tenements of South Harlem.

Strollers in Afro haircuts and brightly colored slacks, old Black ladies clutching their shopping bags, fresh kids sidling down the center of the sidewalk, circling the occasional passer-by like birds of prey, music blasting from the upper stories, the amplified rock beat thumping through the moisture-laden air—this was Harlem on Election Day.

The stoned junkie jived to the beat, like a puppet on wires from the fingers of an epileptic, smiling happily in the embrace of his fantasy. The prostitute lingering at the bus stop, smartly turned out from her sharply creased slacks to tightly wound turban, stared inquiringly over the tops of her huge, rose-tinted glasses, then picked her way past the bucks in front of the Soul Brothers Barber Shop.

Welfare mothers pushed their baby carriages over the asphalt playground in the project, or sat in the sunlight on the wooden benches while the children tugged at their hair and fought amiably among themselves. An old man, tottering on a cane, barely escaped a bus as it swept around the corner of 116th Street. On the back of the bus, blue above the blue exhaust fumes, a sign said simply: "Procaccino—A Mayor for *Everyone.*" Otherwise, it was just another Tuesday in Harlem.

When the votes were officially counted, the citywide totals were:

Lindsay	1,012,633
Procaccino	831,772
Marchi	542,411

Lindsay's citywide plurality of approximately 180,000 votes compared with a Lindsay plurality in Manhattan, alone, in excess of 229,000 votes (compared with 30,000 four years before). The Mayor lost Brooklyn by 45,000 votes and the Bronx by over 13,000 votes. Thus, the Manhattan blitz had paid off handsomely.

An analysis by Louis Harris, based on poll data and a recon-struction of the vote in sample precincts, revealed these break-downs in the vote:

VOTE BREAKDOWN BY KEY GROUPS

	Lindsay	Procaccino	Marchi
	%	%	%
White (79%)	42	35	23
Black (15%)	83	15	2
Puerto Rican (6%)	67	29	4
Jewish (30%)	44	44	12
WASP (6%)	64	10	26
White Catholic (43%)	21	45	34
Italian (15%)	16	50	34
Irish (8%)	19	34	47
Under $5,000 (12%)	48	29	23
$5,000 to $7,000 (19%)	41	33	26
$7,500 to $9,999 (24%)	30	43	27
$10,000 to $14,999 (27%)	35	37	28
$15,000 and over (18%)	59	23	18

The proportion of the total vote received by Lindsay, 42.4 per cent, was the lowest since 1933, when LaGuardia was elected with 39.4 per cent of the total vote. The voter turnout throughout the city, however, was 81 per cent, up sharply from the 73 per cent of the voting lists who went to the polls in 1965 to first elect Lindsay. (Turnout percentages compiled by the mass media tend to be lower than official figures because they often do not tally minority-party vote totals nor take account of those recorded as voting who do not cast a ballot for a particular office, purposefully or otherwise. Also, registration totals have not always been weeded out by Election Day.)

The overall voter turnout was higher than in Cleveland, but there was a large disparity between prosperous, middle-class White areas and Black and Puerto Rican districts. For example, in the 84th Assembly District in Riverdale the voter turnout exceeded 62,000, more than four times the number, 14,659, voting in the 77th Assembly District in the South Bronx, a difference, according to the *City Almanac,* published by the New School for Social Research, "far greater than the difference in the respective numbers eligible to vote." Lindsay's victory, according to the *City Almanac,* was won "by a combination of very heavy pluralities among well-to-do Whites and poor Blacks and Puerto Ricans and a substantial minority of the vote among the middle- and lower-income Whites in Queens, Brooklyn, and the Bronx."

Whereas the Harris breakdowns show that Lindsay's top percentages were scored among Blacks and Puerto Ricans and among affluent WASPS, he managed to carry two out of ten of the votes of White ethnics—comparable to the showing of Black candidates Carl Stokes in Cleveland and Kenneth Gibson in Newark. As in those two other cities, the greatest concentration of bloc voting was among Blacks, even though they were supporting a White candidate in an all-White field. But whereas Lindsay did not do as well as Stokes and Gibson among ethnic Whites (it should be recalled that his political origins are Republican), he ran ten points behind them also in his percentages among Blacks. His victory was undoubtedly due to the split of his conservative opposition between Procaccino and Marchi.

Even so, it was a relatively high turnout of voters in upper-income areas of Manhattan (the focus of his telephone canvassing efforts) that proved more decisive in the end than the more modest turnouts on Election Day of Black and Puerto Rican voters. And in spite of national attention, two in ten of those New Yorkers eligible to vote were content to skip the whole affair.

The "media campaign" mounted by Lindsay did not produce the universal effects on voter interest that some had predicted, although it was notably successful in blunting the sharp edges of anti-Lindsay sentiment. It is fair to say that, where voters are torn between candidates of only moderate attraction and where loyalties are divided beyond traditional party lines, the results of such cross-pressures may be an avoidance of voting which the most powerful media of communication cannot counteract.

If that is true, so-called apathy toward participating in the electoral process in low-income, minority-group precincts is likely to be resistant to one-dimensional approaches to low voter registration and low turnout among registrants on Election Day.

The various images of politics at the grassroots of America range all the way from the Athenian to the Machiavellian. Neither extreme bears much resemblance to reality—a grayish lump of mild public duty mixed with generous portions of public indifference, watched over in the polling places by millions of middle-aged women checking off names in a marvelously monumental duplication of effort.

Time was, perhaps, when well-oiled political machines actually made personal contact with individual voters, organized their support, and efficiently delivered them to the voting booth (even stepping inside to make sure there was no slippage). The middle-class movements of the sixties revived the magic image of "participatory democracy," although Senator Eugene McCarthy's primary vote was poor in most cities and he fared best when affluent, middle-class Americans were organizing one another in the suburbs.

The furious motion characterizing the headquarters of these modern political crusades usually seems to evaporate somewhere between the mimeograph machines, cranking interminably to the squeals and chatter of their volunteer attendants, and the warrens inhabited by city folk. Election Day in New York City—removed from the television cables, milling anticipation, and stale sandwiches at the candidates' main "headquarters"—is about as exciting as U.N. Day in Orange County, California. If any real work was going on, one couldn't find it out there in the precincts.

The trickle of Harlem voters in and out of the neighborhood

public schools during the daylight hours of November 4th, 1969 was scarcely noticeable compared to the holiday crowds thronging the tenement stoops and the gangs of kids tossing firecrackers into the uncollected garbage cans. There was not a political poster in sight. (At the Democratic clubhouse workers explained that since the advent of the poverty program the kids demanded two bucks an hour for that kind of work, and, besides, the Panthers tore the posters down as soon as they went up. The Lindsay people claimed they had seen long sticks with nails on their ends shoved out the back windows of police radio patrol cars during the night, unfriendly cops spearing Hizzoner's picture right off the boarded buildings.)

A block away from Percy Sutton's club on West 130th Street, a lone worker stands on the corner outside P.S. 133. The sour mash fragrance of Heavenly Hill blasts the voter as the clubhouse emissary shoves a long white card into his hand. "This is an official Percy Sutton sample ballot," the card says. "You take this sample ballot into the polling place with you." The card shows how to vote for John Lindsay on Row D, the Liberal line. "Then, Vote Democratic (Column B) for all other offices!" Percy Sutton's name is on line 5B, Borough President, Democratic, and 5D, Liberal, too, but the pitch is to bring the Lindsay voters back to the Democratic candidates for comptroller and president of the City Council. It is all very complicated and confusing, but the election inspectors inside are from Sutton's club, too, and willing to help. They walk in and out of the curtains around the voting machines as if they were going to the pantry.

One of them accosts me and demands what right I have to be within her preserve. She summons a policeman, a slightly built White youth in a uniform that seems two sizes too big for him. He looks uneasy, makes a mild stab at asserting his own authority, then bows to the pressure mounting in the room. "Whatcherdoin here, huh?" With an air of smug triumph I take out a Watcher's Certificate, certified by the chairman of the Independent Party, Richard R. Aurelio, the Mayor's campaign mana-

ger and leader of record for the organization created to give Lindsay an extra line on the voting machine. (The certificates had
been stacked on tables at Lindsay headquarters like handbills
for a ball park event.)

The certificate clearly stated that "the following named person
. . . was duly appointed WATCHER to attend at the Board
of Inspectors at the polling place of the 14th E.D. of the 72nd
A.D. of the City of New York in behalf of said Independent
Body on Election Day, November 4, 1969. (I had filled in the
blanks for the appropriate E.D. as the challenge was being
mounted, a fact that did not escape the attention of either the
policeman or the Democratic inspector.) The policeman gave
me a sidelong glance and began thumbing through his book of
instructions. "Throw him out," the lady commented. "This thing
is no good unless it's been okayed at the club. Look, mister,
go over to the club and get some authority to be in here."

I pointed out to the policeman, in a firm but quiet tone, that
I, the official representative of a political party, was being asked
to go to the headquarters of a rival party to have my credentials
authorized. He continued to thumb through his book of instructions, but now the tone of hostility in the room was swelling.
He motioned me aside a few steps. "Look," he said, "I think
it's probably all right for you to be here, but it looks fishy when
you filled out that thing after you came in. Here, why don't
you take it to another E.D. and give it to them first thing, before
anybody raises a question? Whaddaya say? Be a good guy. If
I let you stay, these dames will be bugging me the rest of the
day. They think they own the joint. Now, why don't you be
a good guy and not make any trouble. Whaddaya say?"

The territorial imperatives felt by party workers are embedded
in the official election laws of New York State. The inspectors
who man the polls for voter registration or elections are all picked
by the Democratic or Republican district organizations (at $26
per day). The four-man Board of Elections in New York City
was not only split between the two parties but, under state law,

could be manned only by members from Manhattan or Brooklyn, the other boroughs not having been part of the foresight of nineteenth-century legislators.

Thus, when John V. Lindsay lost the Republican primary in June, 1969, he also lost the right to official inspectors protecting his candidacy at the polls. He was forced to depend instead on the limited rights of watchers commissioned by the minor parties, or, with State Attorney General Lefkowitz in his corner, on the right to swear in deputies to serve in the state's Election Frauds Bureau. These deputies, many of them bright, young Wall Street lawyers, were farmed out to areas where skullduggery was most feared.

In Harlem, where Percy Sutton's club in the 72nd Assembly District was part of the team and Hulan Jack's club in the 70th was not, the available manpower was sent to keep an eye on the 70th. Thus it was that a young Princeton graduate was stationed in the 28th E.D. and took away a newspaper from the worker stationed in front of the voting curtain, which exposed a large headline in Spanish, "Vote Democratic." There was not much he could do about the "Vote for Jesse Gray" painted in solid colors across the doors on the main entrance to the school.

When the regulars raised a question about the small orange buttons worn by Lindsay poll watchers to identify one another (the law forbids campaign buttons inside the polls), he ruled them permissible. When a machine broke down in the early hours, he heckled the Board of Elections to speed up the repairs. His instructions, he said, were to keep his eye peeled for any unnecessary delays, the *Daily News* poll having reported that Lindsay was favored by 80 per cent of the Blacks interviewed in their sample. One of the countermeasures practiced at Hulan Jack's club, it was rumored, was to spread the false word on the streets that you couldn't vote without being in possession of the routine postcard from the Board of Elections verifying the location of the polling places.

I mounted the long, dark stairs inside the building at 116th and Lenox Avenue leading to the domain of the New Deal Democratic Club, Hulan Jack, leader. I didn't really expect to find a Tammany Tiger in his lair at midday of a tough election. But there he was, alone except for a single visitor and one man with a broom, sweeping languidly around a stack of Procaccino shopping bags in the corner. No workers. No phone calls. Not even any guests. Just Assemblyman Jack, former Borough President of Manhattan, dressed in black, waiting for the roof to cave in.

I told him that I had always heard that the leaders of Harlem campaigned for their man in the streets, talking it up on Election Day.

"Man," said Jack, "have you been out there in the streets? Well, I have and the climate is Lindsay. Ain't no use battling the addicts out there for the Democrats today. Party doesn't mean anything anymore, anyway. It's all television now. Nothing else matters.

"See those buildings over there? When I was a boy we would go over the roofs on Election Day, up and down inside every building, handing out the literature. Why, I wouldn't dare go inside one of those buildings in broad daylight today. Who is going to take a chance on being mugged to pass out campaign leaflets? I send my captains to keep an eye on the polls. What could they accomplish out there on the streets?"

One suspects that party organizations in the big cities, winning or losing, behave at the same level of demoralization the country over. The incentives are gone that could motivate hard work no matter who was the candidate or no matter what the issues. It takes a Robert Kennedy—plus plenty of money—to make contact in the ghetto.

In the Black sections of Indianapolis during the 1968 Indiana primary there was a picture of R.F.K. in a front window on every block, designating the occupant as a Kennedy block captain. Downtown the computer print-outs listing the names and addresses of Black voters went to the flying squads of paid election workers in their rented cars. The block captains steered the beaters through their neighborhoods, calling upon the voters to make good on their debt to the Kennedys. Charisma, plus know-how, plus wherewithal—the combination is rare.

At Wittie McNeil's command post, a few blocks down Lenox from Hulan Jack's abandoned field position, the Election-Day activity for Lindsay was only a faint shadow of a Kennedy operation. The charisma and the money were in comparatively short supply, although someone had sprung for coffee and sandwiches to sustain a half-dozen women and a few high-school kids who were awaiting assignments. McNeil, from a small windowless cubicle, spent most of his time taking phone calls from poll watchers with problems. ("Don't let them get you warm, now. Is the cop a brother? Take his number and get his precinct off his collar. And just sit tight until we get someone over there. You've got every right to be there. Keep it cool until we straighten it out.")

The Lindsay headquarters downtown had recruited Black college students from Morgan State and elsewhere, put them aboard buses at dawn, and deployed them around the city to canvass the housing projects and get out the vote. No one had seen them in the 70th Assembly District, but, then, no one had told McNeil to expect them. ("Maybe you'll find them up at Percy Sutton's club. The help from downtown seems to go that way. I'm not complaining. After all, this is our own independent operation here. But they don't recognize our existence up there.")

Up on West 130th Street, underneath the huge poster of Percy Sutton, a small group sipped on soft drinks out of the clubhouse refrigerator and watched a television soap opera. The folding chairs in the main meeting hall were mostly empty. Assemblyman Charles Rangel had recently left, and explained over the phone that he would be busy until six o'clock getting his campaign accounts in order. Percy Sutton was with the V.I.P.s at Lindsay headquarters downtown. The Election-Day activity, such as it was, appeared to run itself.

A gang of boys swept in off the street and made a beeline

for the refrigerator. Their leader explained that they were part of the Black Citizens Patrol, handing out palm cards as "a constructive form of political action." They were veterans, he said, of Paul O'Dwyer's campaign for the Senate the year before, in which Sutton had also been involved. "Lindsay's got a lot of patching up to do in the Black community. People here have a lot of problems and voting is one of the things they don't have time for. But the people know who they don't want. They don't want any White slavemasters. or Black slavemasters, for that matter. No Space-Age Uncle Toms like Adam Powell or Hulan Jack. Why, Powell showed up drunk to vote this morning. Young people don't go for that. We're going to get the White man's foot off our neck. I might run for something myself next year."

The militant tone was in contrast to the confident complacency exuding from the others, who were like deserving deacons awaiting compliments from the pastor. It was God's will for Lindsay to carry Harlem that day, and He would know whom to reward. That was the luck of politics. Why fight it? Once in a while, the tide was going with you. The boring thing was having to wait until the machines are opened. Until then, there was always television.

It was only five blocks down and three across from there to the faded sign of the Kanawha Club, barely legible through the grime and lowering darkness on 125th Street, a few doors away from the railroad platform along Park Avenue and its trainloads of White commuters heading toward their cocktails and dinners in the suburbs. The polls would be closing three hours from now, and the Democratic organization would be in or out of business for another four years.

The light through the second-floor windows had all the warmth of unshaded bulbs, and no movement was discernible from the street. That was strange, for the Kanawha Club was home base for Frank Rossetti, Democratic leader for New York County, or Chief Sachem of Tammany Hall. It was the party base as well for the 68th Assembly District, on the Upper East Side, where the Italian and Irish stalwarts of a previous era had been forced to make a modest accommodation with the new rank-and-file of Blacks and Puerto Ricans. Today, however, all their chips were on Procaccino.

At the head of the stairs, it became clear that the activity was all in the back. A long bar crossed the room. Standing on top of it, a man in shirtsleeves struggled to reach the fixture hanging down from the ceiling and insert an extension cord running to the automatic coffee urn below. He cursed softly each time the swinging bulb eluded his grasp, and narrowly missed plunging down on to the huge round table set between the bar and a faded oil portrait of Mayor James J. Walker on the wall. At the table, surrounded by a half-dozen glum lieutenants munching on hero sandwiches and Colonel Sanders' Kentucky Fried Chicken, sat Frank Rossetti, as alone with his thoughts as Hulan Jack on the other side of Harlem.

The stacks of cartons against the wall carried the mark of the catering service which had supplied the obvious glut of hero sandwiches. A whole table was covered with them, untouched in their wrappings. A large punch bowl, filled to the brim for the victory never to come, had been covered by a cardboard lid. The five men and one Black woman seated around the table picked at their chicken and waited for the acrobat on the bar to solve the coffee situation. They scarcely noticed the interloper until he asked: Did you know that Colonel Sanders of fried chicken fame had been one of George Wallace's biggest campaign contributors?

Rossetti turned his head toward the questioner as if he had just witnessed a landing from Mars, grunted, and went back to gnawing on a cold chicken leg. The Black lady wheeled. "I'll take Wallace any day," she hissed, "over that hypocrite Lindsay. That's a Black woman talking. You can write it down. I'd rather have Wallace and Maddox any day. At least you know where you stand."

The gray-haired man next to Rossetti, with an Irish twinkle

in his eye, moved in to smooth things over with the reflexes of one who had been to a thousand wakes before, ready to make peace in the kitchen whenever somebody threatened to step out of line. "Have a sandwich," he said, sweeping his hand over the pile of cartons. "We've got plenty. Help yourself."

Rossetti rose to his feet, adjusted his French cuffs, and looked at his wristwatch. "Time for making the rounds one more time," he announced. Two of the men at the tables leaped to their feet, but their faces contained the enthusiasm of frostbite swimmers at Coney Island about to perform for the cameras on New Year's Day. "Did you hear about Wagner?" said another, looking at the front page of the afternoon paper. "Told the reporters he voted for Lindsay."

"Jeez," said Rossetti, "I wish'd I heard that before I voted myself. I might have changed my vote."

Nervous laughter echoed from the entourage, which was not dead sure of the Leader's intent as they marched together out of the Tammany clubhouse toward Armageddon.

The vote and turnout in the 68th, 70th and 72nd Assembly District ended up as shown in the table.

THE FINAL TALLY

		Number of votes				
	Total	Lindsay	Pro-caccino	Marchi	Number Regis-tered	Turn-out
68th A.D.	16,686	9,093	5,340	1,392	21,182	79%
70th A.D.	17,900	13,473	3,238	1,189	24,483	76%
72nd A.D.	18,687	14,742	2,205	996	24,676	76%

The Assembly District with the most Whites and lowest Lindsay plurality, Frank Rossetti's 68th, produced a higher turnout than the predominantly Black Assembly District, the 70th and 72nd, in Harlem. Unlike in Cleveland, in 1969 Whites outvoted

Blacks by a significant margin in New York City. The overall turnout, 81 per cent, was substantially higher throughout the City than in Harlem in spite of special organizational efforts among Black and Puerto Rican citizens in Manhattan.

Whether the standard is that of the Old or New Politics, it is clear that the political mechanisms were operating no more effectively among social minorities in New York City in 1969 than were the other deteriorating institutions of the urban core. About one of every five eligible to vote failed to exercise his franchise on Election Day, and the machinery to increase that proportion by traditional organizational methods had all but disappeared from the scene.

It was John Lindsay's good luck that he avoided defeat not by scoring a breakthrough of participation by the disadvantaged poor. Barely enough went to the polls to have made a sufficient difference had not Lindsay managed to run ahead of his two opponents in the vote cast by Whites. If the turnout of middle-class Whites had been slightly higher and had not Marchi drained off such a large proportion of Procaccino's potential conservative vote, Lindsay would have gone down to defeat with the size of his 1969 pluralities in Black and Puerto Rican districts. A year later, this was to be the fate of Democratic Senate candidate Richard Ottinger in his 1970 race against James L. Buckley and Senator Charles Goodell. Once again Black turnout was poor in New York City, even with a Black candidate on the Democratic ticket running for Lieutenant Governor. And Buckley's victory was the mirror image of Lindsay's good fortune the year before.

Earlier in 1970 liberal Texas Senator Ralph Yarborough failed to win renomination in his state's Democratic primary when expected support at the polls from Mexican-Americans failed to materialize. This was particularly disappointing to him since an ambitious voter registration drive in San Antonio, for example, had seemed to promise otherwise.

The situation among Mexican-Americans in urban centers in

the Southwest and in California is not unlike that already reported among Blacks and Puerto Ricans in such Eastern centers as Cleveland, Newark, and New York. In the next part of this study the registration problem among this significant minority of 12 million Mexican-Americans will be investigated, along with the parallel conditions among the country's nonvoting American Indians.

PART THREE

MINORITY GROUPS IN THE AMERICAN
SOUTHWEST

A political analysis of election data among American Indians on the Papago Reservation in Arizona and Mexican-Americans in the barrios of East Los Angeles, California, and San Antonio, Texas.

Chapter Ten

THE SOUTHWESTERN SYNDROME

The American Southwest is a continent removed from the Black ghettos of Newark, New York, and Cleveland, but the selective character of the political process is even more evident among the descendants of the oldest inhabitants, Indian or Hispanic. The bungalow barrios on the West Side of San Antonio or the East Side of Los Angeles are deceptively attractive to the Eastern eye, accustomed to the grimy exteriors of high tenements or the disemboweled remains of abandoned White neighborhoods. The pastel slums of the Mexican-Americans, with their lovingly cultivated gardens and brightly decorated sidewalls, however, are only a facade behind which overcrowding, poor health, underemployment, and lack of education—all the familiar ills of poverty and discrimination—contribute to their disconnection from mainstream America.

On the reservations assigned to half a million Indian men, women, and children the distant views are often breathtaking and the wide open spaces remain romantically inviting. Then one notices a layer of beer cans lining both sides of the reservation highway, a ribbon of empty metal, a Purple Heart for just one of the psychic wounds suffered by the Red Man at the hands of the White conqueror. In the villages, even the dogs are skinny, or swaying with the bloat of malnutrition. And the progeny of once proud Chiefs are treated like children, irrespective of chronological age, by one of the masterpieces of bureaucratic invention, the Bureau of Indian Affairs.

The culture barriers between the Chicano or Indian and the institutions created by "Anglos," as they say even east of the Pecos, are to some degree even more difficult than those which disadvantage Blacks. The politics of the new frontier, moreover, sometimes takes on a raw hostility that is more carefully masked in older sections of the Northeast.

Because towns and cities are still expanding into open fields and valleys there are more games to be played with annexation, special taxing districts, and political subdivisions. There are municipalities in Los Angeles County occupied only by manufacturing plants which offer no jobs to the adjacent Mexican-American neighborhoods, which are also excluded from their tax resources. Texas cities such as San Antonio are divided into separate school districts with separate tax bases and separate budgets, so that poverty neighborhoods of Blacks and/or Mexican-Americans are tied to inferior public schools while Anglo children go to the best.

A whole separate city, South Tucson, exists within the corporate limits of Tucson, Arizona, an island of Mexican-Americans cut out of the heart of 76 square miles, a kind of Berlin-East Germany situation in reverse. On the desert to the west a wire fence marks the beginning of nearly three million acres of scorched, arid, largely useless land, the Papago Indian Reservation.

Since 1924 all Indians born in the United States have been citizens. But it was not until July 15, 1948 that the Supreme Court of Arizona ruled that Indians in that state were entitled to vote—provided they could pass a literacy test in English. The Papago Reservation and the first government day school go back only to 1917. A small minority of Papago children have gone to off-Reservation Indian boarding schools as far away as Carlisle, Pennsylvania, or Riverside, California. Many did not return, in BIA lingo, "back to the blanket." A study of the nearby Navahos in 1969 found that nearly a third of the entire tribe was functionally illiterate in English.

An Indian's average yearly income is $1,500, less than half the national poverty level. Unemployment on Indian reservations ranges from 40 to 70 per cent. An Indian's average age at death is 44 years. Forty-two per cent of Indian schoolchildren—almost double the national average—drop out before completing school. (The migration of 300,000 Indians to American cities in recent years has removed them from BIA programs and dumped them into some of the worst slum conditions in the nation.)

The average educational level for all Indians in the country under federal supervision is five years, according to *Our Brother's Keeper, The Indian in White America,* edited by Edgar S. Cahn. More than one out of five Indian males have less than five years of schooling. In Oklahoma the average Indian child was 2.2 years behind the educational level of the average Black child.

The superintendent of a mission school for Indian children quoted in the Cahn book explained it this way:

"These kids are learning their values at home unconsciously and operating them at the unconscious level. Then they come to the non-Indian school where the non-Indian values are also taught unconsciously, and there is a conflict.

"Indian motivation is not for personal aggrandizement or for personal self glory, but Indian motivation is that whatever you do, you do for the group. So the Indian youngster at home is taught to be unobtrusive. He works with the group. He adjusts to the group. And then he is brought to the school and he is forced to compete on an individual basis. The dominant value in American culture is material achievement and the schools are geared to that. So the Indian youngster is plopped into this thing, whose values diametrically oppose the Indian system.

"He looks around him, he sees all the norms by which the dominant society measures success, he sees that he does not have them; so why go to school, because the school is the means to an end that is impossible or undesirable to him.''

This conflict of values is exacerbated by textbooks and television shows which brand him an ignorant savage and destroy his self-image. The suicide rate among Indian teen-agers is three times the national rate. Alcoholism is the other symptom of their psychological distress. This conflict of values sometimes involves matters taken for granted by the White man as a spontaneous part of his cultural inheritance, such as the worship of representative democracy.

For thousands of years before the White man came to their hot and dry land in the Sonoran Desert, the Papago Indians practiced their own style of participatory democracy. All of the men of the village attended the nightly meetings to discuss village problems. There was no written law. Since cooperative effort by the group was the key to scratching a living out of fields, diked to trap the precious moisture from the flash floods of July, everyone was permitted to have his say, even if the council lasted until dawn.

The migrant Papago could not afford the Anglo-Saxon luxury of a dissenting minority. He needed a universal consensus among his limited constituency when the time came to clear the washes, move the whole village to the mountains, or to inspire the medicine man to break the magic of a drought.

The object was always unanimity of opinion, arrived at by patient examination of all points of view, a thorough knowledge of the recognized way of doing things, a knowledge cemented by a value system placing compromise reached after a full discussion on a higher plane than any sort of discord.

The concept of politics as a contest for victory between rival factions, the notion of superior status for elected leaders, the fragmentation of common tribal lands into representative districts, and, finally, the vesting of the power to rule in a mere majority—these were the inventions of White men. The White man imposed these new ideas of government as well as new religions upon the Papago, whose caves have revealed the existence of their own culture in the Southwest as long as ten thousand years ago. And in the compulsory schools organized by the White man, the Indian child was encouraged to despise the customs of his ancestors while being drummed with the alien theories of European philosophers of government.

For the Mexican-American, the cultural journey into the American political process is no less bewildering. The rural, feudal origins of the immigrant from Mexico are outside the assumptions of political individualism as perceived by the dominant Anglo. As Edgar Litt, author of *Beyond Pluralism: Ethnic Politics in America,* has observed, "The shared symbols, interests, affection, and real or imagined traits which draw some men together into the group or community are the walls which separate those men from others."

The wall of language is the most difficult to scale when a minority is seeking minimal proficiency in the values of the dominant community. To make matters worse, many Spanish-speaking residents of the Southwest are illiterate in their own language. The social and psychological resources needed for political activity are further reduced by inferior education and low economic attainment. The ethnic enclave, which in one sense gives the Mexican-American the strengths of cultural identification, at the same time keeps him isolated from the process of acculturation. He enjoys little experience or training to guide him toward the skills of political participation.

It is an assumption of the civics courses taught in most Anglo schools that voting is the critical process for articulating the concerns of the average citizen. This assumption is not all that obvious even to those reared with the folk tales of the Boston Tea Party or John Brown's raid at Harper's Ferry. But under the heel of *patronismo,* turned inward toward the consolations of church and family, ground down by the immediate problems of hunger, sickness, and poverty, voting tends to be regarded as a marginal act. Add to this the institutional obstacles erected by a power structure deliberately seeking to exclude minority groups from their proportionate share of influence, and the role of the Indian and Mexican-American in the politics of the Southwest ends up distressingly small.

Chapter Eleven

ARIZONA, A LOST HERITAGE

Of all the states outside the South, Arizona had the lowest percentage of potential eligibles (64.8 per cent) registered to vote
in the 1968 Presidential election and the lowest overall turnout
(51.8 per cent) at the polls. The 200,000 Mexican-Americans and
144,000 Indians who reside in the state constitute most of the
disenfranchised.

Apache and Navajo counties in the northeast quadrant of
Arizona had registration rates 20 to 40 per cent below even the
subpar averages for the remainder of the state. Pinal County,
containing the upper portion of the Papago Reservation as well
as the typical Southwestern small town of Casa Grande, just
off the principal Tucson-Phoenix freeway, had one of the poorest
voter registration levels in the nation—well below 45 per cent
of the adult population.

In adjacent Pima County, at Covered Wells on the Papago
Reservation, only 47 of the 107 Indians eligible voted for governor and congressman in the off-year election in 1966—a ratio
of 43.93 per cent, compared with a countywide turnout of 66.34
per cent. At South Tucson City Hall, 414 out of 769 registered
Mexican-Americans, or 53.84 per cent, voted in the same election.

In the Presidential election two years later, Richard Nixon

and Senator Barry Goldwater carried the county in an 83.77 per cent turnout of voters. The Indians at Covered Wells upped their percentage to 71.87 per cent, still nearly 12 per cent below the county average. (Hubert Humphrey received 84.27 per cent of the vote in this Indian precinct; Goldwater lost the precinct by better than six to one.) In South Tucson the turnout was 73.53 per cent of the registered Mexican-Americans. (Humphrey polled 76.62 per cent of this precinct and Goldwater lost by about five to one.)

Nevertheless, Arizona on May 18, 1970 passed a statute canceling all previous registrations after the 1970 elections and requiring that the books be reopened from scratch. Under the Voting Rights Act of 1965 this ordinarily would have required that in the eight counties of the state with fewer than 50 per cent voting in the 1968 elections the new regulations would first have to be submitted to the Attorney General or to the District Court for the District of Columbia for approval. In 1970, however, the Voting Rights Act was amended and the initiative for compliance passed to the Justice Department to disapprove discriminatory changes in the voting laws. When no such action was forthcoming, the books were cleared and re-registration of minority group members in Arizona proceeded very slowly.

An action was brought in the U.S. District Court in Phoenix challenging the constitutionality of the registration purge, but that court upheld the statute and was in turn upheld by the U.S. Supreme Court. Under the terms of the 1970 Arizona registration law the state list will be purged every ten years. The counties already containing more than a majority who did not vote for President in 1968 were the rural areas in the north and south of the state, where the majority of Indian and Spanish surname residents live, plus Pima County, containing Tucson. The new law, furthermore, closed registration one week earlier than before, eight weeks before an election. The onus of complying over again with registration requirements would probably mean a further dilution of minority-group voting strength in a state where thousands of new residents arrive every year. In Pima County, for example, while re-registration averaged 73 per cent of the 1970 rolls, according to County Supervisor Jim Murphy, the rate in Black, Mexican-American, and Indian precincts was only 50 to 60 per cent. In rural areas, re-registration fell as low as 30 per cent.

Paul Laos, then City Manager of South Tucson, estimated in 1970 that only 35 per cent of the possible Mexican-American voters in that community were on the voting rolls. "I forgot to re-register myself once after being away in Mexico and was taken off the rolls for not voting in a two-year period." He attributed the low figure partly to the Latin tradition of expecting the father to cast his vote in behalf of the whole family, while the women and the young stood respectfully aside. Also, he thought apathy was engendered by "a conservative contentment with the better opportunity here for Mexican-Americans to get beans on their plate plus the sheer difficulty of understanding how local government operates in this country."

Professor Edward Spicer of the University of Arizona pointed out that until 1948 the Indians were regarded officially as wards rather than citizens of the state. On the reservation, Indians can protect themselves somewhat from local prejudice and discrimination, if at the price of isolation from the mainstream. Off the reservation, where one-third of the total number of Indians in the Southwest now lives, an Indian finds himself with inadequate training for urban jobs even after being torn away from his land, his people, and his heritage. The resulting culture shock manifests itself in drinking, withdrawal, and disillusion.

The village of Chui-Chui is in the Sif-Oidak District of the Papago Reservation, twelve miles south of Casa Grande. The mud bungalows have yards littered with junk and the carcasses of abandoned automobiles. The surrounding fields, dotted with mounds of beer cans, are too dry for crops since the well beneath the government-financed windmill went dry. An old mission school building is empty; the children are bused into the public schools of Casa Grande now. The priest no longer lives in the parish house behind the stone Catholic church. The bungalow is occupied by a Mojave Indian from California working in the nearby copper mine, where all but four or five of the workers are Anglos from Casa Grande. There is an anti-poverty representative working with the villagers of Chui-Chui. Some of the women sew dresses in a cooperative venture. At midday, however, some are sound asleep in their bunks. Many of the men are over at the school because it is Election Day in Chui-Chui.

The election is for representatives to the Papagos Tribal Council, a system introduced by the Spaniards and elaborated upon by the Bureau of Indian Affairs to replace the comparative dispersion of the ancient Papago ritual of village pow-wows. The 7,000 Indians on the reservation are divided into eleven districts, each with its own governing body and each with representative rights on the central tribal council. In keeping with the old culture, however, members of the council are expected to return to their home districts for instructions frequently.

This day's election in Sif-Oidak District, however, was made necessary because the results of a previous election had been thrown out by the tribal council assembled in Sells. The elders of the Papago were miffed because an off-reservation immigrant had been nominated by the poverty-program worker and had gone on to win. They simply declared the election null and void, so far have they progressed from the ancient custom of conciliatory dialogue until universal agreement could be recorded.

The stakes of government in this tribe are high this day, because the Papago have been awarded a $1.75 million lease for copper deposits under their land. This for them is a comparatively new development because, unlike for Indians in other sections of the country, it was originally held that they owned no mineral resources found beneath their fields, in accordance with the laws of Mexico under which they had previously lived. The U. S. Court of Claims, which was also adjudicating the true value of the land taken from the Papago to create, the city of

Tucson among other assets, had lately restored the mineral rights to the tribe. And the question now was whether to pay the $1.75 million out in the form of a cash bonus to each individual Indian or to capitalize a plant that might create jobs on the reservation for its Indian inhabitants.

For state and national elections Indians from this part of the reservation must journey all the way to Casa Grande if they want to participate in the White man's political process. It is still a fair journey from Chuppo, Jackrabbit, Kuhatik Anegam, and Cockelhue—the other villages slated to vote for members of the district and tribal councils—to the abandoned schoolhouse in Chiu-Chiu. Before the wells went dry, this had been farming country, with cotton and sugar beets the main crops, and the Papago were spread over the land. Under the ancient rules each village had been autonomous. When one village joined with another on a rare occasion, such as for war, the union was only temporary. The Spanish introduced the call for more centralization and decreed that Indian village governors should be elected every year in the presence of the parish priest. When the Americans came into power in 1854, their idea of government demanded that there should be one head chief for all the Papago, and thus the tribal council was grafted onto a system which had once been informal, egalitarian, and decentralized.

The obligation to vote for these symbols of authority and ambition was not something handed down from the old customs. The ballot conceived by the Papago, nervertheless, was an ingenious accommodation to the problems of literacy. On the wall of the voting place were posted the names of all the candidates, each surrounded by a colored square; yellow, brown, blue, grey, red, etc. Once a candidate runs, he keeps the same color for every election thereafter. The ballot consists simply of a set of these colored squares, and the voter makes an X in the one belonging to the candidate of his choice, dropping it in the box of his village. When the time comes to count them, it is merely a matter of making separate piles according to the color key.

The moderator at the polls on this warm Saturday in February was Vincent Manuel, a handsome figure of a Papago farmer in finely tooled cowboy boots, tailored riding pants, and a bright green silk shirt. An elder from each of the villages sat around the room, able to identify by sight those from his own settlement among the total of 1,200 Papago eligible to vote in this district election. As in polling places the length and breadth of the land, the Indian women folk made sandwiches for the poll-watchers in an adjoining room. Mr. Manuel graciously explained the voting procedures to the White visitors, referred proudly to the democratic traditions of his tribe, and grumbled about the "outsiders" connected with the anti-poverty program who had engineered a temporary electoral coup in the original election a month previous. "We did not permit it," Mr. Manuel said sharply. "These things could not happen if the villagers came out to vote." Low turnout, the final indignity for a people who once would send a deputation to summon anyone who dared not to be present at the council fire, or who once would thrust a lighted cigarette between the toes of any brave whose head might nod as the speeches wore on until council opinion had coalesced unanimously.

The turnout in Sif-Oidak District for this second 1970 exercise in representative local government among the Papago, conducted according to the White man's custom, was hardly more than 16 per cent.

It is hard to imagine a more discouraging manifestation of interest in the forms of community control, until one examines the even smaller figures that have characterized "maximum feasible participation" in elections held in connection with the anti-poverty program or the minimal response to New York City's experiment in decentralized school boards. Is it "apathy" to ignore the trappings of democracy when they have little to do with the substance of meaningful power? Even with nearly $2 million at stake, the Papago people felt little control over the system.

The combination of cultural barriers and marginal rewards has been a powerful deterrent to the political activation of the Mexican-American and American Indian in the governance of the Southwest. But the drive to connect the Chicano and descendants of the original Americans to the electoral system is constantly being renewed and has taken on a new militance with the resurgence of ethnic politics. The registration campaign is the symbolic act of this pressure for recognition, political office, legislative relief, and real power in the community.

What makes the difference between registration campaigns that produce concrete results and those that fizzle out? To cast some light on this crucial question we move now to an examination of two registration efforts among unregistered Mexican-Americans in Los Angeles, California, and San Antonio, Texas.

Chapter Twelve

EAST LOS ANGELES—PARTICIPATION
AMONG MEXICAN-AMERICANS

The slogans of Mexican-American self-consciousness—"La Causa," the cause of justice and equality; "La Raza Unida," the concept of a people unified by cultural pride—are ideas rooted in collective participation. Participation, according to Herman Gallegos, former Executive Director of the Southwest Council for La Raza, "may be the number-one issue of the decade of the seventies." Participation leads to dignity, jobs, equity, and power, he states. "The Mexican-American needs to see how the political system works before devising a strategy to deal with it. He needs a wide variety of organizations—cultural, economic, political—because he needs to learn all the techniques of the power structure by carrying out his own thing. It should not be confused with racism. The search for ethnic confidence among Mexican-Americans is to become a partner in a political process that up to now has been racist toward them in the very real sense of excluding them from control over their own destiny."

The five million Brown Americans in the West and Southwest include one in four families below the poverty line. Because median family size among Mexican-Americans is the highest of all minority groups, a higher proportion than Blacks live in dilapidated housing units. In California, per capita income for the two million Mexican-Americans who live there was $1,380, as against $1,437 for non-Whites in 1969. Most barrio children arrive at school speaking only Spanish and half drop out before finishing the elementary grades. In Texas, 70 per cent do not finish high school. In five state colleges in California in 1969 there were only 247 Mexican-Americans in the graduating classes.

Although Spanish-surname individuals comprise 10 per cent of the state's population, only a single Mexican-American sits in the state legislature as this is written. The state's one Mexican-American Congressman, Edward R. Roybal, represents a district that is now more than 80 per cent Black. When he went to Congress for the first time in 1962, Mexican-Americans lost his representation on the Los Angeles City Council. No Mexican-American has ever served on the Los Angeles County Board of Supervisors although 800,000 make their homes in Los Angeles County. Although California has one of the most liberal registration procedures in the nation (registration is open all year and almost any voter can become a deputy registrar with the power to enroll new voters in his home or some other convenient place), Mexican-American registration is notoriously low, and huge numbers subsequently lose their registration by not voting.

Tony Rios, who heads the Los Angeles Community Service Organization as well as a number of government-funded community development programs in East Los Angeles, explained that the average Mexican-American in California "has always been an isolated immigrant in our neighborhoods. At first, he was isolated in the work camps for his jobs in agriculture, mining, or lumbering. In the barrio, he is afraid and embarrassed to register; he is afraid he will be challenged. Many Mexican-Americans don't feel they are really in the country to stay; they expect to go back. My own mother has been here for over fifty years and only recently did she stop feeling she was going back."

A few blocks down Whittier Boulevard is the storefront headquarters of the Mexican-American Political Association, an activist group which includes many of the young and aggressive exponents of Chicano Power. "Viva Zapata!" posters, a Mexican flag, pictures of John and Robert Kennedy, and a sign proclaiming "Custer Had It Coming" adorn the walls. Abe Tapia, the statewide President from Pico Rivera, conceded that he was "trying to shake up the power structure" in his own 45th Assembly District. "The politicians do not care to register Mexican-Americans," Tapia said, charging that Congressman Roybal maintained his seat with Black and Jewish votes in a tradeoff for letting a Black hold the East Los Angeles seat in the City Council. "You have to educate the community on the issues—housing, education, police brutality—as a preliminary to motivating them to register."

Tapia, who received a college degree from the University of New Mexico, typifies the generation gap that has grown between the new breed of activist Chicanos and the Mexican-American politicians of a previous era. The latter, such as Congressman Roybal and Congressman Henry B. Gonzales in San Antonio, abhor the word "Chicano" after a lifetime spent ridding themselves of the marks of the unassimilated. The new breed downgrades the old guard's liberalism, shocks their social values, and threatens their power base. The infighting perpetuates a tradition of nonsolidarity among Mexican-American politicians in the Southwest, sometimes skillfully exploited by the dominant Anglo.

A survey of Los Angeles City during the 1964 general election showed only 56 per cent of Mexican-Americans registered in comparison to 77 per cent of the Anglo population. The proportion of Mexican-Americans actually voting was 49.9 per cent. Another survey, conducted in 1965-1966 by Dr. Ralph C. Guzman of the University of California, Santa Cruz, showed the registration problem among Mexican-Americans by age and income.

The disconnection of the poor and the young from the electoral

PERCENT MEXICAN-AMERICANS, REGISTERED
TO VOTE—L.A. COUNTY

	Registered
	%
Income over $6,000	73
$3,600-$5,999	49
Under $3,600	40
50 years and over	55
40-49	68
30-39	60
Under 29	40

process is not unlike that previously reported among Blacks and
Puerto Ricans in Newark, New Jersey. Mexican-Americans in
Los Angeles were also asked whether they would favor a political
alignment with Blacks to accomplish their goals. The idea was
rejected by three-quarters of those responding, with the poor
in mixed neighborhoods more likely to favor an interminority
coalition than those living in the barrio. The idea of ethnic unity
centered exclusively among Mexican-Americans, on the other
hand, was endorsed by 81 per cent of those interviewed. The
more disadvantaged the respondent, the more he approved of
ethnic unity.

Tapia, whose MAPA endorsed Black Councilman Thomas
Bradley in his unsuccessful 1969 race against Mayor Sam Yorty,
produced precinct figures to show that East Los Angeles
Mexican-Americans had supported the Black candidate by three-
to-one margins, although defections among the Latinos were
credited at the time with contributing to Yorty's 52.1 per cent
run-off victory. The turnout in these Mexican-American precincts ran just under 60 per cent of those eligible. This must
be compared, however, to a citywide average of 76 per cent.
The kind of Chicano outpouring that had rallied to Senator

Robert F. Kennedy in the 1968 California Presidential primary did not materialize for Councilman Bradley in 1969.

These key elections in 1968 and 1969, as well as the statewide races for Governor and U.S. Senator in 1970, focused major attention on registering the unregistered in California generally and Los Angeles in particular. In addition to the partisan campaigns mounted by candidates, political parties, labor unions, and political action groups, nonpartisan campaigns were sponsored in 1968-1969 by the League of Women Voters and the Mexican-American Community Programs Foundation (MACPF), funded by the Southwest Council of La Raza, a Ford Foundation program to encourage community development and participation in big-city barrios.

In East Los Angeles, the League of Women Voters Education Fund established a Greater East Los Angeles Citizens Committee project as part of an experimental "Inner-City Citizenship Education" program in seven cities across the nation. The idea was to select target neighborhoods which had low registration and poor voting records "to help inner-city people exercise their full political power so their interests will be taken into account when political decisions are made," and "to help League members and through them other 'outer-city' people, particularly suburbanites, to understand through direct communication with inner-city people the problems that confront ghetto dwellers and then do something about them."

Despite noble intentions, the LWV program appears to have floundered in Philadelphia and Boston because of, among other factors, the difficulties of integrating suburban Whites into the intricate politics of the ghetto. A LWV report issued from the East Baltimore Citizens' Center after a 1968 registration drive paints a poignant picture of the frustrations encountered by the League in trying to motivate inner-city residents to participate in the electoral process:

"The East Baltimore Citizens' Center (EBCC) is located in a low-income neighborhood that is almost entirely Negro. In this neighborhood, participation in the electoral process is proportionally lower than in many other parts of the city. . . . What might be accomplished by a small-scale but concentrated effort to register and inform voters in a single precinct in the EBCC's target area? To find out, the EBCC Program Liaison Officer, Neighborhood Liaison Officer, and Steering Committee Chairman developed a plan for a Pilot Project in Voter Registration, Education, and Motivation for the 1968 Primary and General Elections.''

Ward 10, Precinct 7 was chosen as the area of concentration because it was easily accessible to the Center and because 1966 general election figures showed that only 44 per cent of the registered voters had gone to the polls. Training sessions were held at the Center to instruct volunteers how to canvass the fifteen-block neighborhood. Maps and data sheets were prepared. Schedules for all the elections to be held in 1968 and information flyers telling where to register (the Board of Supervisors of Elections, reachable by bus) and answering questions about voting and registering were mimeographed. The Center also purchased a portable machine for projecting a specially prepared League film, ''Voting is People Power.''

''Although four people had originally volunteered, only two people (one VISTA worker and one American Friends Service Committee person) actually helped the EBCC neighborhood Liaison Officer with the canvassing. In addition ten to twelve boys and girls, ages fifteen or sixteen, gave out material on registration, but did not interview. . . .

''Canvassing continued to August 14, the last day registration was open. Most calls were made between 11 A.M. and 3 P.M., although some follow-up calls were made in the evening. Ward 10, Precinct 7 was thoroughly canvassed. A street list of registered voters, copied by volunteers from lists at the Board of Election Supervisors, was used. However, because so many people on this list had moved, the canvassers called at every address, using the street list mainly to make sure they called at all addresses where no registered voters were listed. . . .

"In a typical visit it was mentioned to the resident that elections would be held in September and November. Reasons for the visit were given:

a. There is low rate of voting in the neighborhood.

b. We need to build up awareness of government, which is supposed to meet residents' needs.

c. Neighborhood people need to increase their political power through voting, by electing men who will serve them.

"The resident was asked if he was a registered voter. If not, information on how to register and help in getting registered were offered. A Steering Committee member provided transportation to the office of the Board of Supervisors of Elections when it was requested.

"Residents who were especially interested were asked if they would like to be hosts for small group discussions about election procedures and issues. They were told that the EBCC could arrange for discussion leaders to come to their homes to meet with them and their neighbors, and that EBCC would supply refreshments. . . .

"Records kept by the canvassers show that ten people were registered with direct help from EBCC. . . . Ten new voters registered was considerably less than the number hoped for."

Perhaps forewarned, the inner-city League project in Los Angeles attempted no such neighborhood canvass in the Mexican-American districts chosen as their target area. The director was a White League member from the San Fernando Valley, helped out by a retired teacher from the Peace Corps who spoke Spanish. Congressman Roybal furnished and paid for office space across the hall from his own, a partisan gesture not communicated back to the tax-exempt Education Fund headquarters in Washington. Most of the project's $5,000 budget was spent to hire a bilingual neighborhood resident to man the office, to cover printing costs, and to sponsor Spanish-language broadcasts explaining registration procedures. At the end of six months, the "Citizens Center" was quietly closed in favor of increasing Voters Service efforts in East Lost Angeles.

There were no records of how many new Mexican-American voters were registered during the period from June, 1968, to January, 1969, and no way of telling how many of these were influenced by the East Los Angeles Citizens' Center, But a person connected with the experiment said she thought the long, complicated California ballot, cluttered with referenda on special questions, was too confusing for many Mexican-Americans. "Besides, there is a feeling among Chicanos that politics is corrupt and that the candidates are all working for their own benefit."

The contributions of the League of Women Voters to the distribution of basic information about politics, to stimulating the study of important issues, and to initiating basic reforms in government are familiar to all who have been engaged in the political process at any level. But the traditionally White, middle-class orientation of the League, in spite of its sincere efforts to take a fresh look at its role among the non-White poor, has hampered its effectiveness in activating minority groups. Its nonpartisan approach, moreover, reflects an elitist ethical system that is called upon to compete with the highly charged, polarized appeals of ethnic politics in the ghetto.

In some cities, such as New Orleans, individual League members have managed to provide valuable technical support and education to minority organizations struggling to increase their representation on the voting rolls in adverse circumstances. League materials on organizing registration drives and explaining the electoral process are thorough and well-done. Often the minority registration effort is organized around the fortunes of particular candidates and parties, and League members who have donated their energies and expertise as individuals have managed to skirt the official strictures for nonpartisanship.

VER (Voter Education and Registration)

The Reverend Antonio Hernandez, executive director of the Mexican-American Community Programs Foundation (MACPF), operates from an abandoned Presbyterian Church building on East Whittier in East Los Angeles. The Anglo parishioners began to move away when the Mexican-Americans began to push eastward from the Alloyo, "The Hole," after the Second World War. It is an area of one-story bungalows, with pigs and chickens in the yards and the smell of beans cooking in the kitchens. On the playground outside the tan stucco neighborhood school the ball team consists of seven Chicanos and two Blacks. There are seven public housing projects in the general area. The neighborhood stores advertise anti-cockroach specials. Tony Hernandez, himself an ordained Presbyterian minister, in 1970 was running more than twenty Mexican-American organizations from the stone community center, mostly with money supplied by the Southwest Council of La Raza, and spreading small sums of money around the barrio to aid addicts, support a free health clinic, start a mattress factory, and to help along education, leadership training, and community housing. After the 1968 election, it was Tony Hernandez who coordinated a six-months voter registration drive in East Los Angeles—the umbrella under which the nonpartisan League of Women Voters project and another sponsored by the militant Mexican American Political Association were supposedly sheltered.

Hernandez, who had been working in the community for thirteen years, was the first Mexican-American appointed to the Civil Service Commission by Mayor Sam Yorty. "I took it to open the door," Hernandez recalled. He took on responsibility for the registration drive, he said, to prevent any one organization from dominating it. At the same time, he recognized the danger of fragmentation and duplication in a situation where no less than twelve organizations had expressed interest in enlarging the Mexican-American electorate.

"We had had big registration campaigns before. They swept across the area like a prairie fire and then it's all over. I was interested in finding a model for continuity in a community that is full of mobility. We kept records for the future. We tried to reach out to those who had never been involved before."

LUCHA, an ex-addict group headed by Edward Aguirre, became the central operating organization. College students, young MAPA workers, and neighborhood workers from the barrio were assigned to break down the voting lists, walk the districts, and bird-dog potential new registrants by marking their gates with bright yellow ribbons for the deputized registrars following behind.

Hernandez paid for phones to be installed in twenty homes functioning as registration headquarters in various districts. The phones were needed to round up volunteers for door-to-door canvassing. Because of the distances involved, cars had to be rented to move the forces around. "Perhaps, there was a little joy-riding, who can tell? Every Chicano is dying for his own wheels. They wanted to buy cars. Renting them turned out to be very expensive. We spent $6,000, mostly for the phones and the cars. It all got a little out of hand. I closed it down a month before the run-off election for mayor."

Abe Tapia says MAPA paid out an additional $15,000 to help the Bradley campaign, including sending out canvassers on the issues to follow the VER registrars. Voters were shown how to operate the new IBM punch-card voting machines at card tables set up outside shopping centers and Sears stores, which allocated registration space at their entrances. The thin line between the nonpartisan VER operation and the partisan MAPA follow-up "made the Ford Foundation nervous. So, we decided to let MAPA take over for a while; they are in a position to get some money from labor," Hernandez said.

"When all was said and done, we think there were 27,000 to 30,000 registered in the whole of the East Los Angeles area during that 1968-69 period out of a potential ten times that size.

Of course, it's hard to check out the claims of who is responsible for registering whom.''

The disappointments of those who seek to enlarge the size of the minority-group electorate do not necessarily mean that the cause of reconnecting them to the American political process is hopeless. It is clear, however, that a combination of favorable factors is required, and the absence of one or more of these basic requirements can sometimes cancel out a lot of good intentions.

First, it must be recognized that changing the size and character of the eligible voting population is viewed on the local level as a highly political act, at once threatening the established structure of power and beckoning to those impatient to change the status quo. A clear political objective is indispensable to a successful voter registration campaign in order to mobilize the money and effort required.

Second, the registration of voters demands thorough organization, continual supervision, and concrete evaluation of results. It is a tedious, time-consuming, and laborious undertaking, involving careful planning, skilled administration, sustained application, and sophisticated leadership. The motivation needed to launch and carry through the technical and unglamorous tasks of voter registration must be strong. This usually means the presence of a definable political goal, such as the election of a symbolic or charismatic candidate, a change in the balance of power within local political institutions, or the projected elimination of unfriendly officeholders.

Furthermore, the types of skills needed to conduct registration drives among minority groups include a combination of the technical abilities usually associated with educated, middle-class Whites along with the emotional identification possible only between those of the same ethnic and neighborhood background. Registration, in other words, is an activity that lends itself to broad and active coalitions, while demanding at the same time a firm administrative hand.

Because the morale of a registration effort depends on a capability to measure specific results, as well as the tendency of registration drives to make sweeping, unsubstantiated claims, it is essential to formulate a carefully targeted program. The areas of effort should be precisely identified and the status of voting lists must be carefully researched. The machinery for registration must be analyzed and explained to both the registration workers and their prospective clients.

The cooperation or lack of cooperation by those who control the local institutions in charge of registering new voters can be a crucial factor between the success and failure of the campaign. There is often a margin of interpretation available in registration laws which can sometimes be challenged in the courts and sometimes shaped favorably by negotiations. These ambiguous areas are the most likely shelter for institutional bias. Under sympathetic administration, however, they sometimes can be made to open the door to massive numbers of new voters.

To illustrate the foregoing framework for a productive registration campaign, we turn now to San Antonio, Texas, where unusual efforts were made during January, 1970, to expand significantly the number of Mexican-Americans eligible to vote later that year in the election of a state senator and United States senator sympathetic to Chicano problems and aspirations.

Chapter Thirteen

SAN ANTONIO—ACTIVATING THE CHICANO

San Antonio, Bexar County, Texas, had a resident population of approximately 750,000 in 1970, of which about 48 per cent was Mexican-American and 8 per cent Black. The minority Anglo population, however, constituted a majority on the voting lists by virtue of the fact that, in addition to all the other constraints on minority-group participation in politics, Texas maintained a poll tax until 1966 and, until overturned in the courts after the 1970 elections, the Texas Constitution required every voter to re-register every year before the end of January in order to be eligible to vote in primaries and elections after that date. This usually meant that registration took place before the candidates for various offices that year were even known. Local officials estimated Mexican-Americans to comprise only about 35 to 40 per cent of the city's voting lists.

An analysis of the rates of registration in 104 of the nation's largest cities in 1960 conducted by Stanley Kelley, Jr., Richard E. Ayres, and William G. Bowen ranked San Antonio 99th, with less than a majority overall—42.6 per cent—of those eligible on the voting rolls of Bexar County. The only cities with a worse ratio were Atlanta and Columbus, Georgia, Portsmouth and Newport News, Virginia, and Birmingham, Alabama. Although there was an acceleration of political activity among Mexican-

Americans after the election of President John F. Kennedy, a house-to-house canvass on San Antonio's West Side in 1969 showed that registration in the barrio was still no more than 43 per cent, even after an intensive drive in behalf of three militant Chicanos running for City Council on a "Barrio Betterment" slate.

Another survey by Ralph C. Guzman among Mexican-Americans on the West Side showed that only 38 per cent had actually voted in the 1964 Presidential election, and, among women, the turnout was only 27 per cent of the potentially eligible population. Registration rates were lowest among those under thirty and over fifty. In families with incomes less than $2,760 per year, the rate of registration dropped to 32 per cent, rising to 55 per cent in households with family incomes over that figure. Comparing San Antonio's concentrated ethnic enclave to the dispersed Mexican-American community in Los Angeles, Guzman concluded that the potential political advantage of San Antonio's West Side population seemed "to be swamped by their social isolation and lower economic level."

Kelley, Ayres, and Bowen, however, have suggested an even more critical factor. "Variations in our index of the convenience of the times and places of registration were significantly related to variations in rates of registration. . . . This finding is important, for it suggests that local officials, by varying the convenience of registration procedures, may be able to affect appreciably not only the size, but also the composition of local electorates." In fact, they discovered in statistical tests of twelve variables possibly affecting registration in the 104 cities under study that the most significant relationship of all was between the percentage of the population of voting age that is registered and the date at which the registration rolls are closed.

"Why this is so can be suggested here, if not demonstrated. A longer period in which one may register increases considerably the convenience of doing so, of course, but we doubt that that is all there is to the matter. A late closing date for registration also probably tends to increase rates of registration because it allows the campaign to serve as a reminder to weakly motivated voters that they need to register and as a stimulus to find out from others how they can do so."

Thus, on the roster of institutional biases against the participation of minority groups in the political process, the Texas system of permitting annual registration only between October 1 and January 31—until knocked out in the courts—may very well have ranked as one of the most effective systems of political control in the nation.

The Political Setting
The confluence of interests attempting to buck this structure in San Antonio in the winter of 1969-1970 was unusual: (1) a concerted drive to re-elect Senator Ralph W. Yarborough; (2) the fight to hold the only seat occupied by a Mexican-American in the Texas State Senate, the 26th District in San Antonio; (3) a continuing effort to build up a constituency on the West Side, where 30 per cent of the city's population lives, to reduce the dominant position in the city's local government of the Good Government League, a product of the Anglo business community; (4) an internal struggle within the Democratic party between Congressman Henry B. Gonzales, allied with the Good Government League, and labor leader and County Commissioner Albert Pena, partly over the alliance of the latter with militant young members of the Mexican-American Youth Organization (MAYO); (5) the stirrings in San Antonio's West Side barrio, as elsewhere, for a higher degree of cultural recognition, economic opportunity, and political representation.

A loose federation of those with these parallel but not always identical political aims had been operating in San Antonio since 1968, exchanging information at Dutch treat luncheons held every Friday at Karam's, a Mexican restaurant on the West Side's Zarzamora Street. Any day's gathering might include Commissioner Pena, Herschel Bernard, an active member of the "liberal" wing of the Texas Democratic party who shared offices with Maury Maverick, Jr., Joe J. Bernal, employed by the Diocese in community service work as well as holding the 26th District Senate seat, Councilman Pete Torres, who had first beaten the Good Government League candidate in the 1967 municipal elections, Willie Velasquez and Juan Patlan, two of the young founders of the Mexican-American Unity Council (MAUC), organized with the help of Ford Foundation grants to develop self-help groups in the barrio, and Jose Angel Guiteirrez or Mario Compean, two St. Mary's University graduates who had helped start the Mexican-American Youth Organization (MAYO) in the spring of 1967. (Compean ran on the "Barrio Betterment" ticket for City Council in 1969; Guiterrez led a successful election drive to oust the "Gringo" Board of Education in nearby Crystal City, "Spinach Capital of America," and replace it with members more representative of the migrant Mexican-American field hands, who are the largest population bloc in the Winter Garden of South Texas.)

Interspersed at the tables, munching hot Mexican delicacies, would be county government employees, Model Cities workers, university teachers, union organizers, Democratic committeemen, rank-and-file workers, and any visiting firemen invited to see the surprising sight of a "liberal" caucus deep in the heart of Texas. Quaker-style, speeches were mostly by those who rose on their own initiative to report on the progress of some meeting, educational issue, fund effort, or voter drive. If an informal communications channel is important to grassroots political activity, then the gatherings at Karam's seemed to indicate that the network was crackling on San Antonio's West Side.

Furthermore, in the fluid state of party politics in a state such as Texas and in a city such as San Antonio, where the council-manager system instituted by the Good Government League was ostensibly nonpartisan, even the appearance of working coalitions can result in important political dividends. Senator Yarborough, one of whose key local representatives was "Herky"

Bernard, had carried Bexar County by nearly two to one in a Democratic primary against Gordon McClendon in 1964. Joe Bernal won his Senate seat in 1966 by over 6,000 votes, running against an Anglo. Pete Torres, who made the breakthrough against the GGL in 1967, had survived a run-off in 1969 against another Mexican-American unsuccessfully put up by the GGL to divide the West Side vote. Mario Campean, a neophyte running against Mayor Walter McAllister on a citywide basis, polled a respectable 12,000 votes against the head of one of the city's largest banks. As we shall see, the voter registration drive in which all the above were involved benefited from rulings by the County Tax Assessor, who is responsible for the election rolls in Texas and who must run for election himself. The Tax Assessor's favorable rulings in San Antonio may have resulted from his recognition that his own political fortunes might be affected by those seeking a liberal interpretation of the rules.

Perhaps the most significant political fact about San Antonio as the decade of the sixties came to a close was the awakening of the young Chicano. Some of this was the result of the ferment generated by a new generation of college-educated Mexican-Americans who elected to return to *los barrios* rather than follow the traditional path of assimilation into the Anglo community via a professional or business career. Middle-class Mexican-Americans were even more alarmed at the rhetoric of their "Brown Power" speeches than were middle-class Whites taken back by the Che Gueverra garb of their own offspring. The two phenomena were part of the same revolt against the posture and authority of the adult world, except that the young Mexican-American expressing his fierce pride in La Causa and La Raza was reacting against a cruelly documented reality.

San Antonio had a per capita income of only $2,380 per year, making it reportedly the poorest city of its size in the United States. Forty-four per cent of the inhabitants of the West Side were functionally illiterate. The dropout rate in the Edgewood

School District of 25,000 students was 80 per cent, and nearly half the teachers there were not certified. Housing, health, and community services were all substandard. Nutrition was such as to inspire a network television documentary, "Hunger in America." Youth gangs of chronically unemployed teenagers knifed one another in the streets or sought temporary escape through drugs. Their parents, after a lifetime on the bottom of the socioeconomic ladder, were largely withdrawn into a stultifying web of fatalism.

Herbert J. Kramer, an outside observer of the local scene in September, 1969, concluded in an unpublished report on San Antonio:

"It is unarguable that the Mexican-American in San Antonio occupies the bottom rung of the socioeconomic ladder. A ladder implies that he has the capacity for upward mobility. And indeed, over the past twenty years it can be maintained that opportunity has vastly increased for the Mexican-American to remove himself from poverty and integrate himself into the community-at-large. Segregation of schools, recreation facilities, hotels, restaurants, transportation has long since been outlawed. Even before the civil rights acts were passed, these barriers were voluntarily removed by the city's civic and business leadership.

"More than half the people on the municipal payroll are Mexican-Americans, 10 per cent of them in professional or technical positions. Over the past thirteen years, seven Mexican-Americans have sat on the City Council, three currently. And the administration points with pride to the fact that one Congressman, two state legislators, two county officers, four court judges, and two city judges have Spanish surnames. . . .

"To the inhabitants of the barrio, however, there has been little change for the better in their lives—and the ladder of opportunity has no rungs. In many respects, say the founders and organizers of the Mexican-American Unity Council (MAUC), it is more accurate to say that the majority of Mexican-Americans are not at the bottom, but constitute a separate system. That is, they are affected by the larger system, but are not a part of it. . . .

"Politically, with a low rate of registration and voter turnout, the Mexican-American is under represented. Thus, he lacks political power commensurate with other groups in the community. Activist leaders attribute much of the Chicano's problems to this factor. They feel that because of this powerlessness, most policymakers do not take into account the unique needs of the Mexican-American which, if met, might open the door to his advancement and to participation in the affairs of the larger community. . . .

"Responsible officials all see the Mexican-American as clannish, not aggressive, not ambitious, unmotivated, happy by nature, gentle, loving his family. It is this shimmering, impenetrable curtain of condescension and polite disdain that is as agonizing to the Chicano as the savage discrimination of twenty years age. 'When you are regarded as a slightly dull child,' says one, 'you aren't going to make progress except as a child.'"

This sense of disconnection from the power structure prompted 300 students at Edgewood High School to walk out of their classes in May, 1968, and draw up a petition of their grievances against an inadequate educational system. One consequence was the organization of the Edgewood District Concerned Parents, an unusual step for a group which suffered in silence when teachers fined pupils caught speaking Spanish on school grounds. As a result of this cross-generational involvement, the school superintendent resigned. Although he was replaced by a Mexican-American Professor of Education, West Side schools are still vastly inferior to those in the Anglo sectors of San Antonio. Their condition became the basis of a suit carried all the way to the U.S. Supreme Court against the inequities of school systems tied to the resources of local property taxes.

The impression that the system can be made to budge somewhat when there is concerted action has become a strong motivat-

ng force of the new self-consciousness among Chicanos. More
evolutions have been spawned by hope than by despair. The
more impatient among the young militants sometimes use a vocabulary of violence, especially when goaded by their elders,
but the basic goals are education, housing, economic self-
determination, and social justice. The vast majority are less
interested in overturning the Anglo system than in creating a
system of delivering comparable benefits inside the barrio. "We
want to fuse the Mexican tradition with Anglo expertise and
technical capacities," said Willie Velasquez in 1970, working as
a short-order chef in a Taco stand owned and operated by former
barrio gang members recruited by him when he was executive
director of the Mexican-American Unity Council (MAUC).

The Awakening Mexican-American

It was Velasquez who in September, 1968, received from MAUC
the first payment of a $110,000 grant from the Southwest Council
of La Raza, funded by the Ford Foundation to initiate activities
to benefit the region's Mexican-Americans. High on the Unity
Council's list of priorities in San Antonio was political education:
"Because of the urgency of strengthening the political position
of the Mexican-American in the areas of voter education and
getting out the vote, such a project has been conceptualized and
has first priority with the Unity Council."

The inexperience which was to get MAUC into political hot
water later on was evident in the reference to "getting out the
vote" in this opening declaration of intent. The Southern-based
Voter Education Project, pioneering the way through tax
authorities as well as putting Blacks on the registration rolls,
had learned early in the game that activity on Election Day relating to voting turnout was certain to jeopardize claims of nonpartisan activity, and, along with that, the precious right to classify
contributions as tax deductible.

This thin line, so important to lawyers, obscures the reality of most voter registration drives. The social cost of conducting such a drive—long hours of tedious effort, the most unglamorous of political activities—is too great unless motivated by a high degree of self-interest. Although there is usually a great deal of lip service paid to the nonpartisan aspects of good citizenship—for that is the route to enlist media cooperation and bureaucratic neutrality—the drives are usually focused on selective groups whose political predilections seem safely predictable. Since the poor and disadvantaged offer the highest yield of potential registrants, and since elections sometimes revolve around issues of special relevance to particular racial, social, and economic elements within the broader society, a registration drive focused upon minority groups is by its very nature highly political. When it is not, the motivating drive to activate marginal participants to make that precious extra expenditure of effort is usually lacking. The reward needs to be spelled out in tangible and immediate terms.

One of the stated aims of San Antonio's Mexican-American Unity Council was "to provide the lower-income person with bureaucratic and organizational skills which he can then use to negotiate with the institutions on his own behalf." In distributing funds to neighborhood groups throughout the barrio, the Unity Council first concentrated on the skeletal essentials of organization life: office space, telephones, mimeograph machines, and paid clerical and secretarial help. With this base of organizational sustenance, the myriad problems of the barrio offered ample opportunity for the testing, training, and development of community residents capable of political action on their own behalf.

By the ordinary standards of two-party politics, it is true that such efforts could be justly labeled "nonpartisan." The purpose was not to serve the interests of a particular candidate at a particular point in time, nor to advance the interests of a specific political party structure. One of the groups funded by the Unity Council, the Mexican-American Youth Organization, talked of forming a Chicano third-party—La Raza Unida—but MAYO's interests included the agricultural towns of South Texas, where the established parties were closed corporations of noncompetitive, Anglo conservativism, so that the slogans of ethnic solidarity could be interpreted as a rallying cry for the most basic rights of equal civic opportunity. Before there can be partisan activity there must be some form of political awareness. But the awakening of Mexican-American self-consciousness in San Antonio struck many in the city as in itself a threatening development.

Ironically, one of those who felt most threatened was Congressman Henry B. Gonzales, whose early battles against discrimination as a Texas State Senator and whose liberal voting record on Capitol Hill might have been expected to make him one of the natural leaders of the "Movimiento". But Gonzales, who fought his own way to recognition by the rules of a pluralistic society, was antagonistic to the concepts of the new cultural nationalism. "The very word 'Chicano'," said Albert Bustamante, an aide in the Congressman's San Antonio office, "runs against everything our people have always strived for. We want to be accepted as full-fledged Americans." After years as the unquestioned number-one political success story among middle-class Mexican-Americans in San Antonio, Henry B. found himself going through a trauma with the young not unlike that suffered by Hubert Humphrey in 1968. Those born too late to appreciate the old, liberal victories saw him as the handmaiden of the Anglo Establishment in the Good Government League, "verdido", sold out to the power structure which, in their eyes, was doing nothing about the fundamental problems of the great mass of Mexican-American people.

In his turn, Gonzales denounced the young militants of MAYO as "racial fanatics," "coiled rattlesnakes," and "criminal ruffians." They were stalking horses, he charged, for a new generation of Mexican-American politicians on the San Antonio scene—County Commissioner Albert Pena, whose district covered a large portion of the West Side, State Senator Joe J. Bernal, and independent City Councilman Pete Torres. Not without ambition themselves, they had once been allied to Gonzales, but charged that they broke with him only because of his refusal to permit other stars in his firmament. "The young know what they want and they are going to get it," said Commissioner Pena in his county courthouse office. "I'm an organizational animal and I work at it all the time. We Mexican-Americans have the highest illiteracy rates, the highest unemployment rates, the highest tubercular rates, the highest infant mortality rates. But our registration rate is the lowest. We've been isolated from the governmental process, treated like a conquered people, worse than Japan or Germany. No wonder the young are militant! At first the Chicanos felt it wouldn't do them any good to participate. But now they're organizing and I work with them as closely as possible. I'd rather see them inside the system."

Recruiting New Voters

Of the three "New Politics" officeholders in San Antonio, Torres was scheduled to run for re-election in April, 1969, Bernal in November, 1970, and Pena in November, 1972. Under the peculiarities of the Texas voter registration law it behooved each to cooperate in any way possible with efforts to increase the number of Mexican-Americans on the voting lists at an early date.

In Bexar County, under annual registration then in force, those on the previous year's voting list would receive a form in the mail from the County Tax Assessor whereby they could re-register by mail instead of having to go personally to the county courthouse. Even though many failed to carry out this minimum requirement, a newly registered voter would at least receive the direct mail solicitation once his name was on the Assessor's list. By taking radio spots on Spanish-language stations at the time the forms were circulated, candidates could remind Mexican-American voters that the opportunity to qualify to vote in the next election was conveniently at hand.

As early as the fall of 1968, said Herschel Bernard, "we knew that it was important to get started for the 1970 election, because of the importance of the re-election of Ralph W. Yarborough and the control of the Democratic party. We knew we were laying the base for 1970 as well as the 1969 San Antonio mayorality, because the people we registered then would get a mail-out.

"The special problem of the Texas law in getting new voters is that nobody is interested in October and November, even in a Presidential year, because it is too late to get on the list to vote in the election right at hand. There is nothing to motivate a new voter. Then come Thanksgiving, Christmas, and New Year's. So we have to do all our work in the latter part of January—after hangover time—and before the February 1 deadline. Psychologically it's a bad moment because, although some announce early, filing for office closes two days after the last day for registering."

In this politically charged atmosphere, MAUC announced on December 17, 1968, that it was making a grant of $7,595 to two West Side groups to stimulate voter registration and interest in barrio neighborhoods, plus a grant of $5,935 to the Committee on Voter Education and Registration (COVER) to coordinate a citywide registration drive. Although COVER had existed loosely as a local committee for nearly ten years, it was incorporated specifically for the 1969 registration drive and filed with the Internal Revenue Service for tax-exempt status. Its chairman was the selfsame Mr. Bernard, assisted by a county road foreman from Commissioner Pena's district, a combination not affording very much cover as the word is used by intelligence agents. The Treasury Department refused it tax-exempt status.

The January registration drive offered the Unity Council's newly funded barrio groups something immediate and concrete to sink their teeth into. With seasoned leadership at COVER and youthful energy at MAYO and in neighborhood community organizations, the experiment to see what could be accomplished in a pilot experiment was launched on January 7, 1969, preparatory, perhaps, to an all-out effort for the statewide election year of 1970.

The official voting records of Bexar County for 1968 contained the names of 237,359 persons eligible to vote in the Presidential election, up nearly 40,000 from those eligible the previous year, before the full impact of the repeal of the poll tax had been felt. (Registration had closed before President Johnson's withdrawal, and Texas was also regarded as a 1968 battleground by both major parties.) The fear was that the off-year, with only the local election for City Council at stake, might actually shrink the number of eligibles despite the continued growth of the county.

"Mexican-Americans don't really understand the power of the vote," said Juan Patlan of the Unity Council, "They have trouble believing they can really influence the political system, There are a lot of poor, illiterate people who don't speak any more English than just enough to get by with at work. They are frightened of almost any public activity, afraid of making an ass out of themselves in front of everybody. Maybe they have a relative who got arrested for stealing a hub cap, or another without any naturalization papers. They don't like answering questions about their Social Security numbers, which they are supposed to fill in on the application forms. The Anglo always registers 100 per cent, especially when it is an Anglo versus a Chicano. A lot of people in the barrio don't have telephones or don't read the English-language press. You have to find a way of communicating with them in their own neighborhoods."

Although there was insufficient time for elaborate organization, the Unity Council's newly funded barrio groups took batches of registration forms to their headquarters. A volunteer force of 150, many of them teenagers, was sent canvassing door-to-door. In many of the Edgewood District's twenty-five public schools the children were sent home with leaflets urging their parents to register and vote.

Two weeks before the registration deadline, three of the young barrio leaders—Mario Compean, Chairman of MAYO, Dario Chapa, Chairman of the Cassiano Park Neighborhood Council, and Candelaro Alejos—announced they would personally file as candidates for City Council on a Barrio Betterment platform. Compean, in an act of pure "machismo," filed his name opposite that of eighty-year-old Walter McAllister, nominee of the Good Government League and Mayor of San Antonio since 1961. All three had been active in the registration program coordinated by COVER, preaching Chicano Power, although none had received any compensation for their participation and raised their own political funds separately. Their candidacies, symbolically limited to the West Side even though councilmen all run at large in San Antonio, added to that of Pete Torres, the first ever to outpoll a GGL nominee, gave an added credibility, it was thought, to the one-man one-vote appeal.

COVER kept no day-to-day records of the progress of the 1969 registration drive in San Antonio, and had to await the official tallies in the office of the County Clerk to assess the results. The final figures for Bexar County, 80 to 85 per cent of which is the city of San Antonio, turned out to be 243,946—up 7,489, or about 3 per cent, from 1969. In San Antonio, itself, the increase came to fewer than 3,000 names, only 1.5 per cent of the list eligible to vote in the upcoming municipal election.

On the face of it, this did not add up to a spectacular showing for such a controversial undertaking. Eventually, MAYO and COVER lost their funding from Ford Foundation resources—in part at the insistence of Congressman Henry B. Gonzales. As in the CORE-sponsored registration drive in Cleveland at the time of Carl Stokes's first election in 1967, the political nerve ends jangled by the 1969 project in San Antonio were out of all proportion to the actual political impact.

The sponsors took comfort from the fact that the registration list had not grown smaller in the transition from a Presidential year to an off-year and had now reached an all-time high. But when Henry Appel, a retired Army Warrant Officer who had become Deputy County Clerk and a member of the liberal Friday luncheon group at Karam's, broke the figures down in more detail, there was less cause for celebration. Precinct by precinct, the registration returns on the Mexican-American West Side had fluctuated widely, and some had shown registration losses of more than 5 per cent. Furthermore, when the county's four commissioner districts were analyzed, Commissioner Pena's Area One on the West Side, where a majority of residents were Mexican-Americans and where COVER's efforts had been concentrated, had done little better than the average for the county as a whole and only slightly better than areas where there had been no organized registration activity. The principal gains, moreover, had occurred in Anglo settlements near Kelly and Lackland Air Force bases.

BEXAR COUNTY REGISTRATION RESULTS—1969 VS. 1968

District	Ethnic Breakdown (est.)			1969	1968	Increase
	Anglo	Mex-Am	Black			
	%	%	%			%
One	41	59	—	53,473	51,555	plus 4
Two	65	33	2	79,652	76,974	plus 3
Three	80	11	9	70,504	67,100	plus 5
Four	62	22	16	40,317	40,828	minus 1
Total	62	31	7	243,946	236,457	plus 3

It could not be said, of course, what the outcome might have been without the Unity Council's registration activity. (It is often pointed out that F.D.R. used to win elections with the editorial pages of the nation's press aligned overwhelmingly against him; speculation is rarer as to how great his sweep might have been with an even break in the editorial columns.) The biggest gains, however, were directly related to population growth in the solidly Anglo northern quadrant of the county (Commissioner Precincts

Two and Three). The Black areas on San Antonio's East Side generally lost eligible voters, illustrating a political withdrawal dating back to their comparative disinterest in the 1968 Presidential tickets as well as the barriers against combining two different ethnic groups under the umbrella of a single registration effort.

Three-quarters of a cross section of Mexican-Americans polled in San Antonio in 1965 had expressed opposition to political alignment with Blacks; in turn, most of the city's 50,000 Blacks were segregated in their own ghetto on the opposite side of town from the Mexican-American barrios. Six out of ten Texas Blacks polled in 1970 registered agreement with the statement that "most Texas politicians are bought and paid for by some special interest group."

Regardless of the expenditure of substantial sums of money, energy, and emotional appeal, an untargeted registration effort was simply not effective in doing the job in San Antonio in 1969. Unless canvassers in the field have some concrete measure of their progress, their morale is likely to flag. The wasted motion in trying to identify unregistered voters blindly is prodigious, and is increased by the reluctance of people to admit they are nonvoters. It is always more rewarding to go hunting where the most ducks are likely to be. Without some form of check, there is no way for the supervisor of a volunteer group to differentiate between good, bad, and indifferent performance. The ability to assign definable and manageable quotas not only increases the sense of accomplishment among canvassers but can also be the basis of productive competition between both individuals and groups. Since defeat is an orphan and victory is always claimed by a thousand fathers, a system for keeping track of who might have been on or off target quotas also possesses pragmatic political uses. Registration continues to be a retail type of business even when conducted on a wholesale scale. The problem is to identify, sort, and organize the names and addresses of unregistered voters in a form that lends itself to systematic contact by workers in the vineyard.

A Targeted Approach

Somewhat sobered by the 1969 statistics, the coalition of officeholders, minority group leaders, labor union officials, and party workers with a collective interest in the May, 1970, Democratic primary in Bexar County went about the next year's registration drive with more systematic zeal. Although cut off from Ford Foundation funds via the Unity Council and COVER, the effort was aided by a comprehensive study undertaken by the Political Research and Education Project (PREP) of the Southwest Council of LaRaza. Alternative approaches to identifying unregistered voters—such as house-to-house interviewing and the matching of voting lists against telephone directories and mailing lists—were tested under the rubric of designing "A Regional Strategy for Fair Representation." A Washington computer consulting firm headed by David L. Hackett, longtime friend and former Justice Department associate of the late Robert Kennedy, proposed a program for computerizing lists of unregistered voters by correlating magnetic tapes obtained from the Bexar County Tax Assessor and the publishers of the San Antonio city directory, the R. L. Polk Company. (The latter publishes more or less complete listings of household occupants in street-address order for some 1,400 communities in the United States.) The resultant print-out would produce consecutive street addresses, apartment numbers, and occupants names not on the current list of registered voters.

COVER, still headed by Herky Bernard but financed principally by labor unions backing U.S. Senator Ralph W. Yarborough in his primary race against Lloyd Bentsen, Jr., once again was the coordinating agent for the drive. It left it to the Hackett organization to see if it could negotiate the release of the Polk San Antonio tapes. If so, they were to design a computer program that could correlate it with the tapes of registered voters prepared in the County Assessor's office as well as with precinct and census-block information, so that canvassers could work directly from the computer print-outs.

Meanwhile, Bernard commissioned his forces to undertake an in-depth survey of San Antonio Precinct 222. Precinct 222 was a neighborhood of small, wooden bungalows set among high-tension lines on San Antonio's far West Side. Its population was estimated to be 95 per cent Mexican-American; its street names had the ring of the old country—Calle San Gabriel, Calle La Gloria, Amires Place.

The precinct had gone 86 per cent for Yarborough in 1964, 89 per cent for Humphrey in 1968, and 81 per cent for Pete Torres in the 1969 councilmen's race. There were only 585 names on the 1969 registration rolls; despite the 1969 registration drive, the list of registered in Precinct 222 had actually been diminished by one as compared with the previous year, and COVER was seeking the key to improvement on that showing.

The area was close to St. Mary's University, where COVER could find students willing to work on the survey and eager to earn extra money. Politically, it lay outside the immediate domains of both Commissioner Albert Pena and Congressman Henry B. Gonzales. At the same time it was within the district of the only Mexican-American in the Texas State Senate, Joe J. Bernal, a staunch Yarborough supporter. As Precinct 222 went, so might the hopes of those seeking to increase and activate the number of San Antonio's Mexican-Americans turning out at the polls.

The difficulty of trying to gather the names of the unregistered in a door-to-door survey became apparent. After two weeks of canvassing in Precinct 222's comparatively small area, only half the households had been reached. The necessity for call-backs to check those not at home on the initial visit increased the cost per capita to impractical amounts. Furthermore, surveying in the barrio required extra training, even for Spanish-speaking inter-viewers, because of the timidity of a population consisting of many who were born in Mexico. Even when the names of the unregistered had finally been assembled through this laborious leg-work, there remained the cost of key punching cards to be fed into a computer bank.

A check-out of the same homes against a crisscross telephone directory confirmed the fact that a high proportion of low-income persons, the ones most likely to be unregistered, did not have a phone in the barrio. Telephone listings, moreover, left out the names of most women in these Latin family households as well as the names of voting-age children living at home. Disconnections because of the high rate of transiency in rental apartments or nonpayment of bills added to the likelihood that a canvass geared exclusively to telephone calls would be likely to overlook a substantial number of potential registrants.

When the head count in Precinct 222 was finally completed, the utility of some form of electronic analysis for quickly identifying the unregistered had been confirmed. The number of potential voters turned out to be 1,321 as against the official registration count of 585—for a 44 per cent rate of registration. Fifty-seven per cent of the households contained no registrants at all. For U.S. Senator Ralph Yarborough and State Senator Joe Bernal, expecting to receive eight out of ten votes cast, the theoretical potential in low-registration election districts such as Precinct 222 would be to double their previous pluralities. Since there was an almost exact correlation between the percentage of households containing at least one registered voter (43 per cent) in 1970 and the percentage in which someone had voted in the 1968 presidential election (44 per cent), it appeared that the problem in Precinct 222 was to expand a static electorate. In all likelihood the majority of eligible voters in unregistered homes had probably never been registered at any time.

Employing computer technology to target the unregistered in San Antonio was not without its own set of vexing problems. The County Assessor was at first reluctant to make the registration tapes available to an outside group, and the law on the matter seemed ambiguous. After some pressure by the lawyers involved with COVER, a set of tapes was finally purchased. The R. W. Polk Company was equally nervous, and its San Antonio tapes also had to be bought through a round-about mediary for several thousand dollars. The comparison of the two lists through a computer program making them compatible took longer than anticipated, and COVER inaugurated its drive in December using old-fashioned manual labor.

The original plan had been to make print-outs of the names and addresses of those persons who appeared on the Polk list but not on the county registration list, break that down by precinct, and then by the address numbers on each side of the street in sequence. This would have provided each canvasser with a detailed road guide to every unregistered voter in his assigned territory as well as a method for assessing the most rewarding precincts to be canvassed. The complication and cost of doing all that by computer proved to be beyond the means and resources available to COVER. They finally settled for an alphabetical street listing of the names and addresses of all the unregistered people appearing on the Polk listing, and then relying on volunteer workers to reorganize the material in the most useful form for door-to-door canvassing.

There were also unavoidable errors in the listing originating from the fact that the city directory was revised on a biennial basis, so that approximately 20 per cent of the entries were outdated. The comprehensive listing of household addresses, on the other hand, was valuable to volunteers, who checked them against voting rolls for spotting the addresses and apartment numbers where no registered voter appeared. The discipline and order infused into the registration effort by such systematic tasks and the availability of checkable precinct data was helpful in creating the sense of purpose characteristic of a targeted registration effort.

Because of the national implications of Senator Yarborough's primary race against a far more conservative Democrat, COVER also benefited from outside aid and expertise. Tyrus Fain, a native of San Antonio, who was a former official with Alliance for Progress in Latin America, and who had been one of Senator

Robert Kennedy's organizers in the Southwest during his 1968 drive for the Presidency, was frequently on the scene. Charlotte Roe Kemble, executive director of Frontlash, an affiliate of the United States Youth Council and particularly interested in the registration of low-income groups on a nationwide basis, came to San Antonio personally to help organize students for precinct registration drives.

Frontlash itself was organized in 1967 on the assumption that young people might play a role in counteracting the apparent racial "backlash" that seemed to be developing in many poor and working class communities prior to the Johnson-Goldwater Presidential campaign. Its original funds were a $30,000 grant from the Stern Family Fund. It has since been funded from time to time by the Committee on Political Education of the A.F.L.-C.I.O. The officers, most of them one-time campus activists in a variety of causes, soon took the position described by Charlotte Kemble:

"We believe that it is important for students to have a sympathetic understanding for the problems of working people. The youth of America share many basic interests with the labor and civil rights movements—in reconstructing the cities, in achieving racial justice, in support for quality education, in ending poverty and pollution, in reordering the nation's economic priorities, and in making democracy work. We have concluded that the abolition of poverty is directly related to the achievement of 'participatory democracy' and that young people should use their education and know-how in working to overcome the obstacles to full voting participation. It takes something broader than the peace issue to make young people effective in the movement for social change in America."

Frontlash soon made the discovery that noncollege youth—or students living at home and commuting to community and evening colleges—often made better registration volunteers than those recruited from the campus. Because they had their roots in the communities, they were more acceptable among persons who were nervous about having their names appear on any sort of official government list. They combined that extra special appeal of young idealism with a staying power generated by the realization that they would probably spend their future adult years in the same community as their present political activity. They seemed to be less demoralized by a lack of instant success and less disillusioned by an oversimplified view of the system.

In San Antonio, the young adults of Frontlash brought with them their know-how in the hard, persistent, unromantic work of door-to-door canvassing. "We are effective in this work not just because we train young people in the skills they need, but because we are able to show them, by talking about the issues, how essential it is to become politically aware and involved in order to build the kind of society they want," Charlotte Kemble observed. "They were amazed to find out that the restrictive registration system practiced in Texas was not the same as that in every other state of the union."

The Texas Legislature, after the 1969 registration drive in San Antonio had received statewide notoriety, had changed the law to forestall the bulk mailing of returned registration forms sent to those already on the list. The privilege of enabling deputy registrars to function outside the county courthouse was a matter of local option, and in Bexar County deputies were officially authorized to perform their duties only in a few specific locations. Whether door-to-door registration was even legal was a sticky point, but COVER worked out a system whereby the day's receipts from the precincts would be taken to headquarters, sifted for errors, authenticated by the deputy as if they have been filled out in his office, and then brought in directly to the county courthouse.

"We'd bring in 1,000 or 2,000 every Saturday, clean 'em up on Sunday," explained Herky Bernard, "and then walk 'em in on Monday. Since we had contributors who could give stamps but not money, we'd mail in the dirty ones, usually those who didn't want to give their Social Security numbers, in hopes they might get by. We had to get a special ruling from the Attorney General, at that, to walk 'em in. Somebody tried to say every last one should have a 5-cent stamp on it. The County Assessor finally went along with us, but called up a couple of times to ask us not to screw him up. You need a strong legal arm in situations like this, one capable of raising the question of federal rights and making it stick.''

COVER selected twenty-eight out of forty-five predominantly Mexican-American precincts as the target for its main effort in 1970, as opposed to the shot-gun approach generally followed the year before. Workers were paid to produce the lists, arranging them by precincts and preparing clipboards for canvassers which contained the addresses of persons who most likely had not registered. The neighborhood work was backed up by radio spots on Spanish-language stations, with appeals from such national figures as Cesar Chavez and Senator Edward Kennedy. Hundreds of volunteers, some of junior-high age, were sent out every weekend, provided with lunch and transportation. Trucks, cars, and buses were contributed to the drive. COVER co-ordinated all interested parties, including unions such as the International Union of Electrical Workers (I.U.E.), the Teamsters and the United Auto Workers, the Pena and Bernal political organizations, plus the barrio groups first activated by Willie Velasquez, the Unity Council, and MAYO.

Frontlash operated principally on funds provided by the unions. The Young Democrats, the Catholic Youth Organization, The Chicano Student Coalition, and a variety of neighborhood youth groups participated in the drive under a student coordinator, Martha Martinez. Mrs. Martinez concentrated on a dozen Mexican-American precincts, organizing the block work of some of the youngest of the volunteers from the Edgewood School District. "We needed an intensive recruitment drive," Charlotte Kemble said later, "because volunteers do tire of this kind of work. You have to tap all the community organizations available. Marty had to organize to hit the same houses time after time. It needed a cover of adults to keep the wheels turning and real thorough training is required to leave something behind. We didn't want to be like those middle-class cowboys who swept the South in the early sixties without caring what they left behind. Registration, after all, is only the first step in turning people on to the real grassroots issues. There has to be education and follow-up, something to keep it continuous."

How did it all work out? Herky Bernard, interviewed shortly after the registration deadline, said "I have a feeling it worked, but I couldn't be sure. We aren't even sure whether it really works to go to all this trouble, We didn't have the time to spend to collect the figures as we went along. The last couple of weeks we sent some kids out without any lists at all and brought bunches of cards to the schools for the pupils to bring home. It took a big push to go after the 20 per cent previously registered who didn't mail back their renewals. The clerical problem became overwhelming, especially as far as call-backs were concerned. We just tried to saturate the precincts with the best prospects and hoped for the best."

At first glance, Henry Appel's countywide figures looked considerably better in 1970 than they had in 1969. (See next page.)

Targeted registration, on the basis of these figures, had produced two to three times the percentage increase achieved in Mexican-American precincts in 1969, and this time the greatest gains were clearly in the barrios. And yet, in view of the effort, the overall results were hardly spectacular. Once again, the Northside Anglo suburbs headed the percentages, and this steady population growth was at least partly responsible for the new record registration total for the third year in succession. But there was clear evidence that systematic registration among minority groups could make a difference.

The precincts listed as Mexican-American on the next page were those which contained in the official records more than 50 per cent of persons with Spanish surnames; the Black precincts ran from 75 per cent upwards. COVER sponsored registration activ-

BEXAR COUNTY REGISTRATION RESULTS—1970 vs. 1969

District	Ethnic Breakdown (est.)			1970	1969	Increase 1970-69	Increase 1969-68
	Anglo	Mex-Am	Black				
	%	%	%			%	%
One	41	59	—	59,980	53,473	plus 12	plus 4
Two	65	33	2	84,731	79,652	plus 6	plus 3
Three	80	11	9	73,792	70,504	plus 5	plus 5
Four	62	22	16	41,737	40,317	plus 4	minus 1
Total	62	31	7	260,242	243,946	plus 7	plus 3

HEAVILY CANVASSED PRECINCTS VS. OTHERS—1970-69

	Heavily Canvassed Mex-Am Precincts	Other Mex-Am Precincts	Black Precincts	Pre-dominantly Anglo Precincts
	(28)	(17)	(12)	(114)
1969	38,021	16,442	11,668	125,013
1970	43,844	17,397	12,237	128,549
Change	5,823	955	569	3,536
	15%	5.8%	4.9%	2.8%

ity outside the targeted twenty-eight precincts and in Black areas on the East Side, but this was sporadic and unsupervised compared to the systematic drive in the high-priority Mexican-American neighborhoods. Registration in the Anglo precincts was largely unorganized, although experience in the Deep South has shown that a publicized effort to register minority-group voters often triggers a countervailing reaction within the majority.

The overall increase of 7 per cent in Bexar County in 1970 was lower than the increases in New York City in 1969 and 1970, although the latter enjoyed a system of permanent registration, cutting down on the possibilities for adding names to the rolls, and had a much more restrictive system for neighborhood registration.

On a cost-benefit basis, attacking the problem of low registration by action programs in the field did not appear to result in handsome dividends in San Antonio, other than the utility of registration drives as a gateway for introducing new persons to the experience of political activity. That is not to say that the figures did not show that systematic canvassing in targeted neighborhoods can be made to pay dividends. In saturated Precinct 222, the total of 585 registered voters in 1969 was nearly doubled in 1970 to 908, but the cost of that all-out effort in both manpower and money appeared to be beyond the means of most local registration organizations. The political payoff from having added these extra voters to the rolls, when the time arrived for the May 1970 Democratic primary, will be examined shortly.

The long-term interest of the principal sources of money and administrative talent for the 1970 effort in Bexar County was to increase the participation of Mexican-Americans in the political system. Their short-term interest, however, was to increase registration hopefully to benefit U.S. Senator Ralph W. Yarborough and State Senator Joe J. Bernal, who were fighting for their lives in the Democratic primary.

When the statewide votes were counted on May 2, Senator Yarborough went down to defeat before Lloyd Bentsen. In Bexar County Yarborough unexpectedly lost by the margin of 5,995 votes. He received only 46 per cent of the votes cast, as against 65 per cent of the Primary vote in the county six years before. Senator Bernal squeaked by with a 1,501 vote margin over David Evans in the 26th District, which covers both the Mexican-American West Side and Anglo precincts to the north; Bernal's plurality had been 6,491 votes when he last ran in 1966. Only 39 per cent of the eligible voters turned out, although Texas law permits Republican cross-overs. In the 1968 Presidential election, better than 70 per cent turned out, when Hubert Humphrey carried San Antonio by 32,621 against Richard Nixon.

Early Closing of Registration

The span of more than ninety days between the closing of the registration lists in San Antonio and the first opportunity to cast a ballot, in the party primaries, could have contributed to the deflation of enthusiasm among some new voters. Also, early closings work against late bloomers, whose interest in voting is aroused by the political campaign, which begins long after the voting lists are closed. In striking down the Texas registration law in November 1970, a U.S. District Court estimated that if registration in Texas had been kept open until thirty days before elections, another 1,000,000 Texans might have registered. Other states were then practicing similar early shutdowns. In Pennsylvania the books were closed fifty days before an election; in California fifty-four; in Rhode Island sixty. Only twenty-three states permitted absentee registration.

The acceptable purposes for the early closing of registration, if indeed they ever existed, had been outmoded as seriously as the residency requirements in many states. Although the 1970 Voting Rights Act made thirty-day residence sufficient to vote for President anywhere in the country, it left untouched laws in thirty-three states and the District of Columbia requiring at least a year's residency in order to vote in local contests. Such a requirement did not offer much protection against fraud, since the fact of residence is customarily proved by oath and there are ample criminal penalties for fraud in existing statute law. In an era of rapid communication, a lengthy waiting period is not necessary to forestall dual voting. It was not clear why a period of residency sufficient to vote for President would not be sufficient to vote for Senator, Governor, or Mayor, unless it was assumed that it took a year for new settlers to learn enough about the community to cast an intelligent vote. That, of course, was a highly subjective criterion. But if a way could actually be found to reliably measure the extent of an individual's involvement in a community and his understanding of issues and candidates at the polls, it is by no means certain that time would be the crucial factor.

In March, 1972, the U.S. Supreme Court in *Dunn v. Blumstein* struck down the 90-day residence requirement in the state of Tennessee, touching off a series of decisions in the lower courts in favor of a 30-day limit. This action validated the position that the issues of politics in the United States today are practically universal. The leverage of modern mass media for quick dissemination of campaign material is tremendous. Residence is no antidote against the distortions of television political commercials. In Britain, campaigns have long been strictly limited to a matter of weeks. Shorter residency requirements in this country would seem to be a logical extension of a general feeling that our own campaigns should be shorter. As a practical matter, election contests reach a peak in their final days. There is ample opportunity to acquire all the information necessary to make an intelligent choice at the polls in a matter of days. In any event, long waiting periods in order to qualify for the privileges of the franchise have been recognized by the Court as an anomaly in a mobile society.

Closing the registration books a longer period of time before Election Day than a 30-day residence requirement was obviously no longer practicable. Thus, the Texas and Tennessee decisions opened the way for a nationwide liberalization of the opportunity to register and vote within the limits of a system depending most heavily on individual initiative.

Short periods of required residence, open registration books and a system of permanent eligibility should all be beneficial to the task of improving participation among urban minorities.

Allen M. Shinn, Jr., who in 1970 prepared an analysis of the effects of annual registration for the Mexican-American Legal Defense Fund, pointed out that in 1968 the average rate of registration in four areas that had annual registration (Texas, Alabama, South Carolina, and the District of Columbia) was 19.1 per cent lower than in forty-one states with permanent registration. Similarly, the difference in Election-Day turnout between the two groups of states was around 18.5 per cent.

Shinn found that the significant factor was not the total length of the registration period, but how close the registration period was to important elections. Fairly short registration periods may not be incompatible with high levels of registration, he concluded, provided that a permanent system is used and that the deadline is kept open until the last possible moment before Election Day. The 1972 national elections would provide the first major opportunity to test the practical effect of shorter residency requirements and late-closing registration deadlines on increasing the number of eligible voters nationwide. Democratic Presidential nominee George McGovern planned a mammoth drive to register minority groups and young people under the newly liberalized registration guidelines. President Nixon, in a proclamation authorized by Congress, designated September, 1972, as National Registration Month. Partisan considerations aside, these developments set the stage for a significant test of the American system for qualifying voters.

A bill passed by the Texas State Legislature in 1971, meanwhile, provided for permanent registration, with an additional registration period extending from March 1 through September 30. The bill also permitted registration up to thirty days in advance of the May primary date in Texas. The bill also provided that deputy registrars be allowed to move from place to place, seeking to register voters, and that moving companies and utilities cooperate with election officials in keeping registration lists up to date.

These reforms might have helped to save Yarborough's Senate seat in the 1970 Texas primary, assuming the premise was true that heavy registration would have helped the "liberal" candidates in that election. In that connection it is worth examining what happened to the theory that a record registration total in liberal Bexar County in 1970 was like money in the bank for the cause of Senator Yarborough and Senator Bernal.

Assessing the Outcome

Actually, a variety of factors contributed to Yarborough's defeat. His more conservative opponent made capital among Texas's fundamentalist religious groups of Yarborough's refusal to help buck the Supreme Court decision banning prayers in the public schools. Bentsen organized a Mexican-American committee of his own, and made effective use of Spanish-language television and radio, while Yarborough's media efforts suffered from financial problems in his campaign. Although Yarborough's Washington duties had kept him out of Texas for long stretches at a time and his down-the-line liberalism had set him apart from the Connnally wing of the Party (it was the desire to help make political peace in Texas between John Connally and Yarborough that had brought John F. Kennedy to Dallas in November 1963), his managers seemed supremely confident to the unpredicted end.

Some were prepared to blame his defeat either on Mexican-American defections or polarized reactions to Chicano militancy. In the Twentieth Congressional District of Congressman Henry B. Gonzales, voters were handed slate cards urging them to back Gonzales and Bentsen. Willie Velasquez was vetoed as a member of the Yarborough campaign organization, and most of the Senator's literature in San Antonio played down his association with Chicanos. Commissioner Pena, who was on Yarborough's steering committee, was feuding with the state A.F.L.-C.I.O. president and the Teamsters Union over a variety of labor and civil rights matters, and this schism was reflected in delays in financing and implementing the labor-sponsored get-out-the-vote drive on the West Side. If it were true that Mexican-Americans cost Yarborough his blue-collar Anglo support without producing the backing expected of them, then the COVER operation in San Antonio would have proved to be very expensive indeed.

A spot check of precincts in Bexar County by Tyrus Fain and Henry Appel laid many of these allegation to rest, however. Although it was true that Yarborough's support at the polls fell off badly in Anglo precincts, the drop-off was nearly as serious among Black voters on San Antonio's East Side. Mexican-American voters held up best of all, turning out in higher proportion than six years previously, but one in ten switched over to Bentsen. Better than two in ten, on the other hand, were switching over to Bentsen in the high-income WASP precincts in North San Antonio and the Anglo blue-collar precincts on the southeast.

The table on the next page was prepared by Fain.

A glance at the percentages shows continuous erosion of Yarborough support among all ethnic and income groups, and no signs of a polarized spurt in turnout among Anglo voters. Anglo turnout dropped from 1964, while the interest of minority groups

SAMPLE PRECINCTS, BEXAR COUNTY—1964 and 1970

	Voting for Yarborough			Proportion Voting		
	1964	1970	Change	1964	1970	Change
	%	%	%	%	%	%
Mexican-American Poor; The West Side (13 precincts with over 90% Mexican-Americans)	86.6	76.2	−10.4	43.2	47.1	+3.9
Black Poor; The East Side (7 precincts 85% or more Black)	91.4	71.1	−20.3	29.8	31.6	+1.8
Blue-Collar Workers; The Southeast (12 precincts 80% or more Anglo)	62.5	38.3	−24.2	37.8	35.4	−2.4
High-Income Anglos; The Northside (16 precincts 90% or more Anglo)	40.4	20.0	−20.4	39.0	33.5	−5.5

in Bexar County was rising. Mexican-Americans voted in proportion eight percentage points above the average for the county as a whole and ten points above the average in all of Texas. Statewide, in thirty-three other counties with a population more than 35 per cent Mexican-American, Yarborough had a majority over Bentsen of 15,666 votes. Black voters not only were the most apathetic, but also were nearly as dramatic in their defections from Yarborough as were high-income Anglos. (This was attributed both to post-Kennedy disenchantment with the Democratic party and the impact of the prayer issue on church-going Blacks.) Even though Yarborough received a highly respectable seven in every ten Black and Mexican-American votes, the more numerous Anglos were voting even more monolithically for his opponent. Clearly, something fundamental had befallen the Senator. Bentsen, his underrated opponent, went on in November to defeat George Bush, a former Congressman, who was later appointed Ambassador to the United Nations.

State Senator Bernal, running in tandem with Yarborough, pulled a higher turnout for both himself and Yarborough in Mexican-American precincts than prevailed in other Bexar County races. Bernal, however, averaged better than 90 per cent among his fellow ethnics, as against Yarborough's 76 per cent. Just as importantly, he ran even with or better than Yarborough in Anglo precincts on the North Side, putting to rest the assumption that Chicano militancy was a key issue there. For the 26th Senatorial District as a whole, Bernal's percentage of the total vote was 51, barely enough to win, as against Yarborough's 46. (The voting list was estimated to be 57 per cent Anglo.) But Bernal's narrow margin over his Anglo opponent was in every respect forged in the barrios. In nine precincts in Commissioner Pena's bailiwick in the southwest, Bernal's percentages ran from 91 to 97 per cent, with more than 50 per cent of the voters turning out.

Precinct 222, the locale of COVER's saturation effort, was a disappointment. Only 348 of the newly registered 908 voters came to the polls, as compared with the 390 from a much smaller list who had voted for President (89 per cent for Humphrey). Although all but 5 per cent of the residents were estimated to be Mexican-American, 18 per cent of those voting cast their ballots for Bernal's Anglo opponent. Yarborough ran two points below his Mexican-American average in that experimental precinct.

The mammoth registration effort in Precinct 222, therefore,

had negligible effect on turnout on Primary Day—the 38 per cent average there was below that of the county as a whole. The contrast with the precincts to the south organized by Commissioner Pena's committeemen is testimony to the importance of having workers on the block on Election Day. The defections from ethnic unity are more difficult to explain.

In the city elections of 1971 in San Antonio—following three hard years of registration work—Pete Torres, running for the Mayor's place on the Council Ticket, was soundly defeated. Not only was the Mexican-American vote fragmented by factionalism, but the Anglo wards united against the prospect of a Chicano Mayor.

It is also possible that in increasing the electorate by half, the marginal voters placed on the rolls either did not identify with the concept of collective political action or became confused by their inexperience when it came to casting their votes. A voter registration drive is useless unless it is accompanied by an educational program. The problem with this truism is that voter education is meaningless when divorced from issues of controversy or the partisan considerations of day-to-day politics. And yet these are the very taboos that encircle most of the official guidelines for carrying out a permissible registration campaign.

Logic would seem to dictate that if the government undertook the initiative, onus, and expense of creating and maintaining registration lists containing the names of every eligible citizen, then the funds and energies of private groups in the society could be directed exclusively toward the education of voters. Thus, the line between the nonpartisan act of giving every individual the opportunity to participate in our electoral democracy and the legitimate partisan activity of attempting to motivate them to pursue particular political ends through the exercise of their franchise would be clear and enforceable. The sums presently spent in trying to expand the electorate in the face of archaic and restrictive state registration laws could then be diverted to creating materials for the better understanding of candidates and the enormously complex choices of present-day government.

PART FOUR

NEW THRUSTS FOR PARTICIPATION: THE VOTER EDUCATION PROJECT IN THE SOUTH AND THE EIGHTEEN-YEAR-OLD VOTE

An examination of the history of drives to register Black voters in the South and of the contemporary opportunity for eighteen-year-olds to become part of the national electorate.

Chapter Fourteen

THE VOTING RIGHTS ACT OF 1965 AND THE BATTLE OF NEW ORLEANS

The Voting Rights Act

The fact that statutory changes at the federal level might indeed make a difference in rates of registration at the local level was dramatically documented by the Voting Rights Act of 1965. When the Act was passed, in the seven Southern states covered by its provisions only 33.1 per cent of the Black voting-age population was registered to vote. This compared with 73.2 per cent of the White voting-age population. In Mississippi Black registration came to only 35,000 of a possible 422,256, a shocking 8.3 per cent; in Alabama, the figures were 113,000 registered Blacks in a voting-age population of 481,000, or 23.5 per cent.

The situation had been far worse at the start of the decade. In 1962, however, the Southern Regional Council, a private biracial organization formed "to attain the ideals and practices of equal opportunity for all peoples in the South," launched its first Voter Education Project. "A major purpose of the new undertaking," the SRC said, "was to be research into the causes of low political participation, particularly among Blacks, in the South." The method was to make grants to community organizations to conduct voter registration drives, during which weekly progress reports outlining the local difficulties encountered were filed with VEP headquarters in Atlanta, Georgia.

Most of the grants were for relatively small amounts—$1,000 to $2,000—for periods of from six to eight weeks. Money was supplied on a cost-draw basis rather than in lump sums, furnishing VEP with an effective means of control. The grant letter warned against putting the money to any partisan use, with specific strictures against grantees becoming involved in get-out-the-vote activity after registration had been accomplished. Candidates and others directly connected with political campaigns were not permitted to hold positions of responsibility in VEP-supported registration activities nor to utilize VEP-supported facilities in their own campaigns.

The weekly reports from these early efforts contained stories of discrimination, economic reprisals, and violence against Blacks encouraged to register by the VEP field workers. The application of literacy tests, prevalent throughout the South, was an especially potent weapon in light of the condition of the impoverished Black schools in rural regions. Would-be registrants were handed an obscure and complicated passage from the State Constitution and asked to render an interpretation. The long trip to the county courthouse, moreover, was in itself a strong deterrent, involving not only absence from work, obtaining some means of travel, and the foreknowledge of the hours a registrar might be available, but also running the gauntlet of hostile rednecks lounging in the courthouse square. The results of these early registration drives sometimes ran dishearteningly behind the efforts. In November 1963, VEP abandoned the funding of registration drives in Mississippi.

Nevertheless, in eleven states from Virginia to Texas, 700,000 more Blacks were eligible to vote in the 1964 Presidential election than had been eligible in 1960. The best showings were in Texas and Florida, with 150,000 and 117,000 Blacks, respectively, added to the rolls. In Mississippi the total gain came to a meager 6,500, although White registration had increased by 47,000 during the same period. In all eleven states, the increase in White Registration from 1960 to 1964 amounted to nearly 2,000,000.

The nearly three-to-one ratio of White numerical increases over Black, in addition to an initial White headstart on the voting rolls, could be measured against a four-to-one White advantage in the actual voting-age population. Thus, Blacks were doing proportionately better than Whites despite the obstacles used to discourage their registration and the stimulation of White registration in some areas in response to the threat of Black political activity.

The VEP registration drives had symbolic value in the small towns and rural regions of the South, regions conditioned to a degree of fatalism, even cynicism, over the prospects of equal opportunity for Blacks at the polls. The drives attracted idealistic young volunteers from the North, who helped generate an awareness when they returned home of the need for electoral reform in the South. Within the social structure of the Black South, young ministers such as Martin Luther King, Jr., found the rallying cry for a new crusade in the concern for voter registration and political participation. "It was registration work that sent Dr. King on the historic 58-mile march from Selma to Montgomery in 1965," wrote Vernon E. Jordan, Jr., Director of VEP. "It was this march that led to the Voting Rights Act, and it was this Act that permitted thousands of Southern Negroes to register and vote for the first time."

The Voting Rights Act of 1965 was lobbied through Congress with the help, for the first time, of church groups throughout the South as well as the North whose consciences had been activated by the Southern Christian Leadership Conference working through social action committees. The slow and painful process of case-by-case litigation instituted by the Department of Justice had made little progress against long-standing violations of the 15th Amendment, which declared that the "right of citizens of the United States shall not be denied . . . on account of race, color, or previous condition of servitude."

A state or political subdivision was covered by the Act if both of two circumstances existed: (1) if on November 1, 1964, it applied literacy tests, "good moral character" prerequisites, or similar requirements as conditions to voting; (2) either that less than 50 per cent of its persons were registered to vote on November 1, 1964, or that less than 50 per cent voted in the Presidential election of 1964. In practice, these automatic trigger provisions meant that six states in the South were fully covered—Alabama, Georgia, Louisiana, Mississippi, South Carolina, and Virginia—plus thirty-nine counties in a seventh state, North Carolina.

If a state or political subdivision qualified under the Act, then four consequences followed:

1) It might not use any test or device to limit voting eligibility.

2) The Attorney General might under specified circumstances have federal examiners sent to any county included in the jurisdictions covered by the act. These examiners could qualify persons directly on the registration lists if they were found to be eligible under valid state law.

3) The Attorney General might send federal observers to any county designated for examiners to observe the polling places and the counting of the vote.

4) No state or political subdivision under the act could apply any new voting qualification or procedure without first obtaining either the acquiescence of the Attorney General or a declaratory judgment from the U.S. District Court for the District of Columbia that the new practice "does not have the purpose and will not have the effect of denying or abridging the right to vote on account of race or color." The burden of proving the nondiscriminatory purpose and effect was on the governmental body seeking the exception.

The Battle of New Orleans

In New Orleans, awaiting the day the 1965 Voting Rights Act would go into effect, Bernice Leder, Voting Service Chairman for the League of Women Voters, drilled 100 Blacks to present themselves before A. P. Gallinghouse, the feared Registrar of

Voters for the Parish of Orleans. Until a change in the law, which went into effect in May 1970, giving the City Council control, the Registrar was appointed by the Governor, although the city was required to pay half the expenses for the operation of the office. Gallinghouse, a gruff man with a staff reflecting his own personality, had been appointed in 1961 by Governor Jimmy ("You Are My Sunshine") Davis, an avowed segregationist. This appointment followed a Supreme Court decision the previous year ordering 1,000 Louisiana Blacks who had been removed by a "citizenship test" now cast aside by the Court restored to the voting rolls.

The test had been part of a statewide push by political leaders against the Black franchise following the school integration decision by the Court and the calling of the National Guard to nearby Little Rock, Arkansas, by President Eisenhower. From 1956 to 1958 the number of Blacks on the voting rolls of Louisiana was reduced from 161,410 to 129,644. Between 1956 and 1960 Black registration in Orleans Parish dropped by one-third, and 2,500 names on the list were challenged in a single day in 1959. Until the citizenship test was struck down by the Court, would-be voters were asked to interpret the meaning of such obscure passages from the Louisiana Constitution as: "Prescription shall not run against the State in any civil matter," and "The Legislature shall provide by law for change of venue in civil and criminal cases."

Registrants were required to appear in person at City Hall or one other branch for all of New Orleans' seventeen Wards, except for two on the easternmost extremity of the city, which were served by a special branch. Regulations stipulated that each applicant should bring identifying documents at least ninety days old but not over two years old showing the individual to have been a resident of Louisiana for one year, of Orleans Parish for six months, and of his precinct for three months. Identification was to include signature and correct address either on one document or on separate documents. If the applicant were a married woman who had no documents in her own name, and her husband was registered, then she was permitted to use a marriage license to prove identification and residence. The Registrar's office was open weekdays only, from 9 A.M. to 4 P.M., and during the period from thirty to sixty days prior to an election until 9 P.M. only on Fridays. Re-registration was required if one either moved or married.

Before the 1965 Voting Rights Act was enacted, each application stated that "Applicant shall demonstrate his ability to read and write from dictation by the Registrar of Voters from the preamble to the Constitution of the United States." New forms adopted after the Court decision also required a series of "morality questions." Declarations in the affirmative or negative were requested regarding convictions for misdemeanors other than violations of traffic and/or game laws, or whether the applicant had given birth to an illegitimate child within five years of the date of making application to register or had acknowledged himself to be the father of an illegitimate child.

Not only were such requirements inhibiting in themselves to Blacks unsure of themselves in the world of White officialdom, but they also allowed for considerable leeway on the part of the Registrar and his deputies in deciding who was or was not qualified to go on the rolls. From 1960 through 1964 the number of Blacks registered in New Orleans remained constant at about 35,000 out of a voting-age population of 125,000—a ratio somewhat less than 30 per cent, compared with a White percentage exceeding 60 per cent by the time of the Goldwater-Johnson Presidential election of 1964. (Goldwater, however, polled only 48.9 per cent of the vote in New Orleans, compared to 72.9 per cent upstate in Baton Rouge and 80 per cent in Shreveport.)

The ground had been laid for Black-White cooperation in New Orleans on voter registration during the long local struggle to desegregate the schools. Building on this structure, the League of Women Voters assumed responsibility for coordinating a registration drive in cooperation with thirty organizations, including VEP, the National Association for the Advancement of

Colored People, CORE, and the Council of Jewish Women. The indefatigable Mrs. Leder, head of "Operation Registration," organized registration classes in public housing projects that used exact replicas of the forms in City Hall and a personal counselor technique calculated to condition applicants against possible rebuffs at the Registrar's office. She obtained registration lists never before available to the NAACP and instituted a system at League headquarters for matching the official lists against the city directory and turning them over to VEP workers in the precincts. With the help of young volunteers from the NAACP Youth Council, door-to-door canvassing was undertaken in the most promising precincts.

In the weeks immediately prior to the city primaries of 1965, "Operation Registration" distributed 200,000 sample ballots plus 250,000 flyers that stated "Your Voice is Silent Unless You Register and Vote." Sound trucks toured the city. Voting machines were demonstrated in City Hall during registration hours.

Under pressure from the League, the Registrar reduced the time required between attempts by turned-down applicants from ten days to five days. The League also forced the office to remain open during the lunch hour and, using the new legislation as a wedge, to schedule some special Saturday registration hours for working people. When attempts were made to disuade Blacks from declaring their party affiliation with the then dominant Democrats, they were thwarted.

During the period immediately following the July 1965 Voting Rights Act, "Operation Registration" succeeded in qualifying 5,000 Blacks to vote in New Orleans. According to a report from the League of Women Voters Education Fund, "interest in a school board sales tax election May 3, 1966, added almost 4,000 new registrants to the rolls; but after that election, even with a great deal of effort and organization, relatively few new registrants were added in the period that closed July 13." Over a seventeen-month period Black registration in New Orleans jumped from 35,000 to 53,261— an average of 1,000 per month. The League had spent $16,431, for a cost of slightly less than one dollar per Black voter.

Following this initial spurt in 1965-1966, registration in New Orleans lost momentum. The young leader who had mobilized the NAACP Youth Councils went away to college, an occupational hazard in all such ventures by the young. Bernice Leder, the dynamo of the League of Women Voters, left New Orleans when her husband was transferred to Bethlehem, Pennsylvania. Her successor as Voting Service chairman, Jane Brown, came to town from Seattle, Washington, when her husband took an aerospace job in New Orleans. Explaining the letdown, Mrs. Brown said that the candidacy of George Wallace in 1968 had caused some second thoughts about focusing public attention on voter registration, and the deaths of Martin Luther King, Jr., and Robert Kennedy had taken the starch out of others. Local Black leadership more and more turned its attention to direct political action, making it increasingly difficult for members of the League of Women Voters to satisfy local White members that their skirts were unstained by partisan politics.

The New Orleans League then applied for an inner-city grant from the League's Educational Fund in Washington to develop a program for better recreational facilities and day-care centers in Carrollton Central, a poverty-stricken Black neighborhood in the central city. "We looked on registration," explained Mrs. Brown, "as a means for developing a neighborhood identity rather than as an end in itself." In 1968 the Carrollton registration project put 150 new names on the rolls.

Pete Nichols, a Carrollton registration worker, said that "many Blacks are not interested in participating because of lack of understanding of the system. They get tons of material telling them why they should register as a civic duty, instead of relating each individual's vote to the whole system. I try to start with what one vote in Congress can do for Blacks on particular issues, use it as a parable, so to speak. Even so, it's no good unless you can get someone on each block to approach the non-registered in his own neighborhood. I tried to arrange a meeting of people on the block, and then walked in on them, cold turkey, with the pitch. But some took it as an insult. After knocking themselves out and getting flat turndowns, people get pretty frustrated. Their interest in registration begins to wane.''

In 1967 New Orleans elected a Black State Representative from the 20th District, Ernest N. Morial, who received 30 per cent of the White vote in wards 1 and 2, plus almost solid support from Blacks. Morial's victory in the Democratic primary broke the color line for the first time in the Louisiana State Legislature. Previously, Black legislators had been elected in Georgia, Tennessee, and Texas, part of a growing cadre of elected Black officials all over the South in the wake of the voting drives of the Sixties. The following year Dr. Mack J. Spears, dean of student affairs at Dillard University, was elected to the school board in New Orleans.

With the approach of local elections in 1969 for Mayor and Council in New Orleans, Black groups in the city set their sights on electing their first Black councilman and perhaps playing a decisive role in the selection of a Mayor. At the time Blacks constituted a majority of registered voters in only one of New Orleans' seventeen Wards, testimony both to a lower percentage of total population on the rolls than Whites (approximately 48 per cent versus 63 per cent) and to the relatively unsegregated mixture of neighborhoods in this old southern city. Organizations with such names as the Black Unity Caucus, the Black Political Action Council, SOUL (Southern Organization for Unified Leadership), BOLD (Black Organization for Leadership Development), and COUP (Congress of Urban Problems) sprouted in the soil prepared by the struggle to put the brothers and sisters on the voting roll.

SOUL was organized in the sprawling 9th Ward, which reaches like a salamander's tail toward the growing eastern suburbs of New Orleans. In a registration total of approximately 15,000 in the ward, the split was 8,000 White and 7,000 Black, although Blacks were a majority of the voting-age population. With a $1,300 drawing account from the Voter Education Project, SOUL set itself a target of registering fifty new Black voters per day. "We are interested in making better living conditions for our people by making better citizens of our people," its flyers announced. "A voteless people is a hopeless people."

With no previous experience in voter registration, SOUL looked around for help and found Jane Brown at the League of Women Voters. Mrs. Brown briefed members of the community organization on the techniques of building a card file of unregistered residents, helped them procure voting lists and a city directory, sent them materials to stamp with their own insignia, and, testified one, "seemed to understand how to orient a campaign toward Blacks, not Whites." The resulting literature, illustrated with cartoons and drawings on colored paper, mixed emotion, aphorisms, and reassurance:

"THEY GAVE THEIR LIVES—Medgar Evers, John F. Kennedy, Martin Luther King, Robert F. Kennedy—DO YOU VOTE? Yes, these four great and beloved men are among the thousands of men and women who gave their lives for FREEDOM and to secure A BETTER LIFE FOR ALL AMERICANS. Was their struggle in vain? We say it is not. Today you have the right to make a FREE man's decision in a FREE election. You can pick up where these great men left off, and BECOME A FIRST CLASS CITIZEN, or you can forget what they lived and died for, and remain a nobody, a nothing, a zero. IT'S UP TO YOU. IF YOU DON'T VOTE DON'T COMPLAIN.

"IT IS NOW EASY FOR YOU TO REGISTER! The door is open. Walk through it. NO TESTS, NO INSULTS. Perhaps you have tried to register before and been insulted, or given difficult tests. NOW IT IS SIMPLE TO REGISTER. Because of the Voting Rights Act, and the Civil Rights Act of 1964, you can now register to vote in a pleasant and easy manner. If you need a ride to the registrar's office, call SOUL and the SOUL VOTE BOAT will bring you there. THIS MAY BE THE MOST IMPORTANT RIDE OF YOUR LIFE."

The SOUL boat was a Volkswagen minibus, pressed into service when it was learned, the hard way, that unless prospective new voters were picked up at their doorsteps, they seldom made it to the registrar's office. Nor were volunteer canvassers easy to come by. "It's a seven night a week thing," said a SOUL precinct captain, "and it was hard to get people to spend all that time at night. We found out we needed to pay volunteers in order to make it work. Black people aren't quick to trust Black leadership. They've been sold out too many times. We told them we were trying to unite Black people for strength and to protect the ward against a racist candidate for mayor. But still we had to beat the bushes for volunteers. Some middle-class Blacks in the ward would see the name SOUL and ask what that meant. Some said they were afraid what we were doing would be played up by White politicians. Voter registration is a long and tiresome job, but involvement at the grass-roots level is the only way Black people are going to get what they need in New Orleans in the way of housing, or education or health. We've just got to stick it out."

When the summer was over, SOUL could count 700 hard names of persons taken down and registered, although 20 per day was the high against the initial hopes for 50. The goal for 1969 was a total of 25,000 voters in the ward, but when registration was closed for the mayoralty election the final count in Ward 9 was 16,065—8,139 White and 7,926 Black.

A New Force in Southern Politics

High expectations that become dashed against harsh realities are one of the curses of inexperience in voter registration. A system that places a premium on individual motivation seems to make no allowance for the passivity engendered by generations of hopelessness. The long trip to the Registrar's office in New Orleans was for many Black residents a journey into a dark forest with a sniper in every tree. Those who made it and back were the Green Berets of the Southern electorate and one result, as we shall see, is that unlike urban voters elsewhere in the country, Blacks in Southern cities consistently turned out in local elections in higher proportion than Whites. As Black registration increases, slowly but inexorably, this fact has been having decisive impact on the course of Southern politics generally. In New Orleans, as in Atlanta, liberal mayors have owed their most recent victories to bloc support and high rates of turnout by Black voters.

Maurice E. (Moon) Landrieu, surprise winner over James Fitz-morris in the 1969 Democratic primaries for Mayor of New Orleans carried only 39 per cent of the White vote, according to calculations made by Allen Rosenzweig, local market researcher, as against 88 per cent of the Black vote. Importantly, Black turnout was three percentage points higher (79 per cent) than the White turnout (76 per cent) in helping Landrieu to a winning margin of 12,802 votes in the run-off. Running against a conservative Republican opponent, Ben C. Toledano, in the April 1970 citywide election, Landrieu scored an estimated 99 per cent in Black precincts, which turned out 77 per cent of those registered. This was seven percentage points higher than among White voters, the majority of whom cast their ballots for Toledano. Landrieu was elected handily.

A similar analysis by Charles S. Rooks, research associate on the staff of the Voter Education Project, of the October 1969 elections for Mayor of Atlanta, showed that about 51 per cent of the registered Blacks and 43 per cent of the registered Whites voted in the first round in that city. In the run-off, won by White liberal Sam Massell against a moderate White opponent, Rodney Cook, backed by most of the Atlanta business community, the Black turnout was 56.3 per cent versus 54.1 per cent for Whites. The difference was important, since Massell received 92.2 per cent of the Black vote in the Atlanta run-off as against 27 per cent of the White vote. The 45,000 votes Massell received from Blacks almost equaled Cook's 47,500 votes from Whites, and he won the election by over 11,000 votes.

Why the turnout among both races should be twenty points lower in Atlanta than in New Orleans, especially in view of recent similarities in the political patterns of Georgia and

Louisiana, was not immediately apparent. Outgoing Mayor Ivan Allen had called the first-round turnout a "disgrace" and made a special appeal on television for increased participation. (The turnout had been about 70 per cent when Allen defeated Lester Maddox in 1961.) One factor among Black voters may have been the elimination of the only Black candidate for Mayor in the first round plus the election, without the necessity of a run-off, of a Black Vice Mayor, Maynard Jackson. Among White voters, the defeat of "law and order" conservative, Everett Millican, in the first round could conceivably have accounted for the fact that in many low-income precincts the turnout for the run-off was under 45 per cent. But the vote in these same precincts had been even smaller when Millican's name was on the ballot.

More likely was a replication of the paradoxical phenomenon previously observed among Mexican-Americans in Los Angeles and San Antonio. In the comparatively liberal environment of California, where voting registration is among the easiest in all fifty states, the level of participation among Chicanos was poorer than in the harsh Texas atmosphere of San Antonio, where registration laws were more restrictive. "Liberal" Atlanta, by the same token, seemed to spark less political interest among its qualified voters than was aroused among the veterans of A. P. Gillinghast's obstacle course in old-fashioned New Orleans.

A system of universal voter enrollment by government initiative, some have argued, might likewise cheapen the value of the franchise in the eyes of millions who do not take the trouble to register on their own initiative. The danger of drawing such parallels between the political behavior of Chicanos in Los Angeles and San Antonio or between Blacks in New Orleans and Atlanta is the substance they seem to lend to arguments, rooted in the Puritan ethic of the middle classes, that persons should be kept individually responsible for their own registration. The fact of the matter, of course, is that nonparticipation, as we saw in the survey of nonvoters in Newark, is primarily a psychological condition, engendered by feelings of isolation, powerlessness, personal inadequacy, and discouragement over the delivery of services by the political system. The intensity of such feelings is in itself an index of the disconnection of the disadvantaged poor from the mainstream of life in the "modern" American city. Possibly there is something in the chemistry of up-to-date Los Angeles and booming Atlanta that has made registering and voting seem more of a waste of time to those whom the system has so conspicuously failed. In both the relatively mixed neighborhoods of New Orleans and in the solid barrios of San Antonio, those two least American of U. S. cities, a touch less alienation might have been one legacy of an older, more stable cultural heritage.

The election of a young Black attorney as Vice Mayor of Atlanta, on the other hand, could have been a symbolic milestone in the evolution of the New South. Jackson's run was not unlike that of Carl Stokes in Cleveland—he polled 97.8 per cent of the vote in the Black community, running against three White opponents, and 27.7 per cent of the White vote, better than Stokes's showing among White voters of the North in running for his city's top post. In some of the affluent precincts on Atlanta's North Side, Jackson's percentage of the vote bettered 40 per cent, although he ran more strongly in middle-class neighborhoods than in areas with the highest socioeconomic status.

The coalesence of a Black-White majority for a Black candidate running for high office against a White opponent in a large Southern city, and in a situation where six out of ten persons on the voting lists were White, would scarcely have been predicted a few short years ago. In the 1968 statewide Senatorial primary against Herman E. Talmadge, Jackson had been crushed by more than 450,000 votes; fewer than 50 per cent had voted in Atlanta's Black precincts and fewer than that in other Georgia cities. In some rural counties the turnout approached 70 per cent and Jackson received less than 10 per cent of the vote. In spite of that disappointing 1968 showing, Jackson had carried Atlanta by 6,000 votes by combining Black and White votes, thus establishing his credibility as a candidate there a year later.

If the decade of the sixties marked the first breakthrough for Black voter registration in the South, perhaps the prospects of actual Black power in the decade of the seventies might serve to elevate Black participation above the plateau on which it had paused. Atlanta, on the basis of the 1970 census, joined Washington, D.C., and Newark, N.J., as major U.S. cities with predominantly Black populations. Washington and Newark each had Black mayors. In eleven Southern states there were now 102 counties at least 50 per cent Black in population, if not in the proportion of registered voters.

The existence of a substantial number of Black voters in the South had already exerted a visible influence on state politics. Race was yielding to economics as the number-one issue in many contests for the governorship. In Florida, Georgia, and Arkansas the winning candidates in 1970 took moderate positions in their campaigns, defeating more extremist opponents in both the primaries and the elections. Mississippi, where over 200 Blacks were running for office in 1971, held a Democratic primary for the governorship in which the segregationist candidates ran third and sixth in the first round of voting. Blacks might not yet be in a position to win elections in their own right (the Reverend Andrew Young failed in his 1970 attempt to win the congressional seat including Atlanta), but they do hold a veto power over White candidates in the old racist mould.

Chapter Fifteen

THE BALANCE SHEET

Some of the setbacks in voter registration in the South following passage of the Voting Rights Act of 1965 were the clear result of continuing institutional bias. Even under a Democratic Administration pledged to its implementation, only 64 of the 556 Southern counties covered under the terms of the Act were ever assigned federal examiners for direct voter registration (there were none in Virginia and North Carolina and only two in South Carolina), and not a single county was added to the list in the first year of the Nixon Administration. The outlawing of literacy tests in the seven affected states, moreover, did not prevent registrars from imposing their own tests of residency, such as the requirements to produce utility bills addressed to the applicant as long as a year earlier. Black tenant farmers were sometimes threatened with eviction by their White landlords if they were seen filling out a registration form, and other poor folk were warned that the price of registering might be to lose welfare checks or have credit cut off at the crossroads grocery store.

In the five years between passage of the Voting Rights Act of 1965 and the adoption of an amended Act in 1970 the pace of Black registration in the South nevertheless quickened perceptibly. Compared with the 326,286 Blacks put on the rolls in the seven states between 1960 and 1965, 988,000 were added between

1965 and 1970—or nearly three times as many as in the years immediately prior to the new federal legislation.

BLACK REGISTRATION IN STATES COVERED BY THE
VOTING RIGHTS ACT

States	1960	1965	1969	1970
Alabama	66,009	113,000	295,000	315,000
Georgia	180,000	254,000	370,000	395,000
Louisiana	159,033	163,000	313,000	319,000
Mississippi	22,000	35,000	281,000	286,000
North Carolina	210,450	245,000	296,000	305,000
South Carolina	58,122	143,000	203,000	221,000
Virginia	100,100	169,000	261,000	269,000
Totals	795,714	1,122,000	2,019,000	2,110,000

PERCENT REGISTERED IN STATES COVERED BY THE
VOTING RIGHTS ACT

	Ala.	Ga.	La.	Miss.	N.C.	S.C.	Va.	Total
	%	%	%	%	%	%	%	%
Blacks								
1965	23.5	41.4	31.8	8.3	44.5	38.5	38.7	33.1
1969	61.3	60.4	60.8	66.5	53.7	59.8	59.5	59.5
1970	65.4	64.4	62.0	67.7	55.4	59.6	61.6	60.6
Whites								
1965	78.7	72.8	79.1	57.9	85.2	76.7	57.0	73.2
1969	94.6	88.5	87.1	89.8	78.4	71.5	78.7	83.8
1970	96.9	89.9	88.7	92.2	81.8	79.6	79.7	85.9

Examined from another perspective, however, four out of every ten Blacks at the end of the decade of the Sixties were still unregistered in these target Southern states—after all the confrontations, freedom marches, new legislation, and voter registration campaigns. Although the overall registration percentage of Blacks had nearly doubled, the most significant increases were in states where federal examiners had been sent to register voters directly.

As the percentage of eligible voters began to approach, and even exceed, those among minority-group members in Northern urban centers, the Voter Education Project began shifting some of its emphasis from registration to the education of voters in the practice of exercising their newly acquired grassroots political rights. In addition, VEP also instituted a series of seminars for the growing number of Black elected officials who were the direct outgrowth of the enlarged Black electorate. (Across the South, in 1970, there were 19 Black mayors, 32 legislators, nearly 250 Black city councilman and alderman, more than 90 school board members, about 90 law enforcement officers, and nearly 60 Black elected county officials.)

The importance of the Voter Education Project in the South was that it placed voter registration within the broader context of political education and activation. Vernon E. Jordan, Jr., VEP's first director, who later succeeded the late Whitney M. Young, Jr., as head of the National Urban League, his successor, John Lewis, one of the founders of the Student Non-Violent Coordinating Committee, and Georgia legislator Julian Bond traveled throughout the Deep South preaching the message of Black political participation. Young, charismatic, and dedicated, these registration organizers spread the idea that Southern Blacks had more to hope for than those who had fled North if they only exercised their full political potential. Getting on the voting rolls in Southern states was only the first battle of the campaign. "What we've got to do now," said Jordan, "is maximize that victory, or we may end up like Negroes in the North. How do we maximize our present gains? Our most effective and respected weapon is Black political power, properly exercised, in the Southern political process."

From Voter Registration to Political Action
The state voter education projects funded by VEP published basic texts, simply written and generously illustrated, explaining to Black voters how they could take part effectively in local pre-

cinct meetings and analyzing the powers of county commissioners and local school boards. Unlike the civil rights crusades of the past, Black activism focused on local leadership and local offices. In Mississippi, where 307,000 registered Blacks were eligible to vote in 1971, 83 Blacks already held public office, and Mayor Charles Evers of Fayette was running for the governorship. The Black vote could not control an election, but it might determine the outcome.

The meticulous adminstrative guidelines drawn up and circulated by VEP to distinguish between non-partisan registration and the partisan political activities of a new and self-conscious Black constituency were, of course, a prudent concession to IRS requirements and the wary eye kept by Southern congressmen on this rising new potential in Southern politics. As a matter of fact, in White-dominated jurisdictions where the Black majority in the population had heretofore been barred from voting, the urge was particularly strong for newly enfranchised Blacks to put up and try to elect their own slate of candidates. In a hostile, often dangerous environment, the risk of registering was more likely to be undertaken in the expectation of direct and immediate political consequence. The nomination and election of neighbors of their own race to sensitive political posts was a powerful incentive to those who had been denied this basic right for generations. To try to separate voting registration from running for office was like trying to part a mother from her child.

The connection was even more vivid in small jurisdictions overwhelmingly populated by Blacks, such as Fayette, Mississippi, where Charles Evers had been elected mayor in 1969, or Greene County, Alabama, where Blacks took control of both the County Commission and the school board. In the large, urban centers of the South such as New Orleans, Birmingham, and Atlanta—where ostensibly the sanctions against registering were not as crude as in conservative, rural strongholds—Black registration continued to run below that in some rural sections of Louisiana, Alabama, and Georgia.

The desire of Blacks for a greater voice in their own affairs was thus no longer limited to simply securing the franchise. Along with VEP-sponsored projects in New Orleans, for example, in the summer before the 1969 primaries and 1970 election the Urban League launched its own project to attempt to unify the emerging Black electorate in the Crescent City. Headed by a dynamic, Black community leader, Mrs. Oretha Haley, the New Thrust program of the Urban League sought to combine community organization, voter registration, and voter education in a single viable undertaking. With a budget of $35,000 it concentrated its efforts on the possible election of the city's first Black councilman. Picked as the target area was Councilman District B, the seat held by White Eddie L. Sapir, embracing five wards with the largest concentration of Blacks and including the only one with a majority of Blacks on the voting list. Louisiana's first Black representative, Ernest Morial, had been elected from a portion of the same area in 1967.

The first step was a registration drive from July to October, using student canvassers on a $20 per week stipend. The drive encountered the usual difficulties with rejections at the Registrar's office, and some of the prospects had to go back two or three times. Since City Hall was five to ten miles away from some portions of the District, transportation was provided. Workers collared persons coming into City Hall to pay their water bills, or were sent into Charity Hospital, near City Hall to find prospects who could walk across the street. Registration booths were set up in three public housing projects at the office where tenants went to pay the rent. A corps of fifteen to twenty worked the telephones.

"If we had trouble at the Registrar's office," said Mrs. Haley, "it sometimes turned off a whole block we had been working on. We'd tell them to bring a dozen Christmas cards to prove their residence. We had a community group. BOLD (Black Organization for Leadership Development), which was fighting the location of a new bridge across the Mississippi uptown that would tear down the homes of 3,000 Blacks. Combining that issue with voter registration worked pretty well. But it was hard getting people to go door-to-door.''

A total of 1,093 persons were registered in the five wards, a disappointing showing in a District with more than 15,000 on the rolls.

The next step was the organization of a Black Primary in September, a mock election staged in 48 out of 90 regular polling places (except schools) throughout the District. The polling places and a police officer for every precinct were provided by the city free of charge. Ballots were printed containing the name of the three announced Black candidates for Councilman, and sent to every registered voter. It was hoped that the losers in the mock election might withdraw in favor of the top vote-getter in the Black Primary.

The 2,500 out of 15,000 Blacks who turned out gained experience in marking ballots and familiarized themselves with the intricacies of the New Orleans system (councilmen are elected at-large, although they must live in the District they represent; often they run on slates with mayoralty candidates). But this experiment ran into trouble. One of the three Black candidates announced his withdrawal from the Black Primary one day before the polling. In addition, workers for the White incumbent made phone calls in behalf of the Black candidate they considered to be the weakest. Although the results were inconclusive, and no Black was subsequently elected councilman, Eddie Sapir was the only incumbent councilman forced into a run-off election. In that election, Moon Landrieu carried the District and went on to defeat his Republican opponent in the general election.

"The idea was not to turn around the election," said Mrs. Haley, "but to educate the voter not to be confused or afraid. We didn't elect a Black councilman because numerous candidates canceled each other out. Some were even put into the race to protect the White incumbent. The winner of the Black Primary wasn't on anybody's slate for mayor and voters learned the importance of straight-ticket voting in the outcome of some elections; the incumbent was on the Fitzmorris ticket. The goal was to show that we could have Black representation more responsive to our needs than White representation. I think Black people got the idea that it would be possible once they learned the ropes of the system."

In addition to the institutional discrimination inherent in a system that permits the voters of the whole city to pick councilmen outside their districts, the New Orleans experiment illustrated the distance still to be traversed between the acquisition of the right to vote and the power of Black voters to alter the course of government. Factionalism, confusion, even subversion are part of the growing pains of minority-group political awakening. The education component is important to the governed and governing alike in the Black community. The art of politics is not mastered overnight.

The disconnections among the urban poor have apparently been more crippling than even the isolation of out-of-the-way places, where an informal network of preachers, housewives, school teachers, youngsters, and visiting Civil Rights workers often operated in place of the more formal media. Black political successes in areas of their former disenfranchisement in overwhelmingly Black populated regions, however, have inspired hope in Southern towns and cities where the division is closer.

A 1969 article in *The Carolina Times*, reprinted in the *VEP News*, captured some of the flavor of those years of activity in small settlements across the South:

KINSTON, N.C.—Five years ago, after a Negro-supported candidate lost an election here, a group of black housewives decided to get busy.

They formed the Volunteer Housewives League of Kinston and Lenoir County, centered upon increasing registration to vote.

A black woman, Mrs. J. J. Hannibal, had served for two years on Kinston's City Council in the early sixties. At that time, Negro registration in the county was only some 1,200. Now Negro registration in Lenoir County is more than four times that figure—close to 5,000.

Spurred on by these successes, the housewives continued their registration efforts this summer in the heat of rural, tobacco-growing Lenoir County and came up with some registration techniques that have been borrowed by other eastern Carolina towns.

In the past, the Lenoir County women had used the traditional, time-tested voter registration technique of canvassing—that is, going from house-to-house, block-to-block, road-by-road and neighborhood-by-neighborhood to find out who was registered to vote and who wasn't. This is the method used by black registration workers all over the South.

But in Lenoir County, as in many other localities in the South, all those not registered must be carried to the courthouse to sign up to vote. The courthouse in Lenoir County—as in many other rural counties—is located on a main Kinston street along which Negroes pass during the day.

So the Volunteer League's energetic president, Mrs. Ann Whitehead, came up with an idea. Since the registration office is in a small building adjacent to the courthouse and on the ground floor, just a few feet away from the main street, why not stop passing Negroes on the sidewalk to ask them whether they are registered to vote? If the answer is no, one of the housewives urges the passer-by to step into the registration office to go through the brief procedure of registering.

The approach has been remarkably successful. Even during the hot and busy tobacco harvesting season, the Kinston-Lenior housewives registered well over 100 Negroes a week. Working with a small grant from the Voter Education Project of the Southern Regional Council, the housewives had registered 850 blacks between July 10, when their current effort started and the end of August. Of that number, says Mrs. Whitehead, 314 were brought into the registration office "off the streets."

In addition to patrolling the sidewalk near the registration office, the housewives make regular visits to poolrooms and other downtown places where large numbers of black people are gathered.

The approach saves both time and money. The women are spared the time-consuming task of driving all new registrants to the courthouse and they are saved some of the cost of gasoline for trips back and forth (which can mount up fast in rural areas), although some of this still must be done.

In nearby LaGrange, Ira Branch, operator of a grocery store, keeps a list of customers who are not registered to vote. Customers can sign up at his store for transportation to the registration office at the courthouse.

Members of the League carry an average of two carloads of new black voters to Kinston each week. The customers indicate, as they sign

Branch's list, when it will be convenient to go to Kinston to register.

The League had another big registration push last fall which, with a presidential election approaching, produced heavy black registration gains. But this year is not an election year in North Carolina, and John Edwards, director of the VEP-affiliated North Carolina Voter Education Project, says registration gains as heavy as those being produced by the Kinston-Lenoir housewives are "highly unusual" when no elections are coming up.

In addition to registration work, which is its main activity, the Housewives League has several other projects. These include working with the anti-poverty program in providing homemaking instructions, helping to get welfare benefits to those in need, and helping those in need of housing to get into public housing, Mrs. Whitehead explained. These activities tie in naturally, she added, with contacts made in the course of doing voter registration work.

Members of the Housewives League expected to bring in an even heavier registration when tobacco harvesting was over. They say they have long lists of men who had promised to register when this all-important season had passed.

The Housewives League has many more months of hard work ahead if the black vote in Lenoir County is to be brought to its full potential. The black voting age population is about 10,000, only half of whom are presently registered. The white voting age population is 19,000, of whom more than 17,000 are registered. However, the black voting-age population is concentrated in Kinston, where the Housewives League has been making its strongest effort.

Basically, the Housewives League consists of five housewives and three young people, plus three or four other Lenoir County women who help out regularly. Last year, a sorority gave Mrs. Whitehead the "Finer Womanhood Award" for her leadership role in the League.

The news account of voter registration in Lenoir County illustrated both the inspiration and the frustration associated with voting projects in the South. A comparative handful of persons with an unusual sense of dedication demonstrated their ability to make an impact on a widespread condition of nonregistration. By combining year-round community service with the appeal to become voters, the housewives of Kinston intuitively discovered one of the secrets to making voting drives credible. The practical decision to take registration to the streets was precisely the technique that has produced the most effective results, when allowed by law, in the urban centers of the North. The permissiveness which made possible the open recruitment of Black voters in a small county seat in North Carolina had not come about independently of the Civil Rights legislation of the sixties. In addition, this climate of permissiveness still did not exist in some Black Belt counties of the Deep South, where Black registration has continued to be a mission suitable only for the heroic.

At the same time, as the statistics for Lenoir County confirmed, the full participation by Blacks in the electoral system of the South remained unfulfilled. A study of political participation made by the U.S. Commission on Civil Rights indicated that the White power structure had diluted the Black vote by switching to systems of at-large elections, consolidating counties, gerrymandering, and requiring a voter to vote for a full slate or have his ballot disqualified. Black candidates were thwarted by abolishing offices to which they might stand a chance of election or extending the terms of White incumbents. The Commission found that Blacks had been excluded from party precinct meetings, harrassed by election officials and victimized by inadequate voting facilities. Furthermore, as the Black population continued to flow north and west from the increasingly mechanized agricultural regions, White majorities in the voting-age population continued to be the rule in most of the political jurisdictions below the Mason-Dixon Line.

Of the seven states covered by the Voting Rights Act of 1965, five cast their electoral votes for George C. Wallace in the Presidential election of 1968 and the other two went for Richard M. Nixon. Only one of these, Mississippi, had a non-White population in excess of 30 per cent of the total, and actual registration figures reduced Blacks to even more of a minority position in statewide elections. Whatever the future might bring, a hard core of four in every ten of the Black voting-age population remained outside the system in the South—a proportion not very much different from the percentage of unregistered minorities through-out the nation.

It is possible that what was taking place in the South during the registration drives of the sixties was a closing of the gap between an artificially low number of Blacks on the voting list and the ratio customarily encountered for low-income, minority-group members all over tha United States. After the cream had been skimmed off as a result of extraordinary effort, it seemed that the conventional approaches to further expanding the voting lists might exhibit limited productivity.

A further need to run faster in order to stand still was created by the adoption of the device requiring voters to re-register. That technique was tried, beginning in 1967, in South Carolina and later on in some counties of North Carolina and Mississippi; the theory being that Whites would find it easier than Blacks to repeat the whole process of getting their names recorded on the voting lists. The first astonishing result—in South Carolina—was that Black registration continued to increase while White rolls shrunk, thus adding to the proportion of Blacks in the whole electorate. The extraordinarly high precentages of White enrollment achieved in the South during the Black drives of the sixties may indeed turn out to have included the names of more than a few persons long gone from this earth. Purging such lists cut both ways.

Chapter Sixteen

REGISTERING THE EIGHTEEN-YEAR-OLD VOTER

A dramatic element was added to the voter registration movement in the country in 1970. First, the 1970 amendment to the Voting Rights Act was approved, authorizing the vote for eighteen-to-twenty-year-olds in federal elections. Then the requisite number of states ratified the 26th Amendment to the U.S. Constitution, making the eighteen-year-old vote universal. The sudden addition of a potential new voting cohort of 11.5 million unregistered voters throughout the nation focused special attention upon the laws and regulations, state by state, governing the addition of new voters to the rolls.

Less than half the potential new electorate, 4 million, were students in college. The great majority of the newly eligible were those who had left school to work full-time without a college education, their wives, plus 700,000 unemployed teen-agers and 800,000 eligibles in the armed services: a total of 7.5 million of the 11.5 million between 18 and 20.

Georgia, one of two states which previously had authorized eighteen-year-olds to vote, nevertheless still had a lower percentage of registered Whites than either Alabama or Mississippi and a lower percentage of registered Blacks than Alabama, Mississippi, or Louisiana. U.S. Census reports indicated, furthermore, that the highest percentage of the unregistered nationwide was in the

ESTIMATED VOTING-AGE TOTALS IN '72

| State | 18 and Over | Eligible to Vote in Presidential Election for the First Time | |
		18 to 20	21 to 24
Alabama	2,274,000	198,000	231,000
Alaska/A	200,000	19,000	33,000
Arizona	1,239,000	107,000	133,000
Arkansas	1,310,000	104,000	122,000
California	13,945,000	1,130,000	1,525,000
Colorado	1,558,000	145,000	184,000
Connecticut	2,106,000	152,000	203,000
Delaware	371,000	30,000	39,000
Florida	5,105,000	358,000	450,000
Georga/B	3,104,000	277,000	364,000
Hawaii/C	531,000	48,000	73,000
Idaho	479,000	42,000	47,000
Illinois	7,542,000	587,000	726,000
Indiana	3,509,000	298,000	360,000
Iowa	1,909,000	158,000	173,000
Kansas	1,541,000	133,000	159,000
Kentucky/B	2,206,000	199,000	227,700
Louisiana	2,339,000	224,000	253,000
Maine	666,000	54,000	63,000
Maryland	2,688,000	212,000	291,000
Massachusetts	3,955,000	321,000	400,000
Michigan	5,874,000	504,000	612,000
Minnesota	2,560,000	219,000	256,000
Mississippi	1,403,000	135,000	142,000
Missouri	3,266,000	258,000	307,000
Montana	460,000	39,000	44,000
Nebraska	1,022,000	87,000	98,000
Nevada	348,000	24,000	36,000
New Hampshire	521,000	44,000	52,000
New Jersey	5,025,000	344,000	450,000
New Mexico	636,000	58,000	71,000
New York	12,773,000	925,000	1,193,000
North Carolina	3,463,000	337,000	393,000
North Dakota	402,000	37,000	41,000
Ohio	7,185,000	586,000	722,000

ESTIMATED VOTING-AGE TOTALS IN '72—Continued

| State | 18 and Over | Eligible to Vote in Presidential Election for the First Time | |
		18 to 20	21 to 24
Oklahoma	1,812,000	147,000	181,000
Oregon	1,500,000	120,000	146,000
Pennsylvania	8,161,000	612,000	728,000
Rhode Island	673,000	59,000	75,000
South Carolina	1,706,000	177,000	202,000
South Dakota	434,000	40,000	40,000
Tennessee	2,713,000	232,000	277,000
Texas	7,681,000	678,000	846,000
Utah	689,000	71,000	89,000
Vermont	309,000	29,000	32,000
Virginia	3,197,000	284,000	381,000
Washington	2,371,000	205,000	258,000
West Virginia	1,182,000	98,000	107,000
Wisconsin	2,955,000	255,000	290,000
Wyoming	225,000	19,000	22,000
D.C.	518,000	46,000	65,000
Total United States	139,642,000	11,462,000	14,213,000

A. Previously allowed 19-year-olds to vote.
B. Previously allowed 18-year-olds to vote.
C. Previously allowed 20-year-olds to vote.
Source: Bureau of the Census.

age group twenty-four and under (39.9 per cent), including the four states in which those under twenty-one had been eligible. In the 1968 Presidential election this youngest age group of eligibles also contained the highest proportion of those who neither registered nor voted (48.9 per cent). Broken down by race, the number of Black eligibles from eighteen to twenty-four who did not vote in 1968 came to 61.2 per cent as against 47.2 per cent for Whites.

When it was recalled that the age composition of minority groups such as Blacks, Mexican-Americans, and Puerto Ricans is significantly younger than for Whites, it became clear that the extension of the franchise to eighteen-year-olds greatly magnified the challenge of enlarging political participation among the minority poor. Census data showed that the half-dozen states in which eighteen-to-twenty-year-olds would constitute the largest percentage increase in voting age population were South Carolina, New Mexico, Mississippi, Louisiana, North Carolina, and Virginia. The largest potential for new voters in absolute numbers existed in the key states of California, New York, and Texas.

The speed with which the prerequisite number of states (thirty-eight) ratified the 26th Amendment, including many where the extension of the franchise to eighteen and nineteen-year-olds had been defeated in popular referenda, was more a display of American political pragmatism than a ringing endorsement of an enlarged electorate.

The effect of extending the franchise to youth had been a matter of dispute among experts. Congressional passage of the vote for eighteen-year-olds took place at a time when it was a popular theory that they probably wouldn't differ much from the patterns of their parents; by the time the public opinion polls began to show a heavy preference for the Democratic party among the young (42 to 18 in Gallup; 38 to 14 in Harris) the die had been cast. (Significantly, there were nearly twice the number of political independents among eighteen-to-twenty-year-olds than in the fifty-five to sixty-four age bracket.)

Once the Supreme Court upheld the constitutionality of the legislation authorizing them to vote in federal elections, moreover, the cost and confusion of trying to administer different electorates in national, state, and local elections persuaded most state legislatures to go along with the same age requirements for all elections.

The sudden creation of a vast new cohort of potentially eligible voters on the eve of a Presidential election focused attention as rarely before on the mundane details of registration regulations across the nation. The impatience of the young with the unex-

plained trappings of the past, plus their zeal to put ideas into
action, promised an unusual test of the whole rationale of the
U.S. registration system, as well as of the system for nominating
candidates for public office. At the same time, the success or
failure of efforts to register eighteen-to-twenty-year-olds in time
for them to participate in the primaries and elections of 1972
might in itself tell a great deal about the viability of our registration process. If it failed the young, the fires of reform might
be kindled anew.

The appeal of the idea of young people playing a representative
part in the political system gave a new lease on life to attempts
to change state election and registration laws. Despite the discouraging results from drives to register unregistered adults
above stubborn ceilings, the sudden opportunity to qualify millions of the newly eligible young gave a symbolic lift to arguments
for easing the procedures for voter registration generally.

First returns from campaigns to register the newly eligible on
high-school and college campuses, however, were disappointing.
Well advertised special sessions for making new voters at traditional registration points likewise attracted only mild interest.
A survey of eighteen-to-twenty-year-old registration in December, 1971, by the Young Democrats counted about three million registered, 27 per cent of the potential. A survey by the Youth
Citizenship Fund reported that 36 per cent had registered in 102
cities or counties polled by telephone. (Although 75 per cent
of 171,409 Freshmen at 326 colleges said they intended to vote
in the 1972 Presidential election.)

In theory, the manpower available if young people put the
same energy into voter registration as they had invested in the
campaigns for peace candidates and Civil Rights in the sixties
could be harnessed to register large numbers of adult unregistered
along with the young. The nonpartisan flavor of enrolling the
young would perhaps also be an antidote to the nervousness
engendered among politicans by voter drives tailored specifically
for minority groups.

In 1970, in response to adverse reaction to seemingly militant registration campaigns (such as those in Cleveland and San Antonio) as well as to the massive effort to register Blacks in the South, some members of Congress had sought to limit severely the use of tax-exempt funds for such purposes. Although the most restrictive amendments to the Voting Rights Act were beaten back, provisions were adopted to forbid tax-exempt support of voter registration programs except on a regional basis and only then if no more than 25 per cent of that support came from a single source.

While these matters were being debated before Congressional committees the work of the southern Voter Education Project all but came to a halt in early 1970 while its organizational structure was revised to conform with the new regulations. Foundations which had funded (along with labor unions) most of the registration campaigns after the Voting Rights Act of 1965 took another look as Congress also re-examined the tax laws under which they had been functioning. Until the reopening of the issue through votes for eighteen-year-olds, and notwithstanding that development in some quarters, the steam seemed to be going out of broad-scaled efforts to mount registration campaigns. In the off years just prior to 1972, funds for voter registration all but dried up.

Some of these trends might be defended as a rational reaction to data showing only marginal results in several highly touted registration efforts. Some were a response to the recognition of the partisan aspects of voter drives, whatever the cover or intent, plus the visceral reaction of members of local Establishments who felt their interests had been harmed by supposedly "nonpartisan" voter drives. Action programs to register voters, prudent philanthropists now argued, belonged more appropriately to the partisan political process and the responsibility to fund them should fall to the groups whose interests might be directly served.

A campaign to enroll the young, however, had widespread attraction after a decade marked by campus unrest, youthful dropping out, and rebellion against the value system of adult society. The slogans of participatory democracy and community control seemed less menacing somehow if tied to something as Red, White, and Blue as enabling youngsters to become eligible to vote for Tax Collector.

How intensely young people of the counter-culture would regard voting in elections as relevant to the "new consciousness" of individuality and a noncompetitive life style remained to be seen. Efforts to mobilize campus political action in the off-year elections of 1970 had, for the most part, fizzled. (Although Front-lash, concentrating its efforts in closely contested races, is said to have registered 100,000 new voters in California.)

A study of college youth by Daniel Yakelovitich, Inc., in 1969 and 1970 divulged that seven out of ten students believed "there are serious flaws in our society but the system is flexible enough to solve them." Eight out of ten believed that both Congress and American political parties needed either moderate or fundamental reform. And 84 per cent expressed serious concern about the viability of the present two-party system.

This skepticism among the college-educated, traditionally the most active participants in the American political process, suggested a defection not unlike that among the minorities of the urban ghettos. Isolation, powerlessness, pessimism, withdrawal from a system seemingly unresponsive or corrupt—phenomena usually associated with the attitudes of the disadvantaged poor—were becoming characteristic of a growing number of the affluent young in the new generation. Appeals to good citizenship to induce eighteen-to-twenty-year-olds to exercise their newly acquired franchise might not be any more likely to succeed on the campus than in the slum.

The Presidential candidacy of Senator George McGovern in 1972 caught the imagination of thousands of young people who volunteered to work for him in state primaries even when pundits were pronouncing his cause to be hopeless. The anti-war, anti-establishment stands taken by McGovern offered a concrete avenue of expression for pent-up resentments among the young toward the adult power structure. They brought untiring energy to a grassroots campaign which catapulted McGovern from comparative obscurity to national prominence within the space of a few months.

The drama of the 1972 Democratic primaries, however, obscured the fact that performances were uneven and comparatively small percentages of voters actually took part in these mass-media happenings. The McGovern campaign, moreover, was slow to catch on among Blacks, Chicanos, and other urban minorities. It was difficult to predict in advance just how well the McGovern following might run in a head-to-head contest with President Richard Nixon. If McGovern should fail the young at any point along the way, the consequences might dash a newly acquired taste for active politics. The possibility of major, national success, on the other hand, could be a powerful motivator for groups which in 1968 had felt left out in a choice between Nixon, Humphrey, and Wallace.

The newly eligible youth vote was a prime target for the McGovern forces. Adding those who had come of age since 1968, the pool of potential first-time voters came to 25 million. The announced quota for the McGovern army of grassroots volunteers was to try to register at least 75 per cent of them before Election Day, 1972. As the campaign progressed, the likelihood was that increasing attention would be focused on the impact of new voters on the outcome of elections at every level of government.

Unfortunately, bickering among some organized youth groups competing for the scarce resources available to finance registration drives among the new eligibles was reminiscent of the personal jealousies characteristic of some citizen-group politics of the fifties and sixties, and sometimes equally counter-productive. Selfless dedication to a cause, without regard for considerations of status, recognition, or power, is a quality that seems to be at odds with human nature at any chronological age. And yet the nature of the services required to register voters—requiring massive energy and endurance, and enhanced by a refreshing forthrightness and sincerity—were precisely those qualities most abundant among the young. The probability was that if anybody was going to turn on the young to involve themselves in the political process, it would be their peers. The time for one last effort to launch a model campaign to register the unregistered seemed at hand.

Another by-product of the new political pertinence of those in the age group from seventeen to twenty-one was its possible effect on the educational apparatus. As never before the critical years of high school and college could now be directly linked to the democratic process. Heretofore, the average American's first opportunity to become involved with voting requirements usually had come at a different time and place than his formal education. Now the two could be linked. Rulings in some states (subject to an almost certain High Court test of the whole question) held that students should not be denied the right of establishing their voting domicile in the towns where they attend school. This promised to change the nature of town-and-gown political relationships in extraordinary ways—assuming, of course, that the interest of the students matched the apprehensions of permanent residents in these places.

The correct approach to registering eighteen-to-twenty-year-olds was under study in a number of quarters as the time approached for the 1972 elections. This development was of importance not only to the fate of candidates whose fortunes might be changed by a small swing in votes from traditional patterns, but also as a testing ground for registration techniques and the flexibility of state-by-state registration laws.

In a trial run in Washington, D.C., prior to the District's election of its first delegate to Congress in 1971, the Youth Citizenship Fund made a special effort to put high-school students on the voting rolls. Some of the lessons of that undertaking were incorporated in the following YCF memorandum:

High school students are locked in buildings for several hours each day, five days a week. Their togetherness and immobility make this group by far the easiest to register. If the method of registering the high school students is simple, quick and thorough, more effort may be available for the more difficult groups of college students, employed youth and unemployed youth. In other words, high school students, should not spend a great deal of time registering their own group so that their energy may be expended in other areas of the registration drive.

Regardless of the plan decided upon, a few generalities may be applicable. The sooner some experienced, activist high school students are part of the early planning discussions, the better results may be expected. It is usually wise, however, to avoid students who have a great need to act out an ego need . . .

If your goal is to register students, don't let citizenship education motions confuse the effort. Speakers, films, rallies, dances, seminars, assemblies and the like are very time consuming to organize before the actual registration of the students and usually are unnecessary because they are already sufficiently motivated to register . . .

If students must go away from the school to register, transportation will have to be arranged. Free buses may be available from the school system, churches, military bases, community organizations or wherever. In this case, asking students to pay $.50-$1.00 for the bus ride is usually not a problem. The problem is really one of keeping the ineligible students off the buses because they all want to miss some school for a field trip.

If a field trip to a registration site is called for, then the local teachers association or teachers union may be an ally. Solicit the help of the local president or executive secretary and ask that a small group of teachers be gathered. With the group of teachers, arbitrarily set up a timetable when schools will be asked to go to the registration site. Each teacher in the group may then take the responsibility of contacting a colleague in each of the several schools and arrange for the field trip. In this manner, the board of elections may be notified in advance and the registration carefully spread out to include every school. Also, the teachers are doing all the organizing so that the students organizing energy may be expended on other aspects of the drive.

If students may be registered at school the cooperation of the staff is still a necessity . . . Probably the most effective procedure is to go to social science classes and use class time for registering . . . Registering students in the cafeteria may be another spot . . .

In any plan you need to know who is eligible at each school . . .

A small cadre of students at each school should be responsible for developing the list with names, addresses and phone numbers. The list is necessary to keep track of who is registered and who isn't, likewise others may later reach the parents of the student to see if they are registered. Organizers of a thorough drive will maintain relentless pursuit of each unregistered student as revealed on the list.

Starry-eyed idealism would not be the phrase to describe this young people's strategy for planning the registration of high-school students. Its effectiveness in Washington, D.C. seemed limited in a two-month drive in 1970 just before the election of the District Delegate to Congress. The YCF campaign in seventeen high schools and nine colleges and universities netted a total of 3,461 new voters, eighteen years of age and over, out of a potential ten times that number.

Similar drives were being organized by Frontlash to register students in California, Texas, Michigan, Illinois, New Jersey and New York City, including the production of media materials suitable for use throughout the country. The New York City drive in more than ninety high schools was actively supported by the United Federation of Teachers; more than 20,000 new voters were reported to have been registered by the end of the 1971-72 school year.

Outside the city the rate of registration was directly related to the flexibility of the methods. Registering the young involved all the usual institutional hinderances to qualifying new voters, along with a few special ramifications working particularly against eighteen-to-twenty-year-olds. In Nassau County, New York, where special teams of registrars were permitted to go into every high school and college in the county, it was estimated that 30,000 of the 40,000 potential new voters had been put on the rolls by the summer of 1971. In Westchester County, however, where applicants were required to go to central registry points by their own volition, only 3,000 of 40,000 potential new voters were put on the rolls during the same period. Edwin G. Michaelian, the County Executive, declared that it would be "more educational" for young people to come into the County Building and register on their own. "Young people tell me they want to be treated as adults, not be spoon fed." Michaelian said. Although New York law provided for local registration in cities and towns in late September and early October, that was too late for students going away to school. In addition, special efforts to make registration easy on some college campuses did nothing at all for the large majority of noncollege youth in the eighteen-to-twenty-one-year-old age bracket. Much of the registration effort involving the newly qualified generation threatened to repeat the historical bias in favor of middle-class participation in politics. A Gallup Poll early in 1972 estimated that about 41 per cent of those in the eighteen-to-twenty age group had registered to vote, compared with an 84 per cent rate among those fifty and over. (Gallup estimated the national unregistered at 40 million citizens.)

Some of the perils of generalizing about youth participation in politics have been pointed out by Richard Scammon, co-author of *The Real Majority:*

The fact of the matter is, as Yankelovitch and other researchers have found, there is less of a generation gap in America than there is a class gap. The working class kid whose father is working as a fry cook in a White Tower restaurant, has more in common with his father than he does with the undergraduate at Harvard University from a psychiatrist's family in Scarsdale. I mention these things because it is important to realize you are not dealing with a monolithic group when you talk about the registration of young people.

So much for that. George Wallace ran very well among the blue-collar young in 1968 at the same time that attention was focused on the college-oriented "Children's Crusade" for Senator Eugene McCarthy. An energetic group of young volunteers was part of Conservative James L. Buckley's successful campaign for Senator from New York in 1970. Selective differences in the ease of registering in various states and selective differences in the targets of privately financed registration drives could introduce variables not intended by some of those who introduced and help pass legislation authorizing the eighteen-year-old vote.

Chances are that the groups of young people most likely not to capitalize on the opportunity to vote will not differ markedly from the patterns for the adult population as a whole—and for the very same reasons. The hardest to reach—the school drop-outs, those on the move, those without jobs, those without incentive to invest their time in public affairs—are in the first stage of the grinding cycle caused by poverty and its accompanying social disintegration. It is too much to expect that any except random individuals should be able to find within themselves the motivation to lend legitimacy to their own humiliation. The institutions of our society will have to be revised first. The incentive to participate in the political process may depend on some sign that the institutions of democracy are themselves capable of change.

PART FIVE

UNIVERSAL VOTER ENROLLMENT AND OTHER IDEAS

The systems of national voter enrollment in Britain and Canada are explained and various proposals for a similar system in the United States are set forth. Is the time at hand to break down the institutional barriers preventing free access by minorities to participate in the American political process?

Chapter Seventeen

NONPARTICIPATION AND PARTICIPATION

The Price of Nonparticipation

The facts are unmistakable that millions of Americans are not participating in the most fundamental exercise of the democratic process: enrolling on the list of eligible voters and then turning out to vote on election day. The phenomenon of nonparticipation exists throughout the country, but is most prevalent within those segments of the population most disconnected from the rewards and the values of a system which has always promised unlimited opportunity. The urban poor, the young, Blacks, Mexican-Americans, the American Indian—groups with the largest stake in social change—have the least connection with the political structure which is the supposed instrument of orderly change. The angry and articulate elements among the oppressed and excluded citizenry more and more challenge the assumptions of representative government as practiced in a modern, industrial society. The moral legitimacy of government is weakened when so many in nominal control of a system of self-government are so obviously not involved in its electoral rituals.

—It is not that 100-per cent participation has ever been reached or is even a desirable objective. Compulsory participation, as practiced in dictatorships and attempted in some Western nations, is a mockery of the benefits of involvement. The right not to take part in a selection process offering no acceptable choice is a precious part of democracy. The problem facing America in the seventies not only is the sheer size of the nonvoting population, but also that the size has increased with each Presidential election. The nonfranchised have become a significant proportion of the population, greater even than the number who voted for the winning candidate for President. More serious than that, the ranks of the nonfranchised are disproportionately filled with those most susceptible, in their disaffection and despair, to the dangerous illusions of simplified solutions. Democracy must be its own teacher. Those whose lives are untouched by any sort of involvement have no framework of experience within which to develop the patience and appreciation for the complexities or tradeoffs of evolutionary progress.

It is also clear that one must look beyond the process of registering and voting in order to make major gains in political participation. The data collected for this volume document a history of limited returns, not commensurate with the effort and money expended to increase the numbers of eligible voters within the structure built into the laws of all but one of the fifty States. (North Dakota has no system of voter registration.) This is not to say that registration campaigns are without value. They are often the training ground for the army of volunteer political workers upon which our system depends, and a focal point for the education on issues necessary for a rational democracy. In the case of the re-establishment of Black voting rights in the South, it is unlikely that the gains of the sixties could ever have been won without the leadership of registration organizations at the grassroots level.

There seems to be a limit, however, to what one can accomplish by methods that ultimately rely on initiative by the individual. Despite spectacular successes in some portions of the rural South, where outright repression had kept the lists artificially low and where the support of federal authority could release motivations to participate already felt, voter registration drives in Southern states have not been conspicuously more profitable lately than in Northern urban settings. And the turnout of Black voters in Southern elections, while sometimes better than that of low-income Whites, has frequently been reduced by large numbers of eligibles who stayed at home, even when there was the rare opportunity to vote for Black candidates.

The most successful registration drives, furthermore, have usually been marked by partisan purposes, sometimes only scarcely concealed beneath the trappings of nonpartisanship. It is illogical to expect otherwise. Our survey data showed that most voters were candidate-centered, that political loyalty to a particular party was a powerful albeit shrinking force, and that the strongest feelings about such general concepts as "civic duty" were to be found among those who already were participants in the process.

Partisan sponsorship of individually initiated registration is a logical extension of political competition. The high costs of political campaigns, however, make the high per-capita costs of voter registration a further strain on a process already too dependent upon money raised from contributors who have vested interests at stake. Another main source of registration financing until now—tax-exempt foundations—has been hemmed in recently by restrictive legislation as well as by a prudent regard for the fact that no congressman is unaffected by a newly registered voter.

Voting Lists—The Passport to Participation

The thrust of efforts, therefore, to try to register more voters under the present institutional arrangements in most states might better be redirected. That is not to say that the obligation to register does not continue to be a critical requirement of the American election system. Anyone who has worked for an hour at the polls cannot imagine how the system would function without voting lists. They are the basis for assignments to voting machines or voting booths. Political parties depend upon them to keep track of the hour-by-hour turnout of their supporters.

Although not invulnerable to fraud, they are the essential monitor by which one man casts one vote on Election Day. In a society where even close neighbors are not immediately recognizable to each other, the voting register is the basic passport to participation.

The care with which voting lists are purged of the names of persons no longer eligible to vote varies considerably. American political lore is full of anecdotes regarding the voting, or multiple voting, of ghosts in such places as Cook County, Illinois, and Duval County, Texas. The responsibility for keeping the lists up to date usually falls to the appointees of one or both major parties, who are more or less energetic, depending upon local circumstances. Canceling registration for failure to vote takes place every two, four, or five years, depending upon the state. Scrutiny of the voting lists in some Southern counties has revealed a number of White eligibles considerably larger than 100 per cent of the voting-age White population. In Harrisburg, Pa., the Leage of Women Voters mailed 2,400 letters marked "Do Not Forward" to registered voters in high-turnout areas. Of that number, no less than 1,580—61 per cent—were returned by the Post Office! The League then set thirty volunteers to work helping purge the rolls in the Pennsylvania state capital.

The state of Oregon puts the initiative on the County Clerk to see that the voting lists are kept up to date. A pamphlet containing voter information is mailed to every voter before the date of primary elections. If the pamphlet is returned by the post office, the County Clerk makes a personal check of the registered voter. If the voter cannot be located, he is then purged from the lists. It is the custom in many large cities to mail out notices of polling places to the names and addresses on the registration lists, but few records are kept of whether they are ever received. When law enforcement officers are sent to validate the residences of new registrants, the effect is frequently to intimidate other potential new voters who might find any official scrutiny unwelcome.

Purging the rolls can be a two-way street. Laws in South Carolina and Arizona requiring that the rolls be wiped out every ten years were partly aimed at minority groups who had been enrolled with difficulty in the first place. The right of a county or state to order such new registrations is just one more of those twilight zones of American election law that seemed headed for eventual determination in the Supreme Court.

The cost-benefit ratio of a campaign to sign up unregistered voters has time and again turned out to be unfavorable. The impression often left is one of a frustrating race on a treadmill. The combination of institutional barriers and psychological handicaps is usually too much for the marginal participator in the political process. The effort to surmount the obstacles merely through the employment of more organization, more communication, or more financial backing has continually proved to be disappointing. As the Red Queen advised Alice on the other side of the looking glass, you need to run at least twice as fast in order to make any progress at all.

That is why it is so important to attack the disease rather than the symptoms. And the problem most susceptible to immediate change would appear to be the legal apparatus presently enveloping the registration and voting process in the United States. In the short run, the challenge is to focus judicial attention on the very real inhibitions contained in many of our regulations. Beyond that is the need for state legislatures to overhaul the registration and voting machinery so as to encourage, not thwart, the potential elector. In the long run, a fundamental and drastic revision of the national election system may be in order.

The rights of states in our federal form of government to determine the qualifications required of their own residents to vote have been preciously defended by strict constructionists of the U.S. Constitution. The anti-discrimination passages of the 14th and 15th Amendments did not dissuade the Supreme Court over a period of years from a hands-off attitude toward local arrangements charged by plaintiffs to be patently unfair. A gradual shift in favor of federal intervention was marked by decisions outlawing "grandfather clauses" and striking down the White primary in the South. The Civil Rights legislation passed in 1957, 1960, and 1964 had the effect of eliminating some other forms of anti-Black discrimination. Then followed the historic "one-man, one-vote" decision of 1962 requiring the reapportionment of scores of state and federal legislative districts. The Voting Rights Act of 1965 also survived a series of constitutional court tests before the attack was shifted, with some success, to the floor of Congress. In 1966 the poll tax was outlawed by judicial decision. The 1970 amendments to the Voting Rights Act, while weakening practical federal intervention to protect voting rights in the South, also inaugurated a nationwide eighteen-year-old vote. The 5-to-4 Supreme Court decision declaring the new minimum age to be unconstitutional in respect to state elections was at least a partial reaffirmation of the doctrine of state sovereignty. It did not go unnoticed by members of Congress who, like Senator Sam J. Ervin, Jr., of North Carolina, had been deploring "legislation directly contrary to other provisions of the Constitution which give the states the authority to establish qualifications for voting."

Title II of the Voting Rights Act Amendments also declared the invalidity of language and literacy tests in all fifty states, in effect superseding constitutional or statutory provisions for literacy tests or devices (Idaho's constitution disqualified from voting persons who belonged to organizations encouraging polygamy) in twenty states. This powerful precedent for blanket federal protection of voting rights was defended in a staff memorandum of the U.S. Commission on Civil Rights, on the grounds expressed by the Supreme Court that "the political franchise of voting . . . under certain conditions . . . is regarded as a fundamental right, because preservative of all rights" (Yick Wo v. Hopkins) and "statutes granting the franchise to residents on a selective basis always pose the danger of denying some citizens any effective voice in the governmental affairs which substantially affect their lives" (Kramer v. Union Free School District).

An important point was the showing that, historically, literacy tests had been motivated to render various racial, ethnic, religious, and national origin groups politically impotent. Literacy tests had not existed before the massive waves of non Anglo-Saxon immigration in the nineteenth century. "Diverse groups have been the victims of literacy tests in this nation's history," the Civil Rights Commission memorandum declared, "—blacks, Jews, Irish, Finns, Chinese, Japanese, American Indians, Eskimos, and the Spanish speaking or Spanish surnamed. . . . Our nation is a democracy whose political well being depends upon the participation of all of its citizens in the political process. Artificial, unreasonable and arbitrary restrictions on the right to vote weaken the political health of the Nation."

More subtle forms of influence creating selective differences in the ability to register and vote are more difficult to prove incontestably. Whether the obstacles to registration that effectively hamper universal participation in the political process can likewise be swept aside by Congressional action is one of the pertinent political issues of the seventies. Such action would need to survive constitutional challenges by a Court whose "strict constructionist" membership has been enlarged by President Nixon.

The obstacles to getting one's name and address on the election roll are both legal and pyschological. Our data showed that of two persons with similar disadvantages as to education, income, or race the one who would register and vote displayed no self-evident differences from the neighbor who failed to participate. Although recency of arrival was sometimes a factor, mobility as such was not especially significant. Family backgrounds of participation or nonparticipation more or less washed out in the sample of unregistered surveyed in Newark. The key difference between voters and nonvoters seemed to be their own opinion of themselves, whether or not they felt they possessed the aptitudes for politics, whether or not they felt that the participation of one individual like themselves would make any difference.

Chapter Eighteen

BREAKING THE INSTITUTIONAL BARRIER

The measures required to improve an individual's image of self-worth go to the very heart of our social system. A person's self-image is a product of education, job opportunities, health, nondiscrimination, and sometimes simple human kindness. The reforms that might help the psychologically damaged to become full partners in the democratic process included the entire agenda for alleviating the crisis of our cities. When it is said that urban survival is essential, hopefully survival is defined as something more than vegetating. The social cost of excluding masses of the urban poor from decent shelter, proper health services, satisfying work, and leisure is too enormous to ignore. One of the side consequences is political indifference, the trauma of despair. Beyond that, violence and revolution.

Meanwhile, it is imperative to focus on the institutional barriers that prevent increases in registration. The most obvious, of course, is the historic presumption in the United States that voting is a privilege to be earned by individual initiative rather than a right to be aggressively disseminated by government, itself. The national commitment to full participation, if it is indeed part of the prevailing value system, is not evident in the myriad of regulations confronting would-be voters in the thousands of jurisdictions now placing their own interpretations on the qualifications for the franchise.

The staffing of registration points is usually under the control of local organizations who sometimes have special interest in excluding potential new voters who might threaten the distribution of power. In areas where residents speak a language other than English, the absence of bilingual materials and bilingual registration workers can be keenly felt by timid applicants. The frequency of registration dates, the hours when the public is accommodated, the availability of registration opportunities in locations other than central government offices—all have differential effects on the ability of some to register, particularly those with limited time off from work or limited access to transportation. Complicated registration forms are another inhibiting factor, especially when they include threatening requirements, such as disclosure of past brushes with the law.

Many of the barriers could be removed without any changes in state laws governing the registration process. Many are the product of bureaucratic custom, the most unyielding to change. Appeals to reason or higher authority frequently fall on deaf ears. Those who are the least bit unsure of their ground are easily sent into retreat. What seems to be needed most is an outside monitoring system for these tight little islands of local control.

The lack of uniformity in registration from state to state raises pertinent questions in an era when there has been talk of eliminating the Electoral College in favor of the popular election of the President and instituting a national primary for his nomination. The national character of American elections has its roots in the growth of the mass media, the focus on executive leadership at all levels, and the development of an increasingly mobile population. And yet the bias against mobility has been a central characteristic of most local registration requirements.

The adoption in 1971 of the 26th Amendment, which reduced the minimum age for voting in all U.S. elections to eighteen, put a special spotlight on the divergencies and contradictions among local registration laws. In addition to the 11 million eighteen-through-twenty-year olds in the country who are now potential voters, there were 14 million who had come of age since the 1968 Presidental election. This meant that the total newly eligible voters for the Presidential election of 1972 would come to a massive 25 million—providing, of course, they could be enrolled. In a single test, more than one-sixth of the potential electorate in the country was to be thrown up against the confusion of more than 3,000 different county election boards in fifty states and the District of Columbia.

The first contradiction concerned the 2 million students living and attending school away from the homes of their parents. In Maine the state constitution specifically said "Nor shall the residence of a student at any seminary of learning entitle him to the right of suffrage in the city, town or plantation where such seminary is established." The New York State legislature, in the absence of any such constitutional provision, rushed through a law making it impossible for students to register and vote in a college town where they could not prove a permanent residence. In California, Attorney General Evelle J. Younger ruled that students, unless married, had to vote in the precincts of their parents until the State Supreme Court, in a unanimous decision, ruled otherwise. At about the same time, the Attorney General of Massachusetts, Robert H. Quinn, ruled that in his state anyone between eighteen and twenty-one could vote in the town or city he wanted to, provided a valid claim of residence or intent to establish residence was shown. In his opinion it did not matter whether the residence was a private home or dormitory, and whether the would-be voters were financially dependent on their parents. The state of Florida's Attorney General said that student voters in campus towns should have the same privileges as all new voters.

The Supreme Court of Michigan, in the summer of 1971, declared unconstitutional the registration clerks practice of instructing students to fill out questionnaires telling where they obtained their support, where they spent their vacations, where they held bank accounts, and whether or not they owned or leased property. Such special requirements on would-be student registrants, the Court held, constituted impermissible harassment.

Student bouts with local registrars in college towns highlighted the impact of the discretionary power of local registration officials under the U.S. system of decentralized administration of election laws. This human factor—at the very nerve center of the registration process—has traditionally been the invisible agent of institutional bias exercised against those who might differ in any degree from the demographic norms of those in possession of the registration apparatus.

The following excerpt from a kit on student registration procedure prepared by Common Cause illustrates the application of the techniques of legal confrontation as part of the new politics of the young:

When you go down to the place for voter registration remember that you may be refused and therefore may be in court in the near future. The following procedures will assist your attorneys and increase your chances for success:

1) Select those students who are to go down to test the registration procedures carefully. Be sure they represent a broad spectrum of the student body. Be sure to include in your test group graduate students, married students, students who pay out-of-state tuition, and students who live and do not live in university housing. Moreover, try to select as test plaintiffs those with the closest ties to the local community using the questionnaire included in this packet as a guideline.

2) Inform the employees in the registrar's office you want to register to vote in the next election now that the 26th Amendment has passed.

3) Remember any questions they ask you, and your answers. If they refuse to give you a registration form, ask the person for the reason. Ask for it in writing. If they refuse, remember the answers. (You should have a pencil and a pad with you to write the conversations down as soon as you get outside. Don't write them down inside; it may make the officials reluctant to discuss your problems.)

4) If they give you a form, fill it out (make a copy!). If after you turn it in they ask you any questions, follow the procedure in paragraph No. 3. If they refuse to register you, ditto. Try to get into a friendly conversation with the official, to get more information.

5) If they persist in refusing, ask to see the highest official present;

or ask who you should call or write to to appeal the refusal. If you get to see a higher official, follow same procedure—ask why not registered.

6) Write down the whole experience in narrative form. Be complete. You and we can edit later when you are debriefed.

7) If you decide to negotiate further with the local registrar or registration board be sure to take your lawyer with you.

The merits of the argument as to whether a plumber's helper should be allowed to register and vote when a candidate for a Ph.D. could not were engulfed in the fears of townspeople in such places as Amherst, Mass., and Ann Arbor, Mich., that transient students would "take over" their local governments without the sobering influence of long residence and substantial tax bills. The gray area in the residency laws seemed certain to be tested in the highest courts. But it was a dramatic illustration of the lack of consistency in registration practices and the subjectivity involved in interpreting voter qualifications. Young college students exposed for the first time to time-consuming and excessively complicated procedures entered a kinship with previously disenfranchised minorities.

Neither the registration nor election laws in most U.S. states are generous to the rights of absentees. Absentee ballots are not permitted at all in the voting for some local offices and frequently in the case of party primaries. Such prohibitions not only serve to disenfranchise students away from home, but they also discriminate against businessmen who must travel for their living on registration or Election Day. And they fall with special injustice on men and women serving in the armed forces, large numbers of whom were overseas when the voting age was lowered. Absentee laws should be standardized and made more equitable so that the right to vote can be exercised regardless of one's temporary location. As in the case of excessively lengthy residence requirements, absentee laws reflect a parochial view of politics, passed on from an age when transportation and communication were more limited than they are today.

Aside from the need to create a more uniform and equitable voter registration system, that system must be brought closer to the people. A dozen states in 1972 still prohibited voter registration conducted anywhere except in official headquarters. Twenty-one states did not permit the appointment of citizen deputies to enlarge the range of the registration effort. In a half-dozen states, registration offices still were not open during evenings or on Saturdays. Our data confirmed that off-site registration—in the home, in supermarkets and shopping centers, on street corners—was by far the most effective method to enroll new voters, particularly among minority groups with low rates of registration. A clear majority (61 per cent) of the sample of unregistered voters in Newark said it was at least partly true that "By the time I take care of my everyday problems, I don't have much energy left over to think about politics." Mobile registration, however, has been the exception, not the rule, in this country.

The establishment of year-round branch registration offices in areas of low registration would be one sign of a national commitment to full participation. The careful identification of under-registered areas, however, is not always as simple as it might seem. Election districts generally do not fall within the logical framework of other information-gathering systems, such as Census tracts. In order to extract political meaning from the information available in most metropolitan areas, a painstaking, block-by-block overlay is sometimes required. Targeted registration, the data showed, is the most effective method for recruiting new voters, but it also requires considerable logistical support. Precincts within a few blocks of one another can show surprising variations in rates of registration, even as they show comparable differences in voting behavior. Merely opening a registration office in an area of generally low participation would help by eliminating the need for would-be voters to travel long distances. Significant increases, under present legal patterns, however, probably would require taking the registration machinery directly to those households most out of touch with formal government institutions.

The revision of state laws to authorize door-to-door registration or registration at factories, playgrounds, theatres, transit stations, and other places where people congregate daily would seem to be necessary to create on equal opportunity for all people to vote, irrespective of residence. The speed with which action is possible was illustrated by the record time (three months) between Congressional passage and state ratification of the 26th Amendment. Such occasions have been comparatively rare in our national history. It probably will require an exceptional effort to focus national attention on the inequities inherent in our separate systems of voter registration before the necessary reforms can be ground through the legislative mills in state capitals.

There were signs of stirrings in some of these quarters. A bill was proposed in Florida authorizing mobile vehicles to be sent across the state to register voters. A proposed amendment to the California constitution would reduce residency requirements to thirty days in the state, county, and precinct, keep registration open up to fourteen days before an election, and permit sample ballots in Spanish to be posted at the polls. A bill introduced in the Maryland House of Delegates would authorize the appointment of a deputy registrar upon petition of twenty voters. He could then register voters in churches and shopping centers, or go door-to-door. The Attorney General of Massachusetts asked for a law permitting registration at the local polling place on election day. Under the proposed system the ballots of the newly registered voters would not be counted until the registration information was validated. A proposal in Ohio called for a mandatory, door-to-door canvass by precinct committeemen equally divided between the two major parties. They would be paid ten cents for each new registrant or for each change on the registration rolls resulting from information supplied by them.

A system similar to the one proposed in Ohio has already been instituted in the state of Idaho, where 91.4 per cent of the voting-age population was registered for the 1968 Presidential election and approximately 80 per cent turned out to vote. Local registrars are enlisted for each precinct in the February preceding the election. They set up registration centers in their homes or places of business, and are paid according to the number of voters added to the registration lists. Under these procedures, residents of housing developments, trailer parks, or small population centers can request that one of their residents be commissioned a registrar or deputy registrar with authorization to enroll all the inhabitants. Door-to-door canvassing is also permitted. Registration is allowed right up to the Saturday preceding the Tuesday of the election.

The obvious virtues of this type of voter registration are (1) its simplicity; (2) its localized and decentralized character; (3) the assumption by the government of a major share of the initiative to search out and enroll prospective voters; and (4) its recognition of the principle that registration opportunities should be kept as close as possible to potential voters.

Idaho is a relatively homogeneous state with no large urban centers, a setting more conducive, perhaps, to living-room registration centers. It is worth noting, moreover, that one in ten still was not registered in Idaho even under this model system and two in ten did not bother to vote in the Presidential election.

Universal Voter Enrollment

It is a comparatively small additional step to the idea of Universal Enrollment, with the national government assuming both the responsibility and the initiative for seeing to it that every qualified citizen is registered to vote. "Parliamentary Elections in Britain," a publication of the British Information Service, gives this description of Britain's universal enrollment method:

The register of electors is compiled by electoral registration officers. . . . To ascertain the names of the people in his area who are qualified to be registered, the registration officer either sends a standard form to every separate residence in his area for completion by the occupant, or conducts a door-to-door canvass, as may be thought best suited to the area concerned. Provisional electors' lists are then published and displayed . . . to enable claims and objections to be lodged. . . . The registry must be published not later than 15th February each year and comes in force 16th February. The cost of compiling and printing the electoral register is about 3 million pounds a year.

This makes the registry, like the census, the automatic task of government. The expense is borne by the taxpayer. Not being on the voting lists in this motherland of much of our own political inheritance is as rare as having no postman. Eligibility to vote is simply taken for granted, like a cup of tea in the afternoon.

The Commonwealth adaptation of universal enrollment in Canada calls for a combination of the central government and local political party apparatus to achieve the same end. Under a system in effect since 1935, elections to the House of Commons are under the general supervision of a Chief Electoral Officer appointed by Parliament and serving until he reaches the age of sixty-five. Among his responsibilities is the administration of the Canadian system of enumeration of voters. There are two enumerators for each polling district (roughly 250 to 300 persons). Each of the two political parties with the highest number of votes in the previous election nominates an enumerator for each urban district. These enumerators, acting as a team, enroll the voters in a door-to-door canvass. In rural areas the practice is for the government to appoint the enumerators and make the areas more flexible to allow for a more scattered population.

Enumerators begin enrolling voters forty-nine days prior to the election. They must go to each residence together at least once during daylight hours, and, if they fail to find the prospective voter at home, they must return to the residence at least once during the evening. Where no one is found at home, they must leave word where the enumerators may be reached.

On the forty-second day prior to the election, the enumerators must return a complete copy of their enrollment list to the "returning officer," the individual in charge of the area's overall enrollment. The enumerators must also post the list in a public and conspicuous place. People omitted from the list incorrectly can easily have their names entered on the roll.

Enumerators receive a fee of $32 plus ten cents for each elector on their final list of electors. Spot checks in the last Parliamentary election indicated that 98 per cent of all eligible in Canada were actually registered.

The British and Canadian approaches have produced turnouts of the potential voting-age population in elections for their parliaments approximately fifteen percentage points higher than turnouts for Presidential elections in the United States. Thus, universal enrollment leaves one out of four Britons and Canadians outside the fabric of political participation. It is no panacea for all the problems of voter motivation. Its principal attraction as a model for the United States would appear to be, first, the removal of the financial costs of voter registration from the already extravagent arena of politics, and second, the general fairness of an impartial registration process. In those areas and among those groups most removed from the normal political process the extra effort and expenditures required to enroll these disconnected individuals would be a burden assumed by public authority, not a penalty imposed on top of their other misfortunes. The nation itself becomes the active agent for political involvement. Each individual is guaranteed the opportunity to exercise his franchise.

Universal enrollment has attracted the endorsement of the business-oriented Committee for Economic Development as well as of the Democratic Party National Committee. A 1968 study by the CED's Research and Policy Committee, "Modernizing Elections," focused on the need in the United States for some system of automatic registration:

The vitality of a nation's political process will determine the viability of its government institutions. Confidence in the integrity and equitable administration of government is obviously essential, but fullest opportunity for popular participation leading to action by an informed majority is equally necessary in any democratic society.

If public policies and administrative action are to be solidly based on the consent of the governed, then wide and continuing citizen involvement in political affairs is imperative. . . .

Apathy or disinterest may always prevent total participation, but artificial barriers certainly ought to be removed. No feeling of deliberate exclusion from the political process on the part of any citizen can be tolerated.

CED proposed a system of national registration supervised by a special unit of the postal service. The post office would distribute registration applications to the occupants of every household on a postal route. Preliminary rosters of eligible voters would be established from these returns and published. The rosters would be subject to challenge either by individuals or political parties. Final voting lists would then be issued under the auspices of the federal government.

This idea permitted more discretion by individual residents than the procedures followed in Britain and Canada. The voluntary character of enrolling to vote is cited by some critics of universal enrollment as an important attribute of a democracy. The goal, it is argued, should be to stimulate, not force participation. The problem, the other side of the argument runs, is that, as a practical matter, some volunteers are more equal than others. The debate has its parallel in classical economic theories describing the operation of a self-sustaining free market. It has turned out that compensatory action by central governmental authority is often necessary, paradoxically, to maintain some semblance of individual freedom of choice in the market place. In politics, real freedom of action for the individual can be seriously compromised by unequal educational or economic opportunity systematically perpetuated over the years. For government to compensate for some of that damage by inducing people to vote does not seem to be an ominous threat to individual liberty.

Even more sensitive has been the issue of state sovereignty over setting the qualifications for voting. A "Freedom to Vote Task Force" set up by the Democratic National Committee in 1969, under the chairmanship of former Attorney General Ramsey Clark, skirted this problem by recommending a universal enrollment plan for voters in federal elections, with state and local authorities retaining the option of whether or not to use federal registration lists in their own elections.

The Democratic party's proposal specified that beginning on the first Monday in October of a Presidential year and ending in the third week of that month, enrollment officers would visit every residence in the country and "enroll every qualified person to vote who does not refuse." Modeled after the Canadian procedures, the plan provided for two personal calls at each place of residence, with notification of how to get on the voting list being left behind when no one was at home.

The country's 435 Congressional districts would be the enrolling units, each under a local enrollment director. Teams of volunteer election enrollment officers would be recruited and trained by professionals in comprehensive canvassing and enrollment procedures. Each team would be assigned a limited area in which they would be responsible for enrolling everyone of voting age. Federal appropriations based on a rate of fifty cents for every person of voting age in each Congressional district would cover expenses.

State or local authorities could ask for full registration by federal enrollment officers for purposes of their own elections, paid for under the District budget. If they chose to organize and run their own registration system, and providing they obtained an enrollment exceeding 90 per cent of the voting-age population, then the state or local governments would be eligible to receive the federal funds which would otherwise be spent for federal enrollment. With this carrot dangled before them, states and counties might be induced to perform voluntarily a service which some Democrats, along with some Republicans, contended could not be imposed on them by the Congress.

Each enrollee would be given a voter certificate which he would sign together with the voting registry. If not enrolled before election day, a person could complete an affidavit at the polls and place his ballot in a sealed envelope, to be counted as soon as his enrollment was validated. A person whose name had been enrolled under the federal system but who was not registered for state purposes could vote for President and Vice President only on a special ballot.

This prospect of a dual voting list, made necessary by conceding the point on Congressional power to govern state enrollment, promised to be the Achilles heel of this and other compromise schemes for universal enrollment. The confusion and expense of running elections with two separate electorates had been sufficient to persuade otherwise reluctant state legislators to support the Constitutional amendment lowering the voting age to eighteen in state as well as national elections. The 10 per cent leeway allowed local authorities to qualify for federal registration subsidies could permit discrimination directed against a single minority group. The appointment and control of federal enumerators was a sticky question to dissidents from the power structure of existing party organizations.

The Democratic universal enrollment plan advocated the creation of a National Election Commission, with a nonpartisan National Director and professional staff, to be responsible to a National Review Board of fifteen members, to be appointed by the President from nominations made by political parties and "independent organizations." The budget for the entire operation was estimated to be $5 million per year in the off-years and $50 million in the Presidential years when new enrollment lists would be gathered. Finally, the task force recommended that the date of the Presidential election be declared a national legal holiday. (Election Day is a legal holiday in about a dozen states, but is not always strictly observed.)

Variations of this overall framework for automatic voter registration have been submitted to the Congress by individual Democratic members. A bill introduced by Congressman Morris K. Udall of Arizona and former Congressman Richard L. Ottinger of New York in the 91st Congress changed the name to National Enrollment Commission and recommended that the director be the head of the U.S. Bureau of the Census. Senators Daniel K. Inouye of Hawaii and Fred R. Harris of Oklahoma, former

Democratic National Chairman, picked up the suggestion that anybody should be able to vote by going to the polls on Election Day and having his vote sequestered while his eligibility is validated.

Senator Hubert Humphrey has advocated distributing voter registration forms with income tax forms. Senator Edward M. Kennedy of Massachusetts introduced legislation into the 92nd Congress authorizing individuals to register to vote in federal elections by mailing in a postcard. Compilation of the voting lists would be done by computer. The address listed by the voter on the postcard would be recognized as the one legal residence for voting purposes. No waiting period of residence would be required.

"At a single stroke," said Senator Kennedy, "the system would do away, not only with burdensome registration requirements, but also with unfair residency requirements that operate to bar voters in almost every state."

The compilation of voting lists by computer has attracted criticism from those who have been wary of any amassing of data by government agencies which could become a source of invasion of individual privacy. The specter of a national data bank is not altogether spurious in light of revelations of abuses by private credit organizations as well as questionable activities of law enforcement and military agencies. The gathering of census data, which is of enormous value to scholarly, business, and legitimate government activities, has been circumscribed as a result of such fears. The use of published voting lists for assigning jury duty or collecting back taxes has had a negative effect on volunteer registration, particularly among the disadvantaged. A national registry of eligible voters, on the other hand, would not seem to pose a substantive danger beyond that already created by the existence of city directories and localized voting lists.

The idea of national registration by postcard was further refined in a bill introduced in 1971 by Senator Gale W. McGee of Wyoming. As Chairman of the Senate Post Office Committee,

McGee was in a position to try to steer the proposal to the floor via a favorable vote in this committee rather than being buried in the less sympathetic Judiciary Committee, headed by Senator James O. Eastland of Mississippi.

Under the McGee Bill, the Postal Service would deliver post-card forms to every American household thirty to forty-five days prior to the close of registration. Each eligible voter would fill out a double form and mail it to his local election board, which would put him on the federal election roll and mail back half the card to establish that fact. The new voting qualification system would be run by a National Voter Registration Administration in the Bureau of Census, but all voting records would remain in local hands.

The postcard registration would apply only to federal elections, but no state could require a residency requirement longer than thirty days. There would be a federal bonus paid to any state that made its registration procedures conform to the national system; holding registration open to thirty days before the election and requiring only thirty days residency to qualify.

Opponents of this method of universal registration argued that it would impose federal controls upon the states, create a new federal bureaucracy, multiply the opportunities for fraud, and cost millions of dollars to implement. Some described it as a new form of literacy test, and one not likely to reach either the mobile poor or the mobile young. In March 1972, a coalition of Senate Republicans and Southern Democrats combined to defeat the postcard registration measure, 46 to 42. Of twelve absent senators, three were campaigning in the Presidential primaries and eight had previously supported the bill. The proposal, however, was laid aside until after the 1972 elections.

It would seem that if registration systems are to be altered so as to make registration more convenient and accessible to all citizens, the impetus is probably going to have to come from federal authority. The responsibility for compiling and maintaining voting lists would, in the opinion of those familiar with the mores of U. S. politics, best remain, however, under the jurisdictions within each of the fifty states. The structure to administer a universal enrollment system should be flexible enough to take into account the great variety of state law and practice in the United States. Different procedures should probably be established for urban and rural areas. The protection of the voting list against fraud could undoubtedly be accomplished by a period of general publicity accompanied by a system of voluntary challenges.

The experience with the registration of eighteen-year-olds may have a significant effect on the political prospects of a universal enrollment system in the United States. If it is demonstrated that, after all the hoopla of political platforms, Congressional debate, High Court decisions, and the adoption of a new amendment to the federal Constitution, the franchise was effectively curtailed by local registration procedures, the stage will have been set for a possibly potent lobby. As the Presidential election of 1972 approached, the final outcome could hinge, at least theoretically, on the votes of a new generation of voters. The simplification of voting procedures, like party reforms in the direction of broader opportunity for participation, is the kind of symbolic issue that is easy to grasp. In the political atmosphere of the seventies an issue with appeal not only among the young but also among the awakening minorities throughout the country could sprout into an idea whose time has arrived.

Meanwhile, the grub task of public education and incremental political reform remained to be carried on. For, although the average citizen paid lip service to participatory democracy in public opinion polls and private conversation, the attention span for the dull mechanics of politics that might make a reality of such noble ideals appeared to be more limited. In thousands of jurisdictions across the land the day-to-day works of the electoral apparatus—in those off moments between the temporary excitement of personal political combat—clanked its creaky machinery virtually unnoticed. Public indignation over the inequities, when aroused, diffused itself on a thousand targets. And the system, like a rhino shedding rubber bullets, survived unscathed.

Organizing Institutional Reform

The idea of a citizen's lobby to attack the institutional barricades against full participation in American political life was an essential part of the philosophy behind Common Cause, a privately financed organization headed by John W. Gardner, former Secretary of Health, Education and Welfare. It announced a Voting Rights Project in the winter of 1970-1971 in the following terms:

Its goal is the creation of election laws which assure the potential voter easy and equitable access to the ballot and encourage his participation. . . . The Voting Rights Project will help draft, introduce and lobby for major change in state laws to provide reduced residency requirements, door-to-door registration, registration in factories, shopping centers, schools and apartments. We will seek allies in other organizations to join us in speaking with legislators, testifying at hearings, and generating public support for these reforms. Another area in which we will concentrate is the delegate selection process to be used in various states for the Presidential nominating conventions in 1972. We will strive to make this process more accessible to the average voter.

The national group, with headquarters in Washington, derived some of its thinking from the premise that large numbers of Americans, although concerned about political issues, were not being reached anymore through the traditional political parties. Perhaps they could be activated to support causes not tied to the fortunes of a particular candidate or a specific struggle for political power. There was a hint of Naderism, too, in the enlistment of volunteer lawyers to challenge election laws in various states or to prepare briefs supporting litigation already in progress. The first targets involved residence requirements for voters of all ages with special attention to the rights of young persons away at college. Common Cause members, themselves, were sent an action plan to follow in lobbying with state legislatures and in starting other activities in support of electoral reforms. They also received an inventory of worthwhile bills introduced in the legislatures of their home states dealing with registration, voting, and the conduct of political primaries, along with instructions on where to write key state office holders.

The Voting Rights Project's debut occured when the 26th Amendment went out to state legislatures for ratification in the spring of 1971. How much Common Cause was responsible for the speedy action of the required number of states was difficult to assess. Such experienced forces as trade-union political action committees were also hard at work. And, as previously noted, a consensus coalesced in budget-minded capitals against incurring the extra expense and confusion of trying to run independent elections for those under and over the age of twenty-one. Nor were there any quick, spectacular breakthroughs in liberalizing state-by-state voting laws. Some of the Common Cause leaders were veterans of Senator Eugene McCarthy's 1968 campaign. The unquestioned success of that effort in raising money and volunteers (if not as successful with voters as the claims of some McCarthy enthusiasts) had proved difficult to replicate, however, in state elections in 1970. It remained to be seen whether Common Cause could indeed rally an indifferent public on the relatively dry fare of local election reform.

The strategy of building any campaign for reform around the whole kit of standard election practices throughout the country seemed eminently sound. The political weakness of registration reform was the fact that the constituency which stood to benefit most was, by definition, without power at the polls. In the normal flow of two-party politics, moreover, the Democrats appeared to gain most from the enfranchisement of minority groups usually favorably disposed toward their party. Republican politicians were understandably not in a hurry to cut their own throats.

In the push and haul of passing the 1970 Amendments to the Voting Rights Act, a principal trade-off had been the uniform thirty-day residency requirement for voting for President. Senator Barry Goldwater, testifying in behalf of the provision, recalled that when he was running for President he was struck by the number of persons who had told him they wanted to vote for him but were prevented by the fact that they had only recently moved in to the state. His Republican colleagues felt they had most to gain in 1972 from enfranchising the army of businessmen regularly shifting jobs who, along with their families, constituted part of the nearly two million denied a vote for President because of a change in residence. Together with representatives from populous states where minority-group voters might hold the veto power on their chances for re-election, they helped make up the bipartisan majority for extending the Voting Rights Act another four years.

To assemble similar coalitions for registration reforms in state legislatures might require similar trade-offs, and for that the election process as a whole offered wider opportunities. A suburban legislator interested in keeping the polls open longer hours for the benefit of commuters, for example, might be willing to condone in exchange absentee registration for urban residents. The proliferation of state Presidential primaries stimulated interest in some quarters in making it easier to switch parties or making it harder to cross over on primary day, as the case might be. Once the gates were opened for that purpose other voting changes might pass through. The presence in many state legislatures of a new crop of young members following the reapportionments mandated by the Supreme Court was another sign that the status quo in politics might be subject to change. A popular mandate is a useful springboard for young politicians who prefer not to await the favor of the established structure. And broadening popular participation might seem attractive to such ambitious officeholders irrespective of party interests on a broad scale.

What was needed most was the kind of political focus that can lift an issue out of obscurity and into the spotlight where it cannot be ignored. A working definition of a live political issue might be that no one dares to kill it in committee. Registration reform lacked that kind of appeal on its own. As part of a broader package to open up the political process to maximum participation it might then get the play in the media and on the political platform needed to "go public."

A step in this direction was the Election Systems Project launched in 1971 by the National Municipal League and the League of Women Voters Education Fund, supported by a two-year grant from the Ford Foundation. The League of Women Voters put its members to work in selected communities, sometimes in concert with organizations such as the N.A.A.C.P., to interview election officials, party workers, and individual citizens concerning the local system for registering voters and conducting elections. League members were also to be posted to observe at first hand the actual operation of registration and voting. The stated purpose of this volunteer activity was to point up the obstacles that prevent full exercise of the franchise "by collecting data on the legal, administrative and more subtle factors that influence the participation of citizens in the registration and voting process."

The canvass sponsored by the League Education Fund covered the practices of election officials in 251 communities throughout the country. This study, the League concluded,

documents the fact that the current system of registration and voting functions inefficiently for citizens throughout the United States. . . . Indeed, the system works poorly for *all* Americans. In the case of the minorities, the poor, the uneducated and the aged, who are unable to meet its requirements easily, the system naturally imposes more heavily than it does on the average mainstream America. These groups can be even further excluded from the electoral process by the arbitrary and uneven application of administrative procedures, which, while legal, can be manipulated to serve the political advantage or philosophy of those who control them."

Concurrently the National Municipal League was analyzing the legal problems involved for the purpose of drafting model documents that could be used to simplify voting procedures everywhere. Model state constitutions and city charters previously drafted by the League have had an enormous effect upon state and local committees organized to revise their governmental structures. Similar models dealing with the election laws covering voter registration and administration of the election procedures, it was hoped, might provide the basis for uniform and nationwide improvements in those spheres as well.

In another era, the Flexner Report revolutionized medical education in the United States. In Britain, the Royal Commission has been a prestigious vehicle for institutional change. Detailed examinations of the practical workings of our elections system and of the structural obstacles limiting the free exercise of the franchise were unlikely in themselves to immediately produce dramatic reforms. The Kerner Commission, in a similar context, was unable to alter the institutional basis of racial tension in the country overnight. The important development has been the recognition implicit in these independent studies of the electoral process that the inequities in our election system warranted serious concern, and that remedies were needed that went beyond the reach of ordinary political activity.

The troubled minorities in America—Blacks, Puerto Ricans, Chicanos, Indians—were demanding their turn at political access to the system, the time-honored path trod by immigrant groups in America away from poverty and discrimination. The system that seemed to work for their predecessors, perhaps through the mediating influence of machine politics and a nonbureaucratic administration of loosely drawn laws, had become petrified by the good intentions of reformers seeking to eliminate fraud at the polls. The Anglo-Saxon tradition, furthermore, was steeped with regard for the value of the vote as an end in itself. That concept of civic duty often was simply not part of the cultural heritage of the victims of slavery, tyranny, even genocide.

America had always required the newcomer to assimilate to its ways. Now the rediscovery of ethnic identity as a source of pride and self-worth, rather than a badge of inferiority, called into question the authenticity of the claims made for the whole system of democratic government arranged by the first colonial settlers. The consequence among some minorities was with drawal. The boycott of elections was openly advocated in many situations as a minority voter's only alternative to tweedledee and tweddledum.

Calls for militancy, violence, or revolution among the disadvantaged, on the other hand, were the symptom of how much some had been alienated and how desperate was their despair. Either alternative—withdrawal or violence—would destroy the consensus on which democracy rests. The clear and present danger was not only to the physical and spiritual survival of the groups disconnected from the political process in America, although the situation in that respect was indeed grave. The ultimate peril was to the more favored sectors of society as well. For if the glue of a pluralistic democracy were ever to become unstuck, the debris would bury all.

Less dramatic but equally threatening was a slow attrition of public confidence in the essential fairness of our political system. This was the virus infecting the disconnected young, the next generation responsible for the trying task of making a clumsy system make good on its promise. Democracy could not function without faith in its leadership. The moral demands of youth on the old institutions were in part the familiar pattern of rebellion. This time, however, there were unprecedented numbers of the young living out their convictions. It was not at all clear if these private life styles fitted into a politics of participation.

The great contribution of the young men and women of the 1960s was to refocus America's political priorities on issues emphasizing the quality of life. The genius of the American political system has been its ability to reconstitute itself periodically to pass through times of national crisis. The expansion of the franchise to eighteen-to-twenty-year olds to usher in the seventies might prove to have been one of those critical turning points. The success of the electoral system in involving the new generation as voters and participants would be a measure of the viability of the American political process and a guide to the remaining millions of the disconnected.